Interpreting
the Labour Party

MANCHESTER
UNIVERSITY PRESS

Critical Labour Movement Studies Series

Series editors
John Callaghan
Steven Fielding
Steve Ludlam

Interpreting the Labour Party

Approaches to Labour politics and history

edited by
John Callaghan
Steven Fielding
Steve Ludlam

Manchester University Press
Manchester and New York
distributed exclusively in the USA by Palgrave

Published by Manchester University Press
Oxford Road, Manchester M13 9NR, UK
and Room 400, 175 Fifth Avenue, New York, NY 10010, USA
www.manchesteruniversitypress.co.uk

Distributed exclusively in the USA by
Palgrave, 175 Fifth Avenue, New York,
NY 10010, USA

Distributed exclusively in Canada by
UBC Press, University of British Columbia, 2029 West Mall,
Vancouver, BC, Canada V6T 1Z2

British Library Cataloguing-in-Publication Data
A catalogue record for this book is available from the British Library

Library of Congress Cataloging-in-Publication Data applied for

ISBN   0 7190 6718 9 *hardback*
          0 7190 6719 7 *paperback*

First published 2003

11 10 09 08 07 06 05 04 03   10 9 8 7 6 5 4 3 2 1

Typeset
by Northern Phototypesetting Co. Ltd., Bolton, Lancs.
Printed in Great Britain
by CPI, Bath

Contents

Series editors' foreword

The start of the twenty-first century is superficially an inauspicious time to study labour movements. Political parties once associated with the working class have seemingly embraced capitalism. The trade unions with which these parties were once linked have suffered near-fatal reverses. The industrial proletariat looks both divided and in rapid decline. The development of multi-level governance, prompted by 'globalisation' has furthermore apparently destroyed the institutional context for advancing the labour 'interest'. Many consequently now look on terms such as the 'working class', 'socialism' and the 'labour movement' as politically and historically redundant.

The purpose of this series is to give a platform to those students of labour movements who challenge, or develop, established ways of thinking and so demonstrate the continued vitality of the subject and the work of those interested in it. For despite appearances many social democratic parties remain important competitors for national office and proffer distinctive programmes. Unions still impede the free flow of 'market forces'. If workers are a more diverse body and have exchanged blue collars for white, insecurity remains an everyday problem. The new institutional and global context is moreover as much of an opportunity as a threat. Yet, it cannot be doubted that compared to the immediate post-1945 period, at the beginning of the new millennium what many still refer to as the 'labour movement' is much less influential. Whether this should be considered a time of retreat or reconfiguration is unclear – and a question the series aims to clarify

The series will not only give a voice to studies of particular national bodies but will also promote comparative works that contrast experiences across time and geography. This entails taking due account of the political, economic and cultural settings in which labour movements have operated. In particular this involves taking the past seriously as a way of understanding the present as well as utilising sympathetic approaches drawn from sociology, economics and elsewhere.

Acknowledgements

Nick Randall wishes to acknowledge an ESRC Postgraduate Training Award (R00429634225), which allowed him to conduct the doctoral research on Labour's ideological dynamics on which his chapter is based. In addition he would like to thank Martin Burch, David Coates, Colin Hay, Steve Ludlam and members of the PSA Labour Movements Group for their comments on earlier drafts of chapter 1. Lawrence Black wishes to thank John Callaghan, James Thompson, Nick Tiratsoo and Leo Zeilig, and the audience at a seminar held at the University of Alberta, Edmonton, for their comments and advice about sources. Michael Newman is grateful to Tony Benn for permission to quote from the unpublished version of his diary. Steven Fielding and Declan McHugh wish to thank Peter Clarke, Kevin Hickson, Steve Ludlam, John McHugh and David Marquand for their insights. Steve Ludlam thanks his co-editors for their comments on chapter 10. Colin Hay expresses his thanks to Steven Fielding, Dave Marsh and Dan Wincott for helpful comments on an earlier version of chapter 12 and acknowledges the support of the ESRC 'One Europe or Several?' programme for research on 'Globalisation, European Integration and the European Social Model' (L213252043).

The editors express their appreciation to all those who, as either paper-givers or audience, participated in the Labour Movement Studies' conference 'Understanding the Labour Party' which was held in Manchester in July 2001 and on which this collection is based; in addition, they thank the UK Political Studies Association for financial support and Starbucks for the hosting of their numerous editorial conferences.

Contributors

Lawrence Black is Fulbright-Robertson Visiting Professor of British History at Westminster College, Missouri, USA during 2002–3. He is the author of *The Political Culture of the Left in Affluent Britain, 1951-64: Old Labour, New Britain?* (2003). A volume co-edited with Hugh Pemberton, *An Affluent Society? Britain's Post-War 'Golden Age' Revisited* is forthcoming. He is currently researching British political culture and post-war affluence.

John Callaghan is Professor of Politics at the University of Wolverhampton and the author of *Socialism in Britain* (1990), *The Retreat of Social Democracy* (2000) and *Crisis, Cold War and Conflict: the Communist Party 1951–68* (2003).

David Coates is the Worrell Professor of Anglo-American Studies at Wake Forest University in North Carolina, USA. He has recently edited (with Peter Lawler) *New Labour into Power* (2000), and *Paving the Way: The Critique of 'Parliamentary Socialism'* (2003), the latter being a collection of essays on the Labour Party drawn largely from *The Socialist Register* and written by scholars sympathetic to the perspective discussed in his chapter.

Madeleine Davis is a Lecturer in Politics at Queen Mary College, University of London. The chapter presented here is based on research undertaken for her doctoral thesis, *New Left Review's Analysis of Britain 1964-1990*, completed in 1999. As well as the New Left, she also has an interest in Latin American politics and is the editor of *The Pinochet Case* (2003).

Steven Fielding is Professor of Contemporary Political History in the School of English, Sociology, Politics and Contemporary History and Associate Director of the European Studies Research Institute at the University of Salford. His recent publications include *The Labour Party. Continuity and Change in the Making of 'New' Labour* (2003) and *The Labour Governments, 1964–70. Volume One. Labour and Cultural Change* (Manchester, 2004).

Colin Hay is Professor of Political Analysis and Head of the Department of Political Science and International Studies at the University of Birmingham. He is co-editor of the new international journal *Comparative European Politics* and the author or editor of a number of volumes, including *The Political Economy of New Labour* (1999), *Demystifying Globalisation* (2001), *Political Analysis* (2002) and *British Politics Today* (2002).

Steve Ludlam is a Senior Lecturer in the Department of Politics at the University of Sheffield. His most recent publication, co-written by Martin J. Smith, is *New Labour in Government* (2001). He is convenor of the Labour Movements' specialist group in the UK Political Studies Association.

Declan McHugh is currently working as a parliamentary researcher for a Labour MP. In 2001 at the University of Salford he completed a Ph.D on the development of the Labour Party in inter-war Manchester; he hopes to publish his thesis in the near future.

Michael Newman is Professor of Politics at the University of North London. His books include, in addition to *Ralph Miliband and the Politics of the New Left* (2002), *Socialism and European Unity: The Dilemma of the Left in Britain and France* (1983), *John Strachey* (1989), *Harold Laski: A Political Biography* (1993) and *Democracy, Sovereignty and the European Union* (1996).

Leo Panitch holds the Canada Research Chair in Comparative Political Economy and is the Distinguished Research Professor of Political Science at York University, Toronto, Canada. He is the co-editor, with Colin Leys, of *The Socialist Register* and the recent author of *Renewing Socialism: Democracy, Strategy and Imagination* (2001).

Nick Randall is a Lecturer in British politics at the University of Newcastle. His research interests are the politics of the British Labour and Conservative Parties, the territorial politics of the UK and the issue of European integration in British politics. His publications include 'New Labour and Northern Ireland', in David Coates and Peter Lawler (eds), *New Labour in Power* (Manchester, 2001) and, with David Baker and David Seawright, 'Celtic exceptionalism? Scottish and Welsh parliamentarians' attitudes towards Europe', *Political Quarterly*, 74:2 (2002).

Alastair J. Reid is a Lecturer in History and Fellow of Girton College, Cambridge. His publications include *Social Classes and Social Relations in Britain, 1850-1914* (1995) and, with Henry Pelling, *A Short History of the Labour Party* (1996). He is currently writing a new history of British trade unionism.

Eric Shaw is Senior Lecturer in the Politics Department, University of Stirling. He has written extensively on the Labour Party. His works include *Discipline and Discord in the Labour Party* (Manchester, 1988); *The Labour Party Since 1979: Conflict and Transformation* (1994); *The Labour Party Since 1945* (Oxford, 1996); 'New pathways to Parliament', *Parliamentary Affairs*, 54:1 (2001); and 'New Labour – new democratic centralism?', *West European Politics*, 25:3 (2002).

Mark Wickham-Jones is a Senior Lecturer in the Department of Politics, University of Bristol. He is the author of many works on the Labour Party, most notably *Economic Strategy and the Labour Party. Politics and Policy-Making, 1970–83* (1996).

Introduction

John Callaghan, Steven Fielding and Steve Ludlam

Interpreting the Labour Party is an attempt to take stock of how some of the British Labour Party's leading interpreters have analysed their subject, deriving as they do from contrasting political, theoretical, disciplinary and methodological backgrounds. The book explores their often-hidden assumptions and subjects them to critical evaluation. In introducing this collection, we position the various chapters within a wider context and draw out some of their most striking implications.

It is important to remind ourselves from the outset that all students of the Labour Party – including the authors of this Introduction and those reading it – adhere to some prior analytical–interpretive framework deriving from diverse theoretical positions. This is not something for which anyone should be criticised, for as E. H. Carr stated many years ago (1964), without some such intellectual setting the apparently highly potent 'fact' can have no meaning. It could be argued, indeed, that 'the facts' themselves are often the product of persuasive theories and interpretive arguments. While these propositions might seem uncontroversial when stated in general terms, once applied to a particular subject, in which analysts have invested much time and energy, their implications can arouse controversy. For if scholars are able to agree on certain 'facts', few of them are willing to concede without a fight that their reading of those facts is in any way flawed.

The study of the Labour Party is especially prone to interpretive dispute because it is inherently politicised. Many of those who have written about Labour – for example, Henry Pelling – have at one time or another been party members who identified with one or other of its ideological factions. A number have belonged to groupings, usually, like Perry Anderson and Tom Nairn, to Labour's Left, which have hoped to replace the party in the affections of the working class. More than a few of them – like Ralph Miliband and David Marquand – have been, at different periods in their lives, on both sides of the fence. Those writing from such committed positions have sometimes conceived of the party in teleological terms. That is, they thought it to be an ineluctable force whose destiny was to fulfil a historic mission, the nature of which could be anything from narrowly electoral to broadly anti-systemic. Such an approach is less obvious today, when so few believe in the prospect of establishing a social democratic – let alone a socialist – Britain. Indeed, those who retain some hope that socialism remains possible – in particular those dubbed 'Milibandian' – consider that Labour was never that type of party. In contrast, some observers have eschewed overt political involvement, although their work should not be considered inherently more reliable because of that. For it is impossible not be influenced by the political conjuncture in which one lives, just as it is difficult to see beyond the intellectual, cultural and academic verities of one's day. The appearance of objectivity can never be more than superficial: indeed, it might be suggested, there are none more ideological than those who claim to disavow ideology altogether.

This volume aims to provide insights about what have often been the hidden assumptions of some of Labour's leading interpreters and seeks to explain how they have coloured our picture of the party. The approaches considered here are invariably the result of complex aggregates of theories, methods and empirical evidence. There is often much overlap between different interpretations, for while its authors may make use of broadly the same component parts the novelty of their arguments often lies in their application or arrangement of those elements. Even the same combination of parts can contain important differences of emphasis and so produce contrasting conclusions. In such subtle ways do the motives, political affiliations and moods of the authors express themselves. Moreover, while such factors are sometimes made explicit, there are other influences at work in constructing a particular perspective which are frequently left covered over. The ruling beliefs of the day, the endemic assumptions and intellectual habits of an individual, a generation or a school of thought, may simply be taken for granted. Some, if not all, of these predelictions may not be referred to in the text, escaping the critical attention of both author and reader.

To reiterate, everything written about the Labour Party, whether by scholars, activists or journalists, has strong normative underpinnings. Any full appreciation of the party therefore requires some assessment of the intellectual means through which it has been perceived. When all is said and done, Labour's historic purpose has been to challenge or at least temper, in one way or another, the power of the most dynamic economic and social system in history – capitalism. If such a subject does not arouse partisanship, nothing will.

Rationale for the collection

The chapters gathered here were selected from papers presented to the second conference of the Political Studies Association's Labour Movements Group, held in Manchester in July 2001. This gathering grew out of the group's commitment to create arenas in which researchers, drawn from different academic disciplines and contrasting research agendas, can share their work. It already has a large and diverse membership, composed of adherents to a variety of political, disciplinary and methodological perspectives united in the desire to better understand the Labour Party and the wider labour movement, both in Britain and elsewhere in the world. The group is always keen to attract new members, and its website is an invaluable research resource (Labour Movements Group 2002).

As with this collection, the main purpose of that conference was to highlight how students of the party have analysed their subject. In particular, the organisers hoped to traverse one of the disciplinary divisions that have hitherto hampered the development of a more rounded appreciation of the party: that which demarcates historians from political scientists. This is no new concern. During the early 1960s the first conferences of the Society for the Study of Labour History attracted the participation of political scientists as politically diverse as Robert McKenzie and Ralph Miliband. Despite this, the society went on to embrace traditional historical concerns and methods, leaving little room for such figures (Fielding 2002). More recently, in their individual contributions to the Labour literature members of the Labour Movements Group have brought together the concerns of history and political science to illuminating effect. Despite the advantages of this approach, however, it remains a minority pursuit.

The divide between history and politics has resulted in work that, whatever its intrinsic merits, is often more limited than it might otherwise be. In particular, many political scientists have fallen foul of the assumptions that theoretical elaboration is intellectually superior to empirical research and that all contemporary trends are somehow novel (Callaghan 2002). In contrast, most historians have eschewed the insightful theoretical labours of political scientists and been guilty of promoting a view of the past as a foreign country set apart from the travails of the present day. It could be argued that it would be best to locate analysis of the Labour Party in what Colin Hay (chapter 12) suggests should be a 'post-disciplinary' labour studies that incorporates insights from economics and sociology, along with those of history and politics. This is undoubtedly correct, but for the time being the proper harmonising of the work of historians and political scientists would be a major step forward.

Drawing the two disciplines together would be especially helpful at this present juncture. At the time of writing, Labour is widely referred to as 'New' Labour. This term has given rise to a keen debate about the extent to which the contemporary party forms either a break or continuum with what is described as 'Old' Labour (Bale 1999; Fielding 2003; Ludlam and Smith 2001). While it is not their main purpose, the chapters that follow help frame this debate in both historical and theoretical terms, though of course that does not mean they arrive at a common conclusion about the significance of present-day events.

The chapters

As this collection makes clear, academic analysis of the Labour Party – like the party itself – has never stood still. Over the years, historians and political scientists interested in the party have amended their analytical agendas in response to wider intellectual trends as well as to Labour's own capricious electoral course. This point is elaborated in chapters 1 and 2. Nick Randall (chapter 1) notes the wide variety of approaches to studying ideological change in the Labour Party and identifies five principal explanatory strategies: materialist; ideational; electoral; institutional; and those which synthesise some or all of these. Limitations in many widely read texts are discussed and, echoing the final chapter, by Colin Hay, Randall concludes by calling for a multidimensional approach that would reject, among other things, what he considers the artificial opposition of structure to agency.

Lawrence Black (chapter 2) considers the 'new political history' by way of a comparison with earlier 'realist' analyses of the party which explained its historical development with almost exclusive reference to the social nature of the electorate. He argues that the former view does more than counter social explanations by restoring agency to the party, along with other more directly political factors. For the 'new political history' also questions what it is that the category 'politics' might encapsulate and how it can be represented and contested. The proximity and ordering of party–voter relations are thus problematised, and Black reflects on the imperfect and distorted perceptions which often characterise how academics have understood these relations.

Reflecting the preoccupations of many of those who currently study Labour, the main focus of this collection falls on the party's postwar interpreters. Yet, even given that shortened time frame, there have been many contrasting currents in interpretation that have ebbed and flowed in their influence, as intellectual fashions and political events left their mark. The rest of the chapters of this book can be seen as falling into two main categories. The first involves an assessment of those who can be usefully described as New Left analysts: in their different ways they have promoted a very influential and deeply critical analysis of the Labour Party. This work has broadly assumed that Labour – at least during the 1950s–1970s – impeded the transformation of capitalism into socialism. The most ambitious of these New Left theorists were Perry Anderson and Tom Nairn, who situated Labour in the extremely broad historical context of capitalist development and class formation in Britain since the English Civil War. This analysis was strongly informed by the postwar perception of Britain's industrial decline and its relation to an imperial and post-imperial global financial role serving the interests of the City of London. Madeleine Davis (chapter 3) focuses on the New Left's idea of 'labourism', a venerable notion given new life by this analysis. Mark Wickham-Jones (chapter 6) looks at one of the assumptions underpinning that concept: Labour's supposed isolation from the rest of European social democracy. Both, however, consider the shifting political projects of the New Left in relation to its developing analysis of the Labour Party over the last forty years.

As other contributions show – for example, chapter 8, by John Callaghan – Anderson and Nairn have been hugely influential. Even so, it was Ralph Miliband's *Parliamentary Socialism*, first published in 1961, which best captured the New Left's frustration with Labour. Miliband's biographer Michael Newman (chapter 4) traces the intellectual roots of this powerful critique. He reveals that its argument was widely misinterpreted by contemporaries largely because the author was himself uncertain whether Labour would ever become the vehicle for his kind of socialism. Miliband eventually concluded that the party was fated to remain 'labourist' after despairing of the 1964–70 Wilson Government's policies. From the mid-1960s he therefore dismissed Labour as wholly dependent on capitalism and, indeed, came to see its ability to win the support of most working-class voters as one means by which the status quo was maintained. As Newman also shows, the party's move to the Left during the 1970s and 1980s forced Miliband to revise this view, although he nevertheless remained highly sceptical of the party's potential to engineer fundamental social and economic change.

Since the 1970s David Coates and Leo Panitch have produced numerous works in the 'Milibandian' mould that have made a significant impact on perceptions of the Labour Party. Their contribution (chapter 5) mounts a robust defence of the continuing relevance to both historical and contemporary analysis of this still-controversial perspective. They indicate the extent to which Milibandians have extended their inspiration's original insights by incorporating within their own work the concerns of international political economy. This has imbued them with a perspective far wider than that possessed by most students of the party, who tend to focus on the internal party mechanics and remain trapped within national boundaries. Thus, Milibandians can now claim to possess a unique insight on the wider implications of 'New' Labour policy, based as it is on certain contestable assumptions regarding 'globalisation'.

The second category consists of chapters on figures whose work, while couched in less obviously theoretical terms, proceed from a contrasting set of assumptions that might be regarded as broadly social democratic in orientation. Henry Pelling was one of the leading postwar historians of the Labour Party who wrote a number of founding texts during the 1950s and 1960s. In relation to the more overtly the-oretical work of Miliband that resonated among the radical student audience of the 1960s and 1970s, Pelling appeared the epitome of dull empiricism. Alastair Reid, in chapter 7, rescues Pelling from such a dismissive appraisal and shows how far he defined his early work through an engagement with prevailing ideological currents which traced their origins to the basic concerns of Marxist scholarship. Pelling, who sympathised with the Labour leadership's social democratic outlook, came to conclusions at variance with those of others who, like Miliband, were crit-ical of the party leadership's apparent lack of desire to transform capitalism into socialism. Steven Fielding and Declan McHugh (chapter 9) subject to critical appraisal the work of another – but later – social democratic interpreter. David Marquand's *The Progressive Dilemma*, first published in 1991, has had a profound influence over recent perceptions of party history. Indeed, it has been used to jus-tify 'New' Labour's attempt to increase its appeal to middle-class voters by dis-tancing the party from the trade unions and public ownership. The authors view Marquand's analysis as indicative of a particular moment in the development of social democratic thinking, which has hitherto been less critical of the party's character. They also question some of Marquand's historical assumptions, which are derived from one side of a debate about the inevitability of Labour's rise to the status of a national party during the first two decades of the twentieth century.

Without some understanding of the party's unique and complex relationship with the working class in general and the trade unions in particular, a full appreci-ation of Labour in Britain is impossible. John Callaghan (chapter 8) analyses Ross McKibbin's approach to that relationship which roots the evolution of the Labour Party, and the limits to its growth, in the consciousness and cultures of organised (and unorganised) labour in the first decades of the twentieth century. McKibbin supplies a richly suggestive explanation of why this truly proletarian party was unable to break the electoral hegemony of the Conservative Party until the Second World War. Class and class consciousness are central to this account, although in ways which frustrated 'the forward march' of Labour. Callaghan shows how McKibbin's work draws upon and develops assumptions concerning the 'special path' of working-class development in Britain, and highlights the absence from this body of theory of the sort of rigorous comparative analysis which such arguments presume.

Two chapters deal directly with interpretations of the unions–party link – the labour alliance that has had such a profound influence on Labour's development. In chapter 10 Steve Ludlam outlines the two principal scholarly approaches that have characterised the bulk of postwar work on this link: that of pluralistic theorists and social democrats; and that of Marxist theorists and socialists. He illustrates their main features, and some of their limitations, through an analysis of the unions–party link during the particularly tense period between 1974 and 1983. Thus, Ludlam calls for the disaggregation and sectoral understandings of 'the unions', and for an awareness of the purchase of underlying axioms of liberal political economy. Lewis Minkin's work on the unions–party link is almost unique in its focus. Eric Shaw (chapter 11) performs a great service to students of the party by clarifying Minkin's explanatory mode, analytical categories, and conceptual framework. In doing so he shows how Minkin exposed the fallacies of rational actor models that underpinned the myth of 'baronial' union leaders' domination of the party, and constructed instead a sociological model that reveals the '"rules", roles and relations' which explain how the 'contentious alliance' functions.

In the final contribution (chapter 12) Colin Hay, one of the leading interpreters of 'New' Labour, sketches out an ambitious theoretical framework within which students of the contemporary party might locate their analysis. This takes account of what Hay terms the 'new political science', at the heart of which is 'reflexivity', that is an approach more self-critical about its analytical hypotheses than has hitherto been the case. It might be thought that if past students of the party had practised such reflexivity collections such as this would be unnecessary. Hay's chapter is not, however, meant to establish an agreed agenda for future work on Labour, as no collective programme emerged from the conference. As the reader will have been able to discern, each contributor to this collection, just like those whose work they analyse, has his or her own particular point of view. However, the editors would wish to endorse at least the broad thrust of Hay's perspective. A greater openness to alternative points of view, a more developed self-critical awareness and a willingness to lay one's theoretical cards on the table would indeed be very welcome. The editors wish, in addition, to stress the need to break down apparently 'common-sense' terms such as the 'trade unions', 'labour movement' and especially, of course, the 'Labour Party'. Rather than simply taking them for granted, it would be useful for analysts to think first about what they might mean. Finally, while Hay's own chapter illustrates that theoretical work can greatly illuminate our appreciation of the party, students need to pay due account to historical context, however inconvenient the messy details of Labour's past may sometimes appear.

This collection does not claim to be comprehensive. The work of the historian K. O. Morgan and the earlier historian and theorist G. D. H. Cole, for example, might well have found a place within its covers. There is no contribution on the feminist interpretation of the Labour Party either. It is, however, broadly representative of current scholarship and the diverse postwar corpus of work on the party in which the authors have been schooled. In holding up to critical evaluation those such as Anderson and Nairn, McKibbin, Marquand, Miliband, Minkin and Pelling, we are, in a rather perverse way perhaps, merely paying tribute to their work and acknowledging our intellectual indebtedness to them.

References

Unless indicated, the place of publication is London.

Bale, T. (1999) 'The logic of no alternative? Political scientists, historians and the politics of Labour's past', *British Journal of Politics & International Relations*, 1:2

Callaghan, J. (2002) 'Globalization and social democracy: the limits of social democracy in historical perspective', *British Journal of Politics & International Relations*, 4:3

Carr, E. H. (1964) *What Is History?* Harmondsworth

Fielding, S. (2002) '"New" Labour and the "new" labour history', *Mitteilungsblatt des instituts für Soziale Bewegungen*, 27

Fielding, S. (2003) *The Labour Party. Continuity and Change in the Making of 'New' Labour*

Labour Movements Group (2002) Website: www.shef.ac.uk/uni/academic/N-Q/pol/lmsg.html

Ludlam, S. and Smith, M. J. (eds) (2001) *New Labour in Government*

1

Understanding Labour's ideological trajectory

Nick Randall

The Labour Party is habitually considered the most ideologically inclined of all British political parties, and ideological struggle has been endemic within the party since its foundation. It is no surprise, therefore, that studies of the party have endeavoured to understand why Labour's ideology has shifted repeatedly throughout its history. This chapter considers those efforts.

A large and varied literature is available to explain Labour's ideological movements. Many works address the Labour Party itself. Others examine ideological change in parties in general. Yet others analyse change in social democratic parties in particular. To assess all three strands in the literature requires the application of some form of classification. At the risk of oversimplification, the approach adopted here will be to classify works according to the principal explanatory strategies they adopt. Five strategies are identified and outlined: materialist; ideational; electoral; institutional; and those which synthesise some or all of these four. The five strategies are assessed, and the chapter concludes by outlining an alternative model of Labour's ideological dynamics that might be usefully applied to the study of the New Labour.

Outlines of explanatory strategies

Materialist strategies

The first set of explanatory strategies proposes that Labour's ideological shifts are a product of economic and social determinants. Here three main strands of analysis emerge.

The first strand focuses on the pressure of capitalist interests. Claims that Labour's ideological movements are responses to the structural power of capitalist interests have appealed particularly to Marxist scholars such as Miliband (1972) and Panitch (1976), but are best developed by Coates (see chapter 5 of this collection, by David Coates and Leo Panitch). For Coates (1975: 154), 'the major blockage on the ability of the Labour Party to reform capitalism into socialism by the Parliamentary process, or even to sustain major programmes of social reform, comes from the institutions and representatives of corporate capital'. Forced to co-operate with capitalist interests that control production, investment and employment decisions, Labour governments 'have been clawed to death by the opposition of organised capital' and have surrendered their radical ambitions (Coates 1996: 71). It has also been argued that this structural power of capitalist interests extends to ideological shifts during Labour's periods of opposition. Thus Wickham-Jones (1995) claims that anxiety over business antagonism prompted Labour to pro-actively moderate its economic strategy after 1989.

The second strand focuses on changes in the character of capitalism. The linking of ideological movement to changes in the character of capitalism has a distinguished lineage. Eduard Bernstein, a German socialist, claimed at the end of the nineteenth century that prosperity had curbed capitalism's propensity to generate crisis, and brought the proletariat material advances that drew it away from revolutionary ambitions (see Bernstein 1961). These trends, coupled with growth of the middle classes, Bernstein concluded, required social democrats to moderate their ideological appeals.

Similar arguments recur in relation to Labour. For Crosland (1963: 63) capitalism had been transformed by the mid-1950s, demanding 'an explicit admission that many of the old dreams are either dead or realised'. Prosperity had remedied the abuses and inefficiencies of the capitalist system. In addition full employment, the transfer of economic power to the State, trade unions and managers rendered the ideological totems of the past redundant. Nationalisation and material redistribution were anachronisms; creating genuine social equality and a classless society should become Labour's new mission.

Such claims also re-emerged in later years. Writing in 1989, the authors of *New Times* argued that 'much of the labour and democratic movement still rests upon a world which is fast disintegrating beneath its feet. It still lives in the last house of a terrace which is slowly being demolished and redeveloped' (Hall and Jacques 1989: 24). On this account an epochal shift from Fordism to post-Fordism was generating a new economic, social, political and cultural order which necessitated ideological renovation of Labourism. But most arguments of this genre thereafter were typically more pessimistic, proposing that changes in capitalism created new and fundamental constraints upon social democracy. For Smith (1994) such transformations of the economic environment drastically limited Labour's ideological options. Similarly, Crouch (1997) viewed ideological revision as inescapable given the redundancy of demand management and Fordist production, the internationalisation of capital and the emergence of new occupational groups. John Gray, however, provided the most vivid exposition of how the new international economy impelled ideological change. For Gray (1996: 32), '[e]conomic globalisation removes, or weakens, the policy levers whereby social democratic governments sought to bring about social solidarity and egalitarian distribution', prohibiting full employment through deficit financing, constraining redistribution via taxation and restricting welfare state expenditures.

A third materialist explanatory strategy focuses on changes in the class structure, in particular changes in the class composition of the British electorate and their electoral implications for Labour. For Hobsbawm (1981), the 'forward march of Labour' had been halted by the early 1980s, given social changes to Labour's core electorate. Technological change, the rise of monopoly capitalism and improved living standards reduced the numbers and solidarity of the British working class, requiring Labour to reconsider its ideological position. Others drew attention also to the decline of Labour's core voters (working-class union members and council-house tenants) after 1964 (Heath and McDonald 1987), a trend subsequently confirmed up to the 1997 election (Heath, Jowell and Curtice 2001).

Such analyses of social change have been closely associated with accounts of attitudinal change within the electorate, with claims regarding embourgeoisment being particularly prominent. The basic argument here is that as manual workers achieve relatively high incomes they adopt characteristically middle-class lifestyles. Assimilated into middle-class society, these embourgeoisified proletarians become increasingly moderate politically, demanding parallel ideological responses from social democratic parties.

Within the general literature on political parties, Kirchheimer's 1966 ideologically bland catch-all parties are triggered by embourgeoisment, but within the literature on Labour the classic statement is Abrams, Rose and Hinden's *Must Labour Lose?* (1960). After the 1959 election they concluded that 'the Labour Party's traditional sources of support in the environment, in traditional values and party loyalties have been weakening' (1960: 97). Whereas the Conservatives succeeded in identifying themselves with the affluent society and its ascendant occupational groups, Labour was handicapped by its image as the representative of the working class. Electoral revival therefore demanded ideological renewal.

During the 1980s these arguments returned. For example, Radice (1992) located Labour's problems in its anachronistic image as a working-class party unattractive to upwardly mobile families, particularly those in southern England. Similarly, for Crewe, the non-manual workforce had expanded, but in addition social mobility placed increasing numbers of voters in cross-pressured class locations, leading to a haemorrhage of Labour supporters among the new skilled working class. Thus Crewe (1992: 96) argued: 'If Labour is ever again to form a secure majority government it must pitch camp on the "affluent centre ground".'

Ideational strategies

A second approach to understanding Labour's ideological shifts is to refer to ideational factors. Here two broad sets of explanations emerge.

The first strand has been concerned with dominant ideas. The 'Labourist' critique of the party has identified a dominant bourgeois intellectual tradition in Britain which constrains and moderates Labour ideologically. For Anderson (1992: 33), for example, Britain's exceptional path of development (the absence of a genuine bourgeois revolution; its pioneering role as the first industrial nation; its extensive imperial possessions and a stature as an undefeated nation in two world wars) 'produced a proletariat distinguished by an immovable corporate class consciousness', intent on pursuing its ends within the existing social order. This underpinned Labour's reformist trajectory and generated a traditionalist and empiricist intellectual paradigm which left radical ideas stillborn inside and outside the party.

Saville (1973: 225) similarly laments the British Left's incapacity 'to develop and maintain a critique of contemporary society that seriously grappled with its dominant ideas'.

Others, however, attempt to understand more discrete historical episodes of ideological movement by reference to dominant ideas. Hay and Watson (1998) propose that Labour adopted a particular set of *arguments* about globalisation, and it is these dominant ideas rather than the purported economic changes in themselves that underpin recent ideological changes. Heffernan also argues that dominant political beliefs proved critical during the 1980s: as '[n]eo-liberal political attitudes ... pervaded the body politic, colonising intellectual territory inch by inch', so Labour was impelled to recast its ideology in keeping with its new ideological environment (1997: 46).

The second strand in the ideational approach concentrates on the role of intellectuals. Here Desai (1994) offers the most systematic analysis. To Desai, political circumstances after the 1930s allowed intellectuals a powerful voice in the party. On this account the revisionism of the 1950s originated among the intellectuals of the Fabian Society, *Socialist Commentary* and *Encounter* and prospered because these intellectuals enjoyed the patronage of the leadership, an intellectual ascendancy within the party and a close alliance with union leaders. However, it is Driver and Martell (1997, 1998) who most clearly identify the role of intellectuals in the genesis of New Labour. They have noted the influence of communitarian political philosophers including Etzioni, MacIntyre and Sandel. Moreover, they highlight the ideational influence of Ulrich Beck, Zygmunt Bauman and Anthony Giddens in the development of New Labour's welfare and social policies. Indeed, Giddens, as the principal theoretician of the 'Third Way', is perhaps the chief inspiration for New Labour's most recent ideological departures.

Electoral strategies

The electoral imperatives for ideological movement constitute a third approach. In the literature on political parties, Downs (1957: 295) provides the classic statement: 'parties in democratic politics are analogous to entrepreneurs in a profit seeking economy ... they formulate whatever policies they believe will gain most votes', leading them to contest the electoral middle ground where most voters are located. Accordingly, Labour's ideological shifts can be viewed simply as successive attempts to capture this electoral middle ground.

Alternatively, Przeworski (1985) argues that the de-radicalisation of social democracy emerges from the structure of choices generated by electoral politics. For Przeworski pursuing politics through parliamentary institutions necessitated that social democrats reconcile themselves to the absence of a proletarian numerical majority in each Western nation. This required social democrats to seek multiclass alliances and abandon radical class-based politics. Furthermore, such alliances ruptured the proletariat–party link. Recruiting middle-class allies diluted the class identity of social democracy's working-class constituency: working-class support was lost and the predisposition to ideological moderation was further reinforced.

In the literature specifically devoted to Labour, electoral pressures are taken almost as given, albeit rarely understood, via the systematised approach of Downs and Przeworski. For some, however, Labour's ideological movements are viewed almost wholly in terms of responses to electoral pressures. For example, for Taylor (1997) the party's policy review, undertaken after its 1987 election defeat, sought to secure electoral victory by formulating a set of alternative policies and demonstrating its competence to form a government. For Leys (1997: 17), similarly, ideological changes after 1989 were 'overwhelmingly driven by the need for electoral recovery'.

Institutional strategies

A fourth strategy concentrates on intra-party agents and actors. Here we encounter embourgeoisment again, with claims that embourgeoisified social democratic leaders are responsible for ideological change. The most renowned account is that of Michels (1959: 163), for whom the 'iron law of oligarchy' held that sophisticated organisation (an inevitable response to the recruitment of a mass membership) guaranteed the leadership's dominance over and separation from the membership, impressing 'upon the most revolutionary of parties an indelible stamp of conservatism'. Yet, this became inevitable with the deproletarianising of the party's most capable members who, upon elevation to the party hierarchy, accustomed themselves to bourgeois salaries, lifestyles and outlooks and abandoned their militancy.

Similar arguments occasionally surface in the literature on Labour. For example, Guttsman (1963) considers that after 1918 Labour moderated its position as it attracted individuals from the intelligentsia and the new middle class. Bauman (1972) drew similar conclusions, observing how after 1922 Labour became reliant upon the political expertise of the professional classes. This, coupled with the embourgeoisment of the working class itself, meant that 'the Labour Party began to adopt a conservative attitude towards the structure and the social hierarchy within which the advancement both of the workers as a class and of workers and their sons as individuals was being accomplished' (1972: 286).

Biographies, autobiographies and memoirs of leading party members also focus pre-eminently on the intra-party dynamics of ideological change. For example, Brivati (1996: 138) contends: 'It was Gaitskell more than any single individual who ensured that the British labour movement did not take the Bevanite road.' However, many non-biographical accounts of Labour's ideological movement also stress intra-party factors. For example, Haseler (1969) accounts for revisionism in the 1950s by reference to right-wing dominance of the parliamentary Labour Party (PLP) and the unions, and Gaitskell's own predilections as leader. Both Hatfield's 1978 study of Labour's leftwards shift in the early 1970s and Wickham-Jones's 1996 analysis of the development of the 'alternative economic strategy' draw attention to the machinations of factions and individuals within the National Executive Committee. Similarly, Hughes and Wintour (1990) account for the policy review by reference to the decisions of key individuals in the party's highest echelons.

The party leadership's role in ideological change has also exercised the party's left-wing critics. Miliband in particular proposes that right-wing leaders betrayed the radicalism of the party's rank and file and the British working class. For Miliband (1972: 373) the party's 'leaders are not socialists who for some reason or other have lost their way and who can be brought back to the true path by persuasion or pressure. They are bourgeois politicians with, at best, a certain bias towards social reform.' Miliband conceded that the Left could win concessions. However, the leadership's 'absolute determination to "fight and fight and fight again" to save the party they love – to save it from socialist policies that is' – guaranteed that accommodations were temporary and that radical commitments quickly evaporated (Miliband 1977: 47).

Finally, there are those who have drawn attention to the impulses for ideological moderation that follow entry into the corridors of political power. In particular, Tony Benn, Richard Crossman, Barbara Castle, Brian Sedgemore and Michael Meacher 'have popularized a left-wing version of *Yes, Minister*, in which a devious and conspiratorial Whitehall bureaucracy represents a formidable obstacle to the achievement of Labour's socialist programme' (Theakston 1992: ix).

Synthetic strategies
The approaches considered above are not mutually exclusive. Indeed there have been attempts to synthesise them. For example, within the general literature on political parties Panebianco (1988) proposes that ideological change arises from both exogenous and endogenous factors. For Panebianco, such dynamics have three distinct phases. First, the party is thrown into crisis by an environmental event, for example, electoral defeat. This triggers a second phase where the coalition leading the party is discredited. Finally, a new governing coalition emerges which, to consolidate its control of the party, seeks to change party rules and goals.

Within the literature on social democracy three synthetic accounts which seek to explain differing patterns of ideological change in West European social democratic parties stand out. For Koelble (1991), social democratic parties are faced with new economic conditions, social change and a New Right critique of their governmental practice. However, Koelble proposes that responses to these conditions are mediated by party structures; particularly the extent to which activists and unions hinder leadership-led ideological innovation.

Kitschelt (1994) argues that a new dimension of libertarian–authoritarian party competition has emerged, while the traditional socialist–capitalist axis of electoral competition has ratcheted rightwards. For Kitschelt party responses to this environment are determined principally by institutional factors, particularly the organisational flexibility of the party, the degree of leadership autonomy and the political sentiments of members. However, Kitschelt also introduces ideational factors, suggesting that choices of political strategy are constrained by the party's existing political traditions.

Finally, Hamilton (1989) formulates a complex model that considers characteristics of the state, the labour movement and the economic, political and electoral environments, and intra-party factors. This is best illustrated by Hamilton's explanation of Labour's ideological shifts between 1951 and 1964. At that time party divisions, the intensification of the Cold War and Gaitskell's election as leader all facilitated ideological revision. In addition, an increasingly affluent society was emerging. However, two factors are deemed pre-eminent. Firstly, winning floating votes required ideological moderation. Secondly, revisionists skilfully manipulated the oligarchic characteristics of party institutions to win the institutional supremacy necessary to revise Labour's ideology.

Many accounts focusing on Labour also combine explanatory themes. For example, for Thompson (1993) electoral pressures and cultural changes, particularly a shift from collectivism to consumerism that eroded the labour movement's solidarity, triggered ideological change in the 1950s. For Shaw (1994), however, Labour's ideological shifts since the 1980s are explained by three sets of variables. Shaw argues that the political environment, particularly the rise of the Social Democrat Party (SDP), the vigorous competition for working-class votes and an ideologically buoyant New Right demanded ideological movement. These variables found parallel pressures in the economic environment, particularly globalisation, the redundancy of Keynesianism and the curtailed economic jurisdiction of the nation state. Finally, intra-party dynamics, particularly the marginalising of the Labour Left, facilitated ideological change.

Assessing the explanatory strategies

The merits of these explanatory strategies can now be considered. In the space available here only a very general assessment can be undertaken. Nonetheless, it should be recognised that many of these studies offer important insights for our understanding of Labour's ideological trajectory. Yet, equally, a number of general problems are evident.

The accounts offered above operate with very different explanatory ambitions. Several, implicitly or explicitly, endeavour to provide a comprehensive theory of Labour's ideological shifts. Yet such general theories struggle to provide convincing explanations of the more discrete episodes of ideological change. For example, Marxist scholars have viewed Labour's ideological shifts as instalments in the party's fundamental predisposition towards reformism. However, this focus leaves them poorly equipped to explain the admittedly exceptional but significant periods when Labour's ideology has been reshaped to express more radical ambitions.

In addition we also find that many accounts focus on a relatively narrow range of ideological issues, often economic management and public ownership. Yet it is not clear that factors which explain revision of part of Labour's ideological commitments can explain the broader range of ideological revisionism. For example, economic globalisation may have driven recent ideological changes, but that analysis surely has greater explanatory purchase in relation to the party's economic strategy than it enjoys in relation to ideological changes in areas such as defence, law and order or constitutional matters.

In addition a further general difficulty emerges in the relationship between structure and agency. Materialist, ideational and electoral explanatory strategies account for Labour's ideological trajectory in factors exogenous to the party. But these explanations operate at considerable distance from the institutional processes and agents within the party. Consequently there is a tendency for such works to degenerate into determinist, even teleological, explanations in which actors within the party are seemingly without consequence.

Yet institutional accounts typically bend the stick an equal distance in the opposite direction. Here the interaction of intra-party actors becomes the focus of analysis. But attention to the micro-practices of ideological change typically lacks an understanding of how exogenous constraints and opportunities interact with the ideological intentions of these actors. Accordingly, we are often left with the impression that ideological movement is an autistic process engineered exclusively within the hermetically sealed portals of the party's headquarters, the Palace of Westminster, Downing Street and Whitehall.

Beyond these general considerations, difficulties also arise which are specific to each of the main explanatory strategies discussed above.

I considered above claims that Labour's ideological movements are responses to capitalist pressure. Four observations are pertinent.

- It is unclear that Labour's objectives and the preferences of capital need always irrevocably conflict.
- Such accounts arguably overstate the potency of British capital, which has only exceptionally achieved the common consciousness, coherence and conspiratorial capacities necessary to enforce demands on Labour.
- Such arguments are frequently ahistorical. In particular, the Attlee Government failed to assuage capitalist fears yet succeeded in enacting significant social reforms.
- Even if these considerations are dismissed, an alternative strategy is available to Labour. Thus Labour could respond to capitalist demands not by capitulation but by demonstrating the promise of a radical programme to strengthen the British economy (Hay 1997).

Claims that Labour's ideological shifts are responses to changes in the character of capitalism are also contentious. If we momentarily accept that globalisation has transformed the economic environment it nevertheless seems unduly deterministic to propose that acceptance of neo-liberal economics followed with inevitability. Indeed, Labour's alternative economic strategy was a response to these developments, and since it was never unequivocally implemented in office it seems precipitate to foreclose it as a rational alternative. Equally, although continental social democratic parties have also redesigned their economic strategies the approach of some of them suggests scope for ideological discretion. The Parti Socialiste, for example, has approached globalisation more critically than has New Labour, seeking to protect workers from its pernicious effects (Goes 2000).

If, however, we adopt a sceptical approach to globalisation (for example, along the lines of Hirst and Thompson 1996), there is evidence that leftist governments do not automatically incur the wrath of financial markets, and also that globalisation is not a novel process. Indeed, it might be argued that the UK economy has always been internationally orientated and vulnerable to external shocks. If this is accepted then the economic constraints currently faced by Labour are little different from those faced by the 1964–70 and 1974–79 Governments. This suggests that New Labour's accommodation to neo-liberalism can be no more directly read off the economic environment than can Old Labour's dirigiste economic strategies.

Finally, Coates and Hay (2000) have shown that since 1997 Labour ministers have presented globalisation not as a deterministic process to which political actors were inevitably forced to concede (as was argued in opposition) but as a contingent tendency to be promoted and defended against critics and sceptics. This implies that compliance with the constraints of globalisation is a process that is as much a matter of intellectual conviction as it is an accommodation to material 'realities'.

Explanations focused on changes in class structure are also problematical. Claims that embourgeoisment drives ideological reappraisal share similar myths of a golden past and insistences upon novelty and determinism. As Goldthorpe, Lockwood, Bechhofer and Platt (1968) originally demonstrated, and as Tiratsoo (1991: 50) has argued in relation to the 1950s, the case for a 'fundamental transformation in working class attitudes at this time is remarkably thin'. Enthusiasts for the embourgeoisment thesis overlooked the substantial number of the working class who denied Labour their votes in the past. Furthermore, as Tiratsoo has noted, Conservative electoral victories between 1951 and 1959 were narrow in terms of votes and originated in the collapse of the Liberal vote. Equally, more recent changes to the British social structure may also have been overestimated. Thus Heath, Jowell and Curtice (1992) found 'trendless fluctuation' rather than decisive evidence of class dealignment during the 1980s. Moreover, while they recognised that the growth of the middle class did present problems for Labour, they suggest it explained only half the decline in Labour's vote, the remainder being found in the shortcomings of Labour's general electoral strategy, its image and its reputation for fratricide, in addition to its ideology. Indeed, as their most recent work reminds us, 'support for radical values cannot be read off mechanically from social change' (Heath, Jowell and Curtice 2001: 29).

Nor are ideational explanations without problems. In particular, there is a tendency to overestimate the torpor of British intellectuals (Thompson 1965). The fortunes of British intellectuals have ebbed and flowed (Shils 1972) and at several historical moments intellectuals have provided radical ideas which Labour has adopted. Indeed, it is to be doubted that Labour's relatively radical ideological prospectuses of 1945, 1974 and 1983 can be wholly accounted for without acknowledging the contributions of intellectuals such as Keynes, Beveridge, Stuart Holland and E. P. Thompson.

As Labour is an electoral organisation it would be foolish to deny that electoral pressures affect the party's ideological dynamics. Yet electoral fortunes are determined by various factors aside from ideology. Those minded to employ electoral verdicts as the basis for ideological revision therefore face untangling the contribution of ideological commitments from party campaigning, image, leadership and its capacity to counter-attack its opponents.

It is also not obvious that Labour should respond to electoral unpopularity by ideological reappraisal. In the past this imperative did not always present itself. For example, the Wilson Report (1955) blamed Labour's election defeat of that year upon an organisation which remained 'at the penny farthing stage in a jet-propelled era'. In this the party was merely assimilating contemporary psephological wisdom which held that 'irrational forces' among the electorate required parties to improve organisational capacities to mobilise an already faithful core electorate.

However, even when this electoral strategy was abandoned it did not follow that the party should adopt a Downsian strategy. Politics is a process of persuasion, and opportunities arise for reshaping public opinion through argument (Dunleavy 1991). Thus, alongside preference-accommodating electoral strategies, in which ideologies are transformed to correspond with the beliefs of the electorate, preference-shaping strategies are available which preserve existing ideological commitments and meet the hostility of public opinion with efforts to erode the public distaste for these commitments.

Yet even when Labour has adopted a preference-accommodating strategy there have remained areas of its ideology that were not revised in accordance with this broad strategy, perhaps because these issues lacked electoral salience. For example, if we account for the shift from Old to New Labour in terms of preference accommodation, the party's embrace of European integration is puzzling since, as Tony Blair has acknowledged, the 'opinion polls probably would push us toward a sceptic approach' – an approach which he has denounced as 'folly' (*The Economist*, 8 April 1995).

Przeworski's 1985 account is also contentious. Firstly, Przeworski employs a highly restrictive definition of the working class that seems essential if his electoral trade-off is to function. Secondly, Przeworksi's model isolates working-class interests and delineates them as distinct from those of other classes. Yet it is unclear that full employment and an extensive welfare state, for example, are beneficial exclusively to the working class. Thirdly, Przeworksi relies for a class trade-off not on concrete statistical evidence but on estimates which, as Sainsbury (1990) has suggested, are somewhat eccentric. Indeed, her analysis of the Swedish Social Democrats suggests that it is possible to construct social democratic positions which appeal to both workers and non-workers.

Institutional explanations of the party's ideological trajectory are also problematical. Accounts referring to embourgeoisment of party members are as culpable of sociological determinism as those referring to the electorate. Indeed, embourgeoisment actually promoted the rise of the Labour Left in the 1970s as an influx of young, educated, public service professionals, radicalised trade unionists and feminists formed 'a more assertive rank and file . . . less deferential to parliamentarians (Right and Left!), more determined and persistent in its desire to achieve radical change' (Seyd 1987: 53).

The Left's analysis of leadership dominance enjoys somewhat firmer foundations. Successive studies have shown how party leaders have enjoyed a pre-eminence in party affairs through patronage, loyalty, control of disciplinary and decision-making procedures and habitual support from the trade unions, the NEC and the PLP. Equally, the claim that Labour leaders accept radical commitments under duress and then abandon them at opportune moments enjoys some confirmation. For example, most of the party's leadership were never reconciled to the alternative economic strategy (Wickham-Jones 1996) or to unilateral nuclear disarmament.

Studies of the party membership, however, undermine the claim that the leadership has habitually betrayed the radical instincts of the rank and file. Certainly constituency Labour Parties' (CLP) preferences have been overridden by union conference votes, frustrated by manipulation of conference procedures or wilfully ignored by the leadership. Yet there are also occasions when constituency delegates have willingly endorsed moderation of the party's ideology (Hindell and Williams 1962).

Neither need we accept the Left's view of 'the party as a wasted lion led . . . by the same old donkeys' (Bale 1999: 196), since leadership pre-eminence is neither absolute nor guaranteed. As Minkin (1978, 1991) has shown, party leaders have been forced to accommodate trade union preferences on various occasions. Nor should we neglect clear differences between leaders. For Gaitskell, Kinnock and Blair, for example, party leadership demanded an ideological lead, intolerance of dissent and full use of the resources available to the office in reshaping the party's ideology. Yet, others have been attentive to party unity and have inhibited ideological change. Attlee, for example, between 1951 and 1955, was even-handed in frustrating the ideological ambitions of both the Bevanites and the revisionists. Likewise, as Shadow Chancellor John Smith refused to abandon welfare benefits' increases and redistributive taxation, while as leader his commitment to universalism prevented 'modernisers' developing proposals for targeted welfare benefits.

Finally, evidence for Whitehall resistance is also equivocal. For every Benn, Crossman, Castle and Meacher there are figures such as Attlee, Morrison, Healey, Jenkins and Williams who lionise the neutrality and amenability of civil servants. It is also noteworthy that accounts of civil service resistance exclude the 1945–51 Governments (Theakston 1992). Indeed, the disappointments of later Labour governments can be accounted for by factors other than civil service opposition. For example, if the civil service is blamed for the 1974–79 Government's retreat from Benn's industrial strategy, we are apt to neglect the opposition of the Cabinet and of capital to both Benn and his proposals.

Conclusion: towards an alternative model of Labour's ideological dynamics

Tim Bale (1999: 192) has called for scholars of the party to develop accounts of Labour's past that are 'theoretically rooted, but empirically convincing and constructed'. As should now be clear, there are shortcomings in existing accounts of Labour's ideological dynamics which make Bale's exhortations particularly relevant to this area of the study of the Labour Party.

If we are to follow Bale an alternative model of Labour's ideological dynamics is necessary. Such a model must recognise two important insights at the outset. Firstly, ideological change must be unpacked into two distinct processes. Frequently ideological change is conceived as determining simply the contents of ideological commitments. However, from the work of Heclo (1974) and Kingdon (1984) we can see that before ideological commitments are reshaped there is a prior dynamic which places particular axioms under question and therefore shapes the *agenda* for ideological change. This dynamic need not be identical to that shaping the *content* of ideological changes thereafter. For example, electoral imperatives may prompt reassessment of an existing ideological commitment but the substantive shaping of the new commitment may be better understood by reference to the institutional dynamics of the party.

Secondly, the ontological foundations of an alternative model – its theory of reality – should be considered. Here critical realist theory overrides the rigid dualism between structure and agency, identified above. (A full account of this perspective cannot be offered here; see Archer 1995; Bhaskar 1997; Marsh *et al.* 1997). Suffice it to say that critical realism views the relationships between structure, discourse and agency as irreducible and dialectical. Structures are viewed as imposing objective constraints on and opportunities for political actors. Yet these constraints and opportunities are also mediated by discourse, shaping political agents' interpretation of their social and structural environment and conditioning their calculations. Political actors remain ultimately 'causal', in so far as they are responsible for their own behaviour, but their decisions are conditioned by the constraints and opportunities imposed and afforded by their structural and discursive environment.

From these insights it follows that material factors cannot always be directly and authentically experienced by actors within the party. Moreover, no material condition can impact upon the process of ideological change without a parallel process of interpretation. As Kingdon (1984: 115) notes:

> There is a difference between a condition and a problem . . . Conditions become defined as problems because we come to believe that we should do something about them. Problems are not simply the conditions or external events themselves; there is also a perceptual, interpretative element.

Of themselves, therefore, material conditions rarely determine the content of ideological changes. For example, a rising level of crime, recognised politically as a problem, in itself dictates the adoption neither of punitive penal policies nor of enhanced policies for crime prevention. As such, material conditions serve principally to shape the *agenda* of ideological change.

Belief systems and intellectual constructs are essential to the calculations of actors within the party, allowing them to overcome conditions of imperfect knowledge. However, such dominant beliefs should also not be viewed as direct determinants of the content of ideological changes. Rather they establish constraints on the politically feasible options available to intra-party agents. Dominant ideas preserve particular issues and assumptions from contestation and inhibit alternative ideas entering the agenda of ideological change. Likewise, given their comparative advantage in the intellectual environment, agents face pressure to abandon inherited positions running counter to the pattern of dominant beliefs.

Political parties are office seeking, so that electoral considerations necessarily intervene. Yet intra-party actors face acute difficulties in discovering and interpreting the public's ideological preferences and in drawing ideological conclusions from the electoral fortunes of the party. Furthermore, the imperative to refashion elements of the party's ideology depends on their overall salience within the public's ranking of the most important electoral issues. As such, public and electoral opinion certainly sensitises intra-party actors to the need to reconsider the party's ideological position. Yet, in shaping the content of the ideological changes that follow, public preferences usually provide only broad and vague recommendations and do not preclude other non-electoral considerations.

It is among the institutions, mechanisms, processes and actors of the party that ideological changes are initiated, alternatives considered, policy statements drafted, amended and voted upon. As such, it is here that the content of ideological changes should be seen as being principally shaped. Accordingly the preferences of agents, and the resources available to agents in this process, are of great significance. However, these actors are not autonomous in respect of their environment, nor are they bearers of structures; rather they interpret and respond to their environment.

Finally, the specific contexts in which ideological shifts arise must be considered. The material, ideational, electoral and intra-party environments are dynamic. For example, beliefs rise, achieve dominance, then fall and fragment. Within the party formal and informal relations of power may change. Moreover, the general strategic outlook of the party may shift, with choices between electoral strategies of preference-shaping and accommodation being particularly significant.

Such a model may not provide especially parsimonious explanations. But it does promise more nuanced accounts of ideological change, and it makes available to convincing analysis a wider range of the varied ideological shifts of the party than do existing theories. Indeed, such an approach may prove particularly valuable in reaching fresh understandings of the most recent ideological transformation of the party from 'Old' to 'New' Labour, a transformation that, as Kenny and Smith (2001: 234) suggest, is 'a complex political problem which requires a multidimensional and disaggregated interpretation'.

References

Unless indicated, the place of publication is London.

Abrams, M., Rose, R. and Hinden, R. (1960) *Must Labour Lose?* Harmondsworth

Anderson, P. (1992) *English Questions*, London and New York

Archer, M. (1995) *Realist Social Theory: The Morphogenetic Approach*, Cambridge

Bale, T. (1999) 'The logic of no alternative? Political scientists, historians and the politics of Labour's past', *British Journal of Politics & International Relations*, 1:2

Bauman, Z. (1972) *Between Class and Elite. The Evolution of the British Labour Movement: A Sociological Study*, Manchester

Bernstein, E. (1961) *Evolutionary Socialism*, New York

Bhaskar, R. (1997) *A Realist Theory of Science*

Brivati, B. (1996) *Hugh Gaitskell*

Coates, D. (1975) *The Labour Party and the Struggle for Socialism*, Cambridge

Coates, D. (1996) 'Labour governments: old constraints and new parameters', *New Left Review*, 219

Coates, D. and Hay, C. (2000) 'Home and away? The political economy of New Labour', paper presented at the Political Studies Association Annual Conference, April 2000, London

Crewe, I. (1992) 'On the death and resurrection of class voting: some comments *on How Britain Votes*', in Denver, D. and Hands, G. (eds) *Issues and Controversies in British Electoral Behaviour*, Hemel Hempstead

Crosland, C. A. R. (1963) *The Future of Socialism*

Crouch, C. (1997) 'The terms of the neo-liberal consensus', *Political Quarterly*, 68:4

Desai, R. (1994) *Intellectuals and Socialism – 'Social Democrats' and the British Labour Party*

Downs, A. (1957) *An Economic Theory of Democracy*, New York

Driver, S. and Martell, L. (1997) 'New Labour's communitarianisms', *Critical Social Policy*, 17:3

Driver, S. and Martell, L. (1998) *New Labour. Politics After Thatcherism*, Cambridge

Dunleavy, P. (1991) *Democracy, Bureaucracy and Public Choice: Economic Explanations in Political Science*

Goes, E. (2000) 'Blair and Jospin: two different paths for social democracy?' Paper presented at the Political Studies Association Annual Conference, London, April 2000

Goldthorpe, J. H., Lockwood, D., Bechhofer, F. and Platt, J. (1968) *The Affluent Worker: Political Attitudes and Behaviour*, Cambridge

Gray, J. (1996) *After Social Democracy: Politics, Capitalism and the Common Life*

Guttsman, W. L. (1963) *The British Political Elite*

Hall, S. and Jacques, M. (eds) (1989) *New Times: The Changing Face of Politics in the 1990s*

Hamilton, M. B. (1989) *Democratic Socialism in Britain and Sweden*

Haseler, S. (1969) *The Gaitskellites – Revisionism in the British Labour Party 1951–1964*

Hatfield, M. (1978) *The House the Left Built. Inside Labour Policy-Making 1970–75*

Hay, C. (1997) 'Anticipating accommodations, accommodating anticipations: the appeasement of capital in the "modernization" of the British Labour Party, 1987–1992', *Politics and Society*, 25:2

Hay, C. and Watson, M. (1998) 'The discourse of globalisation and the logic of no alternative: rendering the contingent necessary in the downsizing of New Labour's aspirations for government', in Dobson, A. and Stanyer, J. (eds) *Contemporary Political Studies 1998*, vol. 2, Nottingham

Heath, A. F., Jowell, R. M. and Curtice, J. K. (1992) 'The decline of class voting', in Denver, D. and Hands, G. (eds) *Issues and Controversies in British Electoral Behaviour*, Hemel Hempstead

Heath, A. F., Jowell, R. M. and Curtice, J. K. (2001) *The Rise of New Labour. Party Policies and Voter Choices*, Oxford

Heath, A. F. and McDonald, S. K. (1987) 'Social change and the future of the Left', *Political Quarterly*, 58:4

Heclo, H. (1974) *Modern Social Politics in Britain and Sweden*, New York

Heffernan, R. (1997) 'Ideology, practical politics and political consensus: thinking about the process of political change in the United Kingdom', in Stanyer, J. and Stoker, G. (eds) *Contemporary Political Studies 1997*, vol. 1, Nottingham

Hindell, K. and Williams, P. (1962) 'Scarborough and Blackpool: an analysis of some votes at the Labour Party Conferences of 1960 and 1961', *Political Quarterly*, 33:3

Hirst, P. and Thompson, G. (1996) *Globalization in Question. The International Economy and the Possibilities of Governance*, Cambridge

Hobsbawm, E. (1981) 'The forward march of Labour halted?', in Mulhern, F. and Jacques, M. (eds) *The Forward March of Labour Halted?*

Hughes, C. and Wintour, P. (1990) *Labour Rebuilt – the New Model Party*

Kenny, M. and Smith, M. J. (2001) 'Interpreting New Labour: constraints, dilemmas and political agency', in Ludlam, S. and Smith, M. J. (eds) *New Labour in Government*

Kingdon, J. W. (1984) *Agendas, Alternatives and Public Policies*, New York

Kirchheimer, O. (1966) 'The transformation of the Western European party systems', in La Palombara, J. and Weiner, M. (eds) *Political Parties and Political Development*, Princeton, NJ

Kitschelt, H. (1994) *The Transformation of European Social Democracy*, Cambridge

Koelble, T. A. (1991) *The Left Unravelled – Social Democracy and the New Left Challenge in Britain and West Germany*, Durham

Labour Party (1955) *Report of the 54th Annual Conference*

Leys, C. (1997) 'The British Labour Party since 1989', in Sasson, D. (ed.), *Looking Left. European Socialism After the Cold War*

Marsh, D., Buller, J., Hay, C., Johnston, J., Kerr, P., McAnulla, S. and Watson, M. (1999) *Post-war British Politics in Perspective*, Cambridge

Michels, R. (1959) *Political Parties*, New York

Miliband, R. (1972) *Parliamentary Socialism*

Miliband, R. (1977) 'The future of socialism in England', *The Socialist Register 1977*

Minkin, L. (1978) *The Labour Party Conference. A Study in the Politics of Intra-Party Democracy*

Minkin, L. (1991) *The Contentious Alliance. Trade Unions and the Labour Party*, Edinburgh

Panebianco, A. (1988) *Political Parties: Organisation and Power*, Cambridge

Panitch, L. (1976) *Social Democracy and Industrial Militancy. The Labour Party, the Trade Unions and Incomes Policy, 1945–1974*, Cambridge

Przeworski, A. (1985) *Capitalism and Social Democracy*, Cambridge

Radice, G. (1992) *Southern Discomfort*

Sainsbury, D. (1990) 'Party strategies and the electoral trade-off of class-based parties – a critique and application of the "dilemma of socialism"', *European Journal of Political Research*, 18:1

Saville, J. (1973) 'The ideology of Labourism', in Benewick, R., Berki, R. N. and Parekh, B. (eds) *Knowledge and Belief in Politics – the Problem of Ideology*

Seyd, P. (1987) *The Rise and Fall of the Labour Left*

Shaw, E. (1994) *The Labour Party Since 1979. Crisis and Transformation*

Shils, E. (1972) *The Intellectuals and the Powers and Other Essays*, Chicago

Smith, M. J. (1994) 'Understanding the "politics of catch up": the modernization of the Labour Party', *Political Studies*, 42:4

Taylor, G. R. (1997) *Labour's Renewal: The Policy Review and Beyond*

Theakston, K. (1992) *The Labour Party and Whitehall*

Thompson, E. P. (1965) 'The peculiarities of the English', *The Socialist Register 1965*

Thompson, W. (1993) *The Long Death of British Labourism*

Tiratsoo, N. (1991) 'Popular politics, affluence and the Labour Party in the 1950s', in Gorst, A., Johnman, L. and Lucas, W. S. (eds) *Contemporary British History 1931–1961: Politics and the Limits of Policy*

Wickham-Jones, M. (1995) 'Anticipating social democracy, pre-empting anticipations: economic policy-making in the British Labour Party, 1987–1992', *Politics and Society*, 23:4

Wickham-Jones, M. (1996) *Economic Strategy and the Labour Party. Politics and Policy-Making, 1970–83*

2

'What kind of people are you?' Labour, the people and the 'new political history'

Lawrence Black

Like their subject, historians of Labour have tended to be attached to tradition and sceptical of novelty – in short, rather conservative. Newer tendencies are nonetheless evident. These result, in part, from changes in Labour. New Labour's constitutional reforms, its engagement with issues of national identity and communication skills have been concurrent with recent work on the party's past in such areas (Chadwick 1999; Ward 1998; Wring forthcoming). These historiographical shifts have been accompanied in terms of method by what for the past decade or so has been known as the 'new political history'. This embraces work associated with the 'linguistic turn' and more generally a rethinking of the category of 'the political' (Lawrence 1998: chapter 3; Stedman Jones 1983a).

These developments have raised numerous questions about established ways of understanding Labour's history. It questions the extent to which politics can be seen as the upshot of social forces – an assumption familiar in studies relating Labour's fortunes and character to (primarily) the industrial working class, one famously advanced in Eric Hobsbawm's essay 'The forward march of labour halted?' (Hobsbawm 1981). This 'electoral sociology' approach is evident in arguments about the growth of class politics as an ingredient in Labour's rise, notably in work by McKibbin, Hobsbawm (Kirk 1991) and Laybourn (1995). It features, too, in debates about Labour's 'decline' since the 1950s, in political science literature about class dealignment, fragmentation of values and the diminished size of the working class. Common to both are the ideas that voters' attitudes are essentially shaped by economic and social structures, that they are politically socialised by those structures and that successful parties must respond to such developments (Hindess 1971).

Balancing this stress on the influence of social and economic change has been a recent emphasis on political factors – party, policies and ideas. Curtice (1994: 41–2) has argued that the British party system was in important ways immune to social change and that 'rather than the helpless plaything of sociological forces, post-war British politics has been vitally shaped by political choices'. Labour's early growth, post-war difficulties and renewal as New Labour were, then, much more of its own making. By this model voters made an 'instrumental' or 'rational choice' of the party whose policy or governing performance was most likely to advance or had best defended their interests. Akin to electoral sociology, a close relationship between voters and parties is supposed. Attempts to interrelate expressive and instrumental interpretations have made the manner in which Labour addressed social change the factor that influenced attitudes towards the party (Fielding 1995a: 19–31; Heath, Jowell and Curtice 1985: 170–5).

The 'new political history' shares much with the latter approach. It emphasises parties' attempts to build constituencies of support by the interpretation they place on change and 'interests'. As Lawrence and Taylor (1997: 18) maintain, critical here is that voters' interests and identities are not assumed to pre-exist their political expression and that parties should be seen as attempting 'to construct viable forms of social and political identity'. Schwarz (1998: 154) argues that 'in part the job of politics is to speak to those whose social positions are widely divergent and to project an imaginary community in which the people would wish to imagine themselves'. Parties are not reactive, but active agents. Language is important in this, but so are political communication, internal and informal party culture, and how these define and construct a party's audience – in short, political culture.

Besides theoretical shifts, regional studies stressing the specificity of social structures and the contingencies of local politics (like organisation or electoral marginality), and excavating a sense of popular politics in practice have further suggested that social explanations will not alone suffice in explaining political character and patterns (Savage 1987; Tiratsoo 2000).

But the 'new political history' does more than counter social explanations by restoring agency to party and political factors. Most ambitiously, at issue is what the category 'politics' encapsulates and how it is represented and contested. Germane to this chapter, the proximity (besides the ordering) of party–voter relations are problematised – although in the hands of Lawrence and Taylor (1997) electoral sociology's influence over historians is more rigorously critiqued than is rational choice (despite this also supposing a close fit between voters and party). Equations of the two are destabilised by seeing politics as a mutative category – whose methods, audiences and contexts were fluid. Situating 'politics' more broadly acknowledges its limits, its often non-pivotal place in everyday life and the dissonance as much as the dialogue between politics and the popular.

The 'new political history' alerts historians to the manifold relations between politics and the people. If parties are more than reflectors of social change, voters are more than passive receptors of ideas. The ability of parties to construct or mobilise support was not limitless. Parties were not at liberty to construct politics irrespective of their supposed audience and were also constrained by their lack of resources and by the resistance of voters to party appeals. Close correlation between party and people is further tempered by their partial knowledge of each other. Berrington (1992) suggests that there was a 'dialogue of the deaf' between political elites and the electorate, each working with perceptions of the other informed by myth, hunch and assumption.

Voting, then, might be regarded as a compromise, representing some, not all, 'interests'. Hobsbawm (1982: 27) has argued that 'modern political choice is not a constant process of selecting men or measures, but a single or infrequent choice between packages, in which we buy the disagreeable part of the contents because there is no other way of getting the rest'. (Hobsbawm adds that while his argument 'applies to all parties . . . non-communist ones have generally made things easier for their intellectual adherents by refraining from formal commitments on such subjects as genetics or the composition of symphonies'.) For historians, votes are then a weak guide to how well a party's version of events is received, since many voters have an imperfect knowledge of parties – and even where voters are more conversant with parties votes cannot be read as a full endorsement of everything a party stands for. Thus parties may enjoy electoral success with a fragile, rather than mass, popular following. Organisation and communication were in this respect as vital components of political discourse as were policy and rhetoric.

Given this relative autonomy of politics, it follows that what a party says about social change is a more reliable guide to that party and its vision of its constituency than to social change. Also, how parties conceived of the people was at least as important to understanding politics as was what the people were *really* like. As Lawrence (1997: 97) suggests, 'the perception of social reality among an imperfectly informed elite [of politicians] mattered far more than the objective processes of structural change taking place around them'.

This is not far removed from a 'high politics', or 'primacy of politics', approach. In this the 'centre of attention', as one of its practitioners – Bentley (1996: 13) – has outlined, are the preoccupations of leading politicians. This focus on the 'people at the top', policy-making circles and parliamentary elites, while confined to a narrow sample of opinion, was conscious, like the 'new political history', of the self-defining aspect to politics – that it was more than a signal of external social factors. It was the intellectual universe and assumptions of politicians (including the notion that politics was ultimately a meter of social change) that were vital.

As Morgan (1983: 285–7) comments, this approach 'applied most naturally to the established Gilbertian world of the Conservative and Liberal parties'. It was of less value for understanding Labour, which conceived of itself as a grass-roots movement, countering 'from below' this very establishment and privilege. In other ways, institutional studies of Labour centring on the balance of power between Left, Right and unions, or emphasising how Labour has become mired in 'parliamentarism', have been similarly sourced (from party conference, parliament and leading figures and thinkers) and have duplicated something of the 'high' approach.

One interpretation of Labour thus questioned is the left-wing critique that Labour(ism) thwarted the radical potential of the working class. In accounts, like Miliband's 1961 *Parliamentary Socialism*, of Labour's limited progress towards socialism, popular opinion is a strong, silent presence. *Pace* Miliband, recent work on Labour and popular attitudes, like Fielding, Thompson and Tiratsoo's *England Arise!* (1995: 211), has asked why the view 'that the people's politics may have inhibited Labour's attempt to build socialism has never been seriously countenanced' by historians. Such revisionism has been characterised by critics as 'blaming the working class for the failings of the Labour leadership' (Thorpe 1997: 4).

The 'new political history' is, then, useful in understanding Labour within a less reductive framework than either the 'high' (emphasising elite influence) or 'from below' (privileging subaltern forces) approaches and in more novel terms than the Left–Right positions adopted within Labour. Attentiveness to the interactions of popular and 'high' politics also entails a more catholic range of sources.

But for all that there remains common territory, as Pedersen (2002: 40–4) suggests, between the 'new political history' of Lawrence and Taylor and recent developments in 'high politics'. The focus on political culture stems from more than just the linguistic turn or critiques of Marxist and social-based accounts of politics. Moreover, anticipations of the newer approaches – notably alertness to the fragility of voter–party relations (if uncertain of how to treat this) – are evident in older accounts. I illustrate this by mining an intentional mix of historical works to probe the novelty as much as the uses of newer approaches. In addition, proposing a more contingent relationship between Labour and the people, something I contend was more generic to politics than historians have generally allowed and more than simply a function of differences between labour movement and working-class culture, I argue that Labour has often imagined the people to be a brake on its progress.

Labour and the people

Touring England in 1954, journalist and social commentator Harry Hopkins encountered classic immigrant city politics in Liverpool: 'rafts bound together by strands of race, religion, sectional interests and jealousy, afloat on an ocean of ignorance and apathy'. His critical observations on voters were shared by and acquired from local politicians. Of a Labour MP on a depressed housing estate – who otherwise could 'not be accused of a lack of sympathy with the working-class tenants' – Hopkins asked: 'Why not plant trees?' The MP replied: 'Trees? Oh, they'd pull 'em up in no time. Why, you cannot even keep a light bulb in a corridor two minutes' (1957: 133–4, 124).

Such expressions of disappointment in the people, for their failure to live up to the vision and hopes socialists had of them, were legion. Labour's relations with the people were troublesome for a party claiming to be *The Voice of the People* (Labour Party 1956). As one local activist bluntly put it, Labour canvassers had to 'learn to suffer fools gladly or they would go crackers' (Lamb 1953: 190–2).

Disaffection with the people – the supposed agents of socialism or the beneficiaries of Labour's efforts – is recognisable in Bevin's annoyance at their 'poverty of desire' (Drucker 1979: 21) or Douglas Jay's refrain that 'the man from Whitehall really does know better what is good for the people than the people themselves' (1937: 317). It is also an age old disaffection. Bevin's phrase was borrowed from John Burns who in a 1902 pamphlet – 'Brains Better than Bets or Beer' – argued that 'the curse of the working class is the fewness of their wants, the poverty of their desires' (quoted in Waters 1990: 47).

Sometimes it wasn't so much their *lack* of desire as what the workers *did* desire that concerned socialists. The mass media (a particular villain) was held to be not only deceiving people, but pandering to their trivial interests. *The Daily Chloroform* and the *Obscurer* were popular papers in Tressell's symbolically titled setting for *The Ragged Trousered Philanthropists*, 'Mugsborough'. In 1921, former Independent Labour Party (ILP) activist Shaw Desmond's equally instructively titled *Labour: The Giant with Feet of Clay* quoted Robert Blatchford arguing that what 'was troubling the factory girl was not the downtrodden proletariat or theory behind International Socialism, but . . . what the Duke said to the Duchess in the conservatory' (1921: 38).

Labour was as uneasy as the Conservatives at the prospects of mass democracy after 1918. Ramsay MacDonald had long worried at the fitness of Britons to participate in democracy, believing them too swayed by emotion or mass psychology. Social progress required reform of the people – 'You can't make a silk purse out of a sow's ear' was how he put it in 1919 (quoted in Macintyre 1977: 483). Labour was also disappointed not to reap greater electoral benefits from the expanded suffrage – in *The Faith of a Democrat* (1928) Philip Snowden complained: 'the people for whom [the socialist] works and sacrifices are often indifferent and seldom show any gratitude' (quoted in Macintyre 1977: 479).

If *The Ragged Trousered Philanthropists* is any guide – as its enduring popularity with the Left suggests it to be – such was their disdain at popular ignorance that socialists were prone to doubt the entitlement to vote of many. 'With feelings of contempt' for his workmates' conversation, the socialist Owen berated Cross (for admitting 'I don't never worry my 'ed about politics'): 'You are not fit to vote' (Tressell 1991: 21–7). Such prejudices were still aired privately after 1918. For a member of the Socialist Vanguard Group, a 1940s' Labour sect, it seemed contrary to socialism that 'the ignorant masses should be able to veto the decisions of the more intelligent few' (Hadfield 1946). More common were calls to make voting compulsory, in despair at apathy. A Labour canvasser in Lowestoft during the 1950s felt that this would allow time for 'the important work of political education', and dissentients concurred with the aim of establishing voting as a 'social obligation' (Lowestoft Labour Party 1958).

Even at the apogée of Labour's success in the 1940s, *England Arise!* has argued, popular attitudes proved resistant to the sorts of moral transformation the party's socialism attempted and envisaged. Popular pastimes were subject to criticism. In the affectionate 1951 account *This Football Business* – applauding the 'brilliant football' of 'Middlesbrough and Spurs' – Huddersfield MP (and fan) Bill Mallalieu outlined less sports-friendly thinking, prone to surface on the Left. Reviewing 'the spectators', he noted that some thought 'watching is a sign of decadence, that watching other people play instead of playing oneself is demoralising, that the post-war increase in the number of spectators is a sign that Britain is riding down the circus path of Ancient Rome' (1951: 4–5). Mallalieu's Bevanite colleague Ian Mikardo was more forthright, condemning gambling (and by inference gamblers) in *A Mug's Game* (1950). Baker (1996: 99, 119) claims that the Attlee Governments 'did not always consider that which interested the working class', like greyhound racing, 'to . . . be in the best interests of the working class', and they 'despaired of some aspects of the way of life of those they "represented"; politically but not socially'.

Nor did the Second World War always have the radical effect commonly supposed. In Wesker's 1960 play *I'm Talking About Jerusalem*, Ada announces that she
and Dave will give up politics after the war:

> I'm not so sure I love them [the people] enough to want to organize them . . . Six years
> . . . working with young girls who are . . . lipsticked, giggling morons . . . Dave's expe-
> rience is the same – fighting with men whom he says did not know what the war was
> about. Away from their wives they behaved like animals . . . the service killed any illu-
> sions Dave may have had about the splendid and heroic working class. (Quoted in
> Hayman 1970: 25)

Evidence suggests that these critical impulses peaked in the 1950s. Denis Healey
asked an audience during the Suez crisis: 'What kind of people are you to allow a
liar and a cheat to be your prime-minister?'(quoted in Epstein 1964: 140) Such
sentiments were most apparent in the Left's unease at popular affluence – consumerism, home ownership, television and 'pop' culture. For Dick Crossman, 'the
luxuries, gadgets, entertainments and packaged foodstuffs which so many workers
enjoy in our affluent societies' were 'irrelevant . . . immoral . . . vulgar' (quoted in
Dodd 1999: 171). No less than did poverty, affluence excited the Left's disdain. Dis-
approval of poverty slid easily into condescension of prosperity, those experiencing it and the popular tastes it was inferred to have revealed. J. B. Priestley's
derogatory synonym for the consumer society, 'admass', was shorthand also for the
masses' susceptibility to it. The equation was made countless times in Priestley's
New Statesman columns: 'If our papers are trivial . . . it is because our people are
trivial' (quoted in Black 2003: see chapters 4, 5 and 8).

The Left struggled to articulate a politics of pleasure. Dodd (1999: 172–3) has
suggested, noting the popularity with the Left of Hoggart's *The Uses of Literacy* and
its lament for passing working-class values, that Labour 'preferred its supporters
. . . heroically labouring rather than frivolously playing'. The Left's cultural and
leisure preferences, and its strictures on what the people needed, carried little
authority (and not a little authoritarianism) given the expansion of popular
choice. Need came more easily to its vocabulary than choice. 'Wrong' choices and
people's right to make them (rather than the 'right' choices being an obligation)
were the price of highly prized liberties in a liberal, pluralist society, not least in a
Cold War context (Weight 1994).

From the socialist mind emerged a familiar figure – the 'affluent worker' – a con-
sumerist progeny of the Labour Aristocrat, born as the empire passed away, but still
a signifier of the corrupting effects of capitalism and the corruptibility of the people
(Black 2003 124–54). As a construction of the socialist imagination the 'affluent
worker' was a recurring demon. The secretary of Oldham Labour Party estimated
in 1908 there were 'many hundreds of mill-workers in Oldham who own their own
houses, also have shares in mills and it is this class of workers that our opponents
play on'. To 'know that the working class in Oldham are . . . the best paid in Great
Britain' was to 'understand why we don't move so quickly' (Olechnowicz 2000: 10).

The idea that materialism corrupted or waylaid workers from exercising their
rightful political consciousness was accompanied by a host of less attractive

characters making clear socialist suspicions of the people: in the 1950s, 'Jimmy Green' (green by both name and political nature); and, between the wars, 'Henry Dubb' ('Quair' 1953: 139). The gendering of these epitomes relays something of the pre-1918 assumptions current in party culture, although women (notably as consumers) were regularly singled out for criticism. Francis (1997: 217) argues that Jay's 'Whitehall gentleman' revealed 'hidden assumptions about the essential "infantilism" of women'. According to Macintyre (1977: 487–8) Dubb 'represented the apathetic mass whom Labour could never convert', but also 'consoled the elect in their conviction that they were right and their audience manifestly dim-witted'. Despite projecting a less-than-flattering image of cloth-capped voters, Dubb featured in Labour propaganda. 'Labour's Own Press Campaign', securing *Daily Herald* sales, showed Dubb being clubbed on the head by a press baron – the cerebral consequences of buying the baron's paper (Labour Party and Trades Union Congress 1929).

Disappointment at post-war social change was a *leitmotif* of activist nostalgia. Arthur Barton depicted 'Uncle Jim' in his 1967 novel, *Two Lamps in Our Street*:

> He saw slums wiped out . . . council houses multiplied . . . a forest of television aerials and car of sorts at every other house . . . the bairns' bairns come down the street in pseudo-Edwardian finery where their ragged parents had played. And he puzzled over the emptiness of heart and mind that a security beyond his modest hopes had brought . . . An old fighter whose victory had turned sour . . . 'What went wrong, hinney?' he asked. (Quoted in McCord 1979: 260–1)

Annoyance at what the people *didn't* do, rather than what they *did*, remained common. Labour's *Leeds Weekly Citizen*'s columnist 'Candida' (1953) argued that on price rises the Conservatives were able to 'trick' the people, because too many 'expect so little of life and ask far, far too little'. It is in this context that Hobsbawm's review of Miliband's *Parliamentary Socialism* in *New Left Review* should be read. Agreeing that parliamentarism and its leaders ('sheep in sheep's clothing') constrained Labour's radicalism, he added that 'a fundamental weakness of the movement' was 'the damned modesty of the British worker's demands' (Hobsbawm 1961: 64–6).

If laments peaked in the 1950s, they were not extinct in later years. O'Farrell's blithe account (1998) of the 1980s' Labour Party shows that a range of prejudices and assumptions about lifestyle continued to flourish. Tony Benn was heard to express 'disgust at the vulgar decoration of recently purchased council houses' (Dodd 1999: 171). All told, this mode of thought calls to mind Brecht's 1952 poem *The Solution*:

> Stating that the people
> Had forfeited the confidence of the government
> And could win it back only
> By redoubled efforts. Would it not be easier
> In that case for the government
> To dissolve the people
> And elect another? (Quoted in Rosen and Widgery 1996: 95)

Short of so doing, what *could* Labour do if the people didn't behave as the party hoped? As argued here, it could castigate them. Those blaming voters for Labour's election defeat in 1959 reminded Hugh Gaitskell 'of Oscar Wilde's remark: '"The play was a great success, but the audience was a failure"' (Labour Party 1959: 106). The State, Jay's Whitehall experts, offered another recourse from the people's perceived shortcomings. Orwell highlighted the dilemma this posed: 'In the popular regard Labour is the party that stands for . . . a free health service . . . free milk for schoolchildren', he noted in 1949, 'rather than the party that stands for socialism' (quoted in Shelden 1992: 436–7). His fear was that without deeper popular support, Labour would be tempted to introduce change summarily. To Michael Young, the 1945 manifesto's chief author, Labour did seem to be erring from its supporters towards bureaucratic solutions, and he suggested a vacant cabinet seat to represent the 'unknown constituent' (*Guardian*, 16 January 2002). Herbert Morrison worried about the popular response to Labour's efforts and whether 'human imperfections will convert the dream of the reformers into just another bit of bureaucratic routine' (quoted in Fielding 1995b: 24). Public ownership, notably in 1950s' debates about commercial television, was in Labour's mind a device not only for economic democracy but for the cultural control and improvement of the people – to protect them (and Labour) from their own tastes (Black 2001).

England Arise! proposes that Labour was less bureaucratic than critics (Left and Right) have suggested. However, the Left's officiousness was not only a feature of its statism. A 1919 ILP poster, for instance, illustrated socialist change in terms of 'a grammar lesson' – the shift from 'my wealth' to 'our wealth' – that required the 'possessive case' be 'correctly used' (Independent Labour Party 1919). Clever as this was, the Left could easily come across as syntactic pedants or as self-righteous. Equally, attempts to encourage participation in civil society came up against the indifference of the majority and a generally unfavourable political culture. The fate met by alternative left-wing offerings hints at this. Travel, sports or cultural projects – from Clarion cyclists to Wesker's Centre 42 – invariably floundered against commercial competition and majority opinion or functioned as marginal sub-cultures alongside rather than counter to the mainstream.

Another response was to incorporate into its strategy the fallibilities Labour perceived in its audience. Tiratsoo (2000: 295–6) argues that as early as the 1920s Labour was aware of its limited appeal among urban workers and of the need to compound this with other support. Shifts in Labour's publicity (television, pollsters and modern marketing) from the 1960s took place as its circumspect opinion of voters lessened resistance to new techniques. Much as Labour disliked it, so it was argued, 'the average Labour-inclined ITV-viewing voter has got to be got at in the style to which he has become accustomed – simply, repetitively, irrationally' (Rowland 1960: 351). The weaknesses Labour perceived in its audience were to be an axis of its publicity (Black 2003: 155–87).

Theories

The New Left also theorised Labour's shortcomings in relation to those of the working class. Perry Anderson's article 'Origins of the present crisis' (1992: 33–7) proposed that 'in England a supine bourgeoisie produced a supine proletariat', with 'an immovable corporate class consciousness' but 'almost no hegemonic ideology'. This defensive consciousness and the paucity of theory were embodied in Labour, and its limitations were then for Anderson those of the material with which it worked. In short, 'the density and specificity of English working-class culture . . . limited its political range and checked the emergence of a more ambitious socialism'. Anderson's approach has been influential, notably on Stedman Jones's early work. Stedman Jones held that 'with the foundation of the Labour Party', in 1900, 'the now enclosed and defensive world of working-class culture had in effect achieved its apotheosis' (1983b: 238).

Concluding *Classes and Cultures*, McKibbin (1998: 534–5) echoes those themes. The reforming scope of the Attlee Governments was 'so circumscribed', McKibbin argues, because 'the expressed wishes of Labour voters were not much less circumscribed'. Labour's 1945 voters remained culturally conservative, more content with commercial culture than alternatives, and had little interest in reforming 'civil society'. Labour's failure was to not create a more conducive political culture – either constitutionally or by challenging the institutions and the mores at large in civil society.

Labour's social base, in short, governed its actions. This framework leaves little space for the frustrations expressed when Labour's ambitions conflicted with its constituency's, outlined in this chapter. But it does explain why, elsewhere, McKibbin (1990: 34–5, n.104) finds the 'popularity' of *The Ragged Trousered Philanthropists* 'almost inexplicable', given its critical tone towards working-class attitudes. Yet this was the very source of its popularity – that Tressell's socialist character Owen voiced the doubts many on the Left harboured about the masses, their tastes and struggles with these. 'Leninist tract' Tressell's work may be, but such cultural elitism and moral (not to mention political) vanguardism were not confined to Marxist circles.

The pervasiveness of these critical sentiments derives from their eclecticism. Fabian faith in the dispassionate expert and non-conformism are well-established parts of Labour's cultural make-up. Collini (1991: 83) has traced 'the slightly patronizing tone and somewhat aggressive personal austerity' that were 'distinctive features of many of the Labour Party's intellectuals . . . until at least the 1950s' to ideas of altruism and service that from the late Victorian period 'enjoyed a long life among "progressive" members of the educated class'. Another Victorian liberal inheritance was a belief in elite, 'high' culture above commercial, mass, popular culture (Waters 1990: 191–5).

Orwell's *The Road to Wigan Pier* (1937) mordantly imprecated the personal foibles (like dress or diet) of socialists, which he felt derived from Liberal non-conformism. The Left, as Wilson (1983) has it, long wore questions of fashion uneasily – whether discarding them as simply trivial and superficial or, donning the critical theory of the Frankfurt School, applying them in critique of mass culture. Its puritanism meant that 'the charge of socialist dreariness' stuck. Socialist bugbears have been various – Hollywood, alcohol, debt and suburbia, among others. Samuel (1988) has highlighted attempts to escape materialist living, moral fads – the 'simple life', temperance, social purity – in socialist sub-culture, arguing that socialists were a 'people apart', convinced that they knew better – moral absolutists not pluralists. For Macintyre (1977: 484) Labour had a positivist view of human evolution from a primitive to rational mindset, which would account for its rhetorical references to the herd-like masses. For Fielding (2001) Labour's politics by mid-century adhered to a particular vision of the electorate – optimistic, worthy, but highly partial and disabled by post-war social change. Widgery (1989: 115) complained that at the close of the 1970s the Left was defining 'the political' too narrowly, and lacked 'cultural variety in communicating its ideas' to appeal to emotional besides economic interests.

Popular(?) politics

As the New Left demonstrated, Labour was not unique in exhibiting these critical qualities. Across the Western European Left, post-war affluence was commonly sniffed at (Sassoon 1997: 196). In America, too, Richard Ellis (1998: 73, 275) has highlighted a recurring tendency towards 'illiberal egalitarianism' in Left, radical movements from abolitionism through progressivism to the 1960s' New Left. Whilst reformers 'blame oppressive institutions for the current degradation . . . of people', this 'often seeps through to disdain for the people themselves, who appear quite content to live lives that to egalitarians seem shallow and inauthentic, materialistic and selfish'. Thumbing one's nose at the masses, however characteristic of protest culture, rarely assisted a mass movement.

In Britain mistrust of voters was not hard to detect among Conservatives. In 1933 Austin Hudson, chair of the Conservative London Metropolitan Area, bemoaned the party's supposed supporters: 'It is amazing to me to find the number of wealthy men and women who would be prepared to lose quite large sums of money at cards, yet who will not even subscribe £1 a year to assist those . . . fighting a battle in which they are so vitally interested'. Hudson had 'reckoned without the apathy of the average "Conservative"' (*The Times*, 4 April 1933). In Davies's pithy account of popular politics in the Calder Valley during the 1997 election – one voter tells: 'I'll be voting . . . I'll decide how when I've got five minutes' – a Conservative admitted that 'calling the electorate naïve' (which Davies felt explained much about that party's defeat) 'was not, for an aspiring politician, too clever' (1998: 203, 277, 299).

If particularly pressing for Labour's claim to be the people's party, elitism and disparagement of 'the people' were clearly endemic to British political culture. It was ingrained in the benign façade of the constitution (Colls 1998). Bagehot's *The English Constitution* of 1867 held government to be best rendered by 'the educated "ten thousand"', in comparison to whom the people were 'narrow-minded, unintelligent, incurious' (1983: 63, 246–51). Crossman (1963: 56–7) introduced a 1963 edition of Bagehot. Though optimistic that the 'passivity of the people' might soon pass, he noted post-war affluence had seen new concentrations of power occur 'unnoticed by an indifferent electorate which behaves with that deference Bagehot claimed to be the essential precondition of political stability in a free society'.

If, as Taylor (2000) proposes, Labour was more attached (as a moderniser) to the constitution than has been assumed, it certainly absorbed some of its prejudices. Morrison, with Crossman among the party's chief constitutional reformers, discloses some in his doting account *Government and Parliament*. In the section 'Public opinion', Morrison (1959: 169) inclined towards 'a respect and not a contempt for the general body of good citizens.' But (echoing MacDonald's misgivings) where the people became 'swept by an emotion' which 'leads them to wrong conclusions' (regarding his decision as home secretary to end the Mosleys's detention) Morrison turned to the 'less sympathetic language' of Liberal William Harcourt. Harcourt advised that, 'to be firm when the vulgar are undecided, to be calm in the midst of passion . . . are the characteristics of those who are fit to be the rulers of men'.

If socialists were 'people apart', this was augmented by the otherness of politics itself. For Berrington (1992: 72) this boiled down to the fact that 'the politician *is* a politician' and thus 'will be psychologically untypical of the electorate', because while 'for ordinary voters, politics is often peripheral; for the MP it is the chief, perhaps the only, interest in life'. As a function of the minority character of politics *per se*, this was true of elites and activists alike. Political sociologist Rose (1965: 94) estimated that one in every 250 electors was a party activist. Based around a study of Brighton's Kemptown district, Forester (1973 and 1976: 99) found 'constituency Labour parties' to 'have only played a limited role in the community'. Roberts's account of early twentieth-century Salford likewise stressed politics' limited presence. The 'Conservative Club, except . . . at election times, didn't appear to meddle with politics at all' and was more 'notable . . . for a union jack in the window and . . . brewer's dray at the door' (Roberts 1973: 16–17, 28). Most paid scant attention to the Marxist 'ranters' because 'the problems of the "proletariat", they felt, had little to do with them'. Despite this (and thereby emphasising how Labour's electoral support was not contingent upon a strong appreciation of its policies) Labour's support grew after the war and its 1923 triumph was wildly celebrated.

The limits to formal participation curbs reading politics as a barometer of social change or popular interests. Rose (1965: 93) hazarded that 'the proportion of the adult population actively participating in politics' was 'scarcely higher' than it had been before 1832. Labour might aspire to regard 'electors, not as voting fodder to be shepherded to a polling station . . . but as partners in a common enterprise', as Tawney put it (Forester 1976: 57), but apathy made this hard to manage. Labour was frustrated by the 'apolitical sociability' – the notion that 'it was the Labour Party which dragged "politics" into everything, which took everything so "seriously"' – which McKibbin holds (1998: 96–8) was characteristic of middle-class mores and an inter-war Conservatism that contrived to 'not talk about politics much'. Yet while McKibbin's (revealing) opinion that 'never to talk about politics or religion is . . . never to talk about two of the most interesting subjects in human history' might appeal to historians of politics – would, historically, most Britons share such enthusiasm?

Historians might decode 'apathy' in terms of activists' frustration or popular mistrust of party (or, as McKibbin infers, in terms of Labour's reticence). They might also situate it in terms of the limits to popular interest in politics or to a participatory political culture. In his account of inter-war leisure Jones (1986: 162–3) notes how attempts to pose a popular alternative to the pub, football ground and racecourse failed because 'the majority of workers . . . had neither heard about socialist recreational organizations nor bothered themselves with Labour's attitudes to the theatre or cinema'. Assessing Labour's encouragement of involvement in town planning decisions in the 1940s, Tiratsoo (1998: 152–3) has concluded that it was not only 'the character of the local planning process', but that 'popular attitudes acted to constrain rather than facilitate Labour plans'.

Popular attitudes notwithstanding, parties often did not measure up to voters' expectations. Local elections in April 1970 saw *The Times'* letters' page illuminated by grumbling: '[A] lot is said about the apathy of the *constituents*. What about the apathy of the *candidates*?' A new voter (the voting age was cut to 18 in 1969) wondered, 'with such apathy on the part of the parties . . . how can they . . . complain about a similarly unimpassioned response on the part of the electorate?' Birmingham Borough Labour Party's chief organiser Richard Knowles found this 'less than fair', and retorted that 'the candidate and his friends are doing voluntary work for the community'. An Edgware voter was 'surprised that so many appear mystified by this apathy', as his 'experience . . . living in London for . . . 70 years' was that it was 'hard to find what difference either party makes to the day to day life of the private citizen' (*The Times*, 11, 13 and 14 February 1970).

Labour politicians discerned the gap between politics and everyday life. 'We must face it', Gaitskell (1954: 3, 10) admitted, 'politics is still looked upon in many quarters as a slightly odd, somewhat discreditable . . . occupation.' Bus conductors, Labour's soon-to-be-leader noted, announced Parliament Square by crying '[A]nyone here for the gas house?' Yet, ultimately, he 'suspected that the public view of [politics] as insincere . . . is due more than anything to a failure to realise the nature of party system'. In other words, Gaitskell believed the limits to politics lay in popular thinking not political discourse. Differences between political and popular interests had ramifications. Squaring the interests of members and voters was a thankless task for party leaders. Jefferys (1999: xiv–xv) has noted that (excepting MacDonald before 1931) the 'popularity among the party faithful' of Labour leaders has been 'in inverse relationship to the standing of a leader among the voters at large'. Wilson and Blair commanded more popular support, but less party affection, than Foot or Hardie.

As evident are tensions between Labour as a people's voice and as a socialist voice or, as Lawrence (1998: 263) has pointed out, between a desire to represent the people and to improve them. Belief in humans' capacity to improve presupposed a current need for improvement. Labour's progressive dilemma was to articulate reform without criticising (and risking losing the support of) those they hoped reform would benefit – this often made building alliances of support difficult. Prescriptive and ethical language allowed the Tories to paint Labour as bureaucratic, interfering or moralising, where they were able to pose as dealing with people as they *were* not as they *might* or *ought* to be; though, as Green (1997) and Jarvis (1997: 140) maintain, Conservatives were also uncertain and untrusting of the fickle mass electorate – their popular support hard won more than innate.

Such criticisms were not the only or dominant attitudes within Labour, but a significant undercurrent across time and all quarters of the party. Macintyre (1977: 488) notes such sentiments in the 1920s were less prevalent amongst Labour's ex-Liberal, Trade Union and left-wing cohorts. Nor were non-conformist impulses absent from working-class culture. Rather this chapter, acknowledging that the Left could be frustrated by popular opinion and apathy, emphasises its frustration with what it alleged to be the people's complacencies and ambitions (or lack of), and contends that these disclose less about the electorate than about the ways Labour imagined them.

That earlier studies, like Forester's or Drucker's mapping of Labour's world, anticipate more recent concerns in their awareness of the complexities of relating parties and voters and how Labour's own culture has shaped visions of the people, suggests that the 'new political history' is not so novel. There is in it a strong trace of what Green (1997: 177) refers to as 'the primacy of politics' – insisting on the self-determining qualities of politics. Lawrence and Taylor (1997: 18) admit that the 'need for parties to mobilise and forge stable coalitions of interests is not an idea which is absent from the electoral sociology model', but that invariably this 'assumed that voter interests . . . are predetermined . . . only requiring recognition and expression by the parties'.

Traces of the newer approaches are evident in the old. Beer's classic study *Modern British Politics* argued parties 'aggregate the demands of a large number of groups in the electorate' and, while 'under pressure from such opinion', also (with the mass media) went 'a long way toward creating these opinions' (1965: 347–8, 406). Regarding parties akin to advertisers 'bidding' for consumers, Beer alleged that voters 'demands . . . did not arise autonomously from the immediate experience . . . but very largely from the interactions of that experience with interpretations offered by organizations, especially the political parties'. Miliband's *Parliamentary Socialism* (1961: 339), too, while in many ways a traditional 'high' study, argued that Labour's difficulties at the end of the 1950s lay in its own 'fear of the electorate . . . never had Labour leaders been so haunted by a composite image of the potential Labour voter as quintessentially *petit-bourgeois* and therefore liable to be frightened off by a radical alternative'.

Whilst perhaps not so new, these approaches offer historians superior ways of understanding Labour. Rather than supposing it some unique organisation, peculiarly 'British' or warranting a specific approach ('Labour history') it situates Labour in a broader re-thinking of political history.

References

Unless indicated, the place of publication is London.

Anderson, P. (1992 [1964]) 'Origins of the present crisis', reprinted in his *English Questions*

Bagehot, W. (1983) *The English Constitution*

Baker, N. (1996) '"Going to the dogs". Hostility to greyhound racing in Britain: puritanism, socialism and pragmatism', *Journal of Sports History*, 23:2

Beer, S. H. (1965) *Modern British Politics*

Bentley, M. (1996) *Politics Without Democracy, 1815–1914*

Berrington, H. (1992) 'Dialogue of the deaf? The elite and the electorate in mid-century Britain', in Kavanagh, D. (ed.) *Electoral Politics*, Oxford

Black, L. (2001) '"Sheep may safely gaze": socialists, television and the people in Britain, 1949–64', in Black, L., Dawswell, M., Doye, Z., Drake, J., Homer, A., Jenkins, J., Minion, M., Powell, G. and Tracey, L., *Consensus or Coercion? The State, People and Social Cohesion in Post-War Britain*, Cheltenham

Black, L. (2003) *The Political Culture of the Left in Affluent Britain, 1951–64: Old Labour, New Britain?*

'Candida' (1953) 'Poverty is again being inflicted on thousands', *Leeds Weekly Citizen*, 21 August

Chadwick, A. (1999) *Augmenting Democracy: Political Movements and Constitutional Reform during the rise of Labour, 1900–24*, Aldershot

Collini, S. (1991) *Public Moralists: Political Thought and Intellectual Life in Britain 1850–1930*, Oxford

Colls, R. (1998) 'The constitution of the English', *History Workshop Journal*, 46

Crossman, R. H. S. (1963) 'Introduction' to Bagehot, W., *The English Constitution* Curtice, J. (1994) 'Political sociology 1945–92', in Catterall, P. and Obelkevich, J. (eds) *Understanding Post-War British Society*

Davies, P. (1998) *This England*

Desmond, S. (1921) *Labour: The Giant with Feet of Clay*

Dodd, P. (1999) 'The arts of life: Crosland's culture', in Leonard, D. (ed.) *Crosland and New Labour*

Drucker, H. M. (1979) *Doctrine and Ethos in the Labour Party*

Ellis, R. (1998) *The Dark Side of the Left: Illiberal Egalitarianism in America*, Lawrence, KS

Epstein, L. D. (1964) *British Politics and the Suez Crisis*

Fielding, S. (1995a) *Labour: Decline and Renewal*, Manchester

Fielding, S. (1995b) '"To make men and women better than they are": Labour and the building of socialism', in Fyrth, J. (ed.) *Labour's Promised Land: Culture and Society in Labour's Britain*

Fielding, S. (2001) 'Activists against "affluence": Labour Party culture during the "golden age," c.1950–70', *Journal of British Studies*, 40:1

Fielding, S., Thompson, P. and Tiratsoo, N. (1995) *'England Arise!' Popular Politics and the Labour Party in 1940s' Britain*, Manchester

Forester, T. (1973) 'Anatomy of a local Labour Party', *New Statesman*, 28 September–5 October

Forester, T. (1976) *The Labour Party and the Working Class*

Francis, M. (1997) *Ideas and Policies Under Labour 1945–51*, Manchester

Gaitskell, H. (1954) *In Defence of Politics*

Green, E. H. H. (1997) 'The Conservative Party, the State and the electorate, 1945–64', in Lawrence, J. and Taylor, M. (eds) *Party, State and Society: Electoral Behaviour in Britain*

Since 1820, Aldershot

Hadfield, J. (1946) 'Applications file', September, Socialist Vanguard Papers, MSS 173, Box 18, Modern Records Centre, University of Warwick

Hayman, R. (1970) *Arnold Wesker*

Heath, A., Jowell, R. and Curtice, J. (1985) *How Britain Votes*, Oxford

Hindess, B. (1971) *The Decline of Working Class Politics*

Hobsbawm, E. (1961) 'Parliamentary cretinism?', *New Left Review*, 12

Hobsbawm, E. (1981) 'The forward march of Labour halted?', in Mulhern, F. and Jacques, M. (eds) *The Forward March of Labour Halted?*

Hobsbawm, E. (1982) *Revolutionaries*

Hopkins, H. (1957) *England Is Rich: An Exploration, in Circuits, after Daniel Defoe*

Independent Labour Party (1919) 'A grammar lesson', Bristol Records Office, BRO/32080/TC5/5/8

Jarvis, D. (1997) 'The shaping of Conservative electoral hegemony 1918–39', in Lawrence, J. and Taylor, M. (eds) *Party, State and Society: Electoral Behaviour in Britain Since 1820*, Aldershot

Jay, D. (1937) *The Socialist Case*

Jefferys, K. (1999) (ed.) *Leading Labour: From Kier Hardie to Tony Blair*

Jones, S. G. (1986) *Workers at Play: A Social and Economic History of Leisure, 1918–1939*

Kirk, N. (1991) '"Traditional working-class culture" and the "rise of Labour"', *Social History*, 16:2

Labour Party (1956) *The Voice of the People*

Labour Party (1959) *Report of the Fifty-Eighth Annual Conference*

Labour Party and Trades Union Congress (1929) *A Great Press For Labour*

Lamb, S. (1953) 'How to learn the canvassing art', *Labour Organiser*, October

Lawrence, J. (1997) 'The dynamics of urban politics, 1867–1914', in Lawrence, J. and Taylor, M. (1997) (eds) *Party, State and Society: Electoral Behaviour in Britain Since 1820*, Aldershot

Lawrence, J. (1998) *Speaking For the People: Party, Language and Popular Politics in England, 1867–1914*, Cambridge

Lawrence, J. and Taylor, M. (eds) (1997) *Party, State and Society: Electoral Behaviour in Britain Since 1820*, Aldershot

Laybourn, K. (1995) 'The rise of Labour and the decline of Liberalism: the state of the debate', *History*, 80:259

Lowestoft Labour Party (1958) *Contact: Journal of Lowestoft CLP*, vols 1 and 2, British Library

Macintyre, S. (1977) 'British Labour, Marxism and working class apathy in the 1920s', *Historical Journal*, 20:2

McCord, N. (1979) *North East England: An Economic and Social History*

McKibbin, R. (1990) *The Ideologies of Class*, Oxford

McKibbin, R. (1998) *Classes and Cultures: England 1918–1951*, Oxford

Mallelieu, J. P. W. (1951) *This Football Business*

Mikardo, I. (1950) *A Mug's Game*

Miliband, R. (1961) *Parliamentary Socialism*

Morgan, K. O. (1983) 'The high and low politics of Labour', in Bentley, M. and Stevenson, J. (eds) *High and Low Politics in Modern Britain*, Oxford

Morrison, H. (1959) *Government and Parliament: A Survey from the Inside*, Oxford

O'Farrell, J. (1998) *Things Can Only Get Better*

Olechnowicz, A. (2000) 'Unions first, politics after: Oldham cotton unions and the Labour

Party before 1914', *Manchester Region History Review*, 14

Orwell, G. (1937) *The Road to Wigan Pier*

Pedersen, S. (2002) 'What is political history now?' in Cannadine, D. (ed.) *What Is History Now?*, New York

'Quair' (1953) 'Quair's page', *Labour Organiser*, July

Roberts, R. (1973) *The Classic Slum*

Rose, R. (1965) *Politics in England*

Rosen, M. and Widgery, D. (eds) (1996) *The Vintage Book of Dissent*

Rowland, C. (1960) 'Labour publicity', *Political Quarterly*, 31:3

Sassoon, D. (1997) *One Hundred Years of Socialism: The Western European Left in the Twentieth Century*

Samuel, R. (1988) 'A spiritual elect? Robert Tressell and the early socialists', in Alfred, D. (ed.) *The Robert Tressell Lectures 1981–88*, Rochester

Savage, M. (1987) *The Dynamics of Working-Class Politics: The Labour Movement in Preston 1880–1940*, Cambridge

Schwarz, B. (1998) 'Politics and rhetoric in the age of mass culture', *History Workshop Journal*, 46

Shelden, M. (1992) *Orwell: The Authorised Biography*

Stedman Jones, G. (1983a) *Languages of Class: Studies in English Working-Class History 1832–1982*, Cambridge

Stedman Jones, G. (1983b [1974]) 'Working-class culture and working-class politics in London 1870–1900', reprinted in *Languages of Class: Studies in English Working-Class History 1832–1982*, Cambridge

Tanner, D. Thane, P. and Tiratsoo, N. (eds) (2000) *Labour's First Century*, Cambridge

Taylor, M. (2000) 'Labour and the constitution', in Tanner, D., Thane, P. and Tiratsoo, N. (eds) *Labour's First Century*, Cambridge

Thorpe, A. (1997) *A History of the British Labour Party*

Tiratsoo, N. (1998) 'New vistas: the Labour Party, citizenship and the built environment in the 1940s', in Weight, R. and Beach, A. (eds) *The Right to Belong: Citizenship and National Identity in Britain, 1930–60*

Tiratsoo, N. (2000) 'Labour and the electorate', in Tanner, D., Thane, P. and Tiratsoo, N. (eds) *Labour's First Century*, Cambridge

Tressell, R. (1991) *The Ragged Trousered Philanthropists*

Ward, P. (1998) *Red Flag and Union Jack: Englishness, Patriotism, and the British Left, 1881–1924*, Woodbridge

Waters, C. (1990) *British Socialists and the Politics of Popular Culture 1884–1914*, Stanford, CA

Weight, R. (1994) 'The politics of pleasure: the Left, class culture and leisure in England, 1918–1960', *Journal of Urban History*, 20:2

Widgery, D. (1989) *Preserving Disorder*

Wilson, E. (1983) 'All the rage', *New Socialist*, 14

Wring, D. (forthcoming) *The Marketing of the Labour Party*

3
'Labourism' and the New Left

Madeleine Davis

This chapter assesses the contribution made to analysis of the Labour Party and labour history by thinkers of the British New Left. In part constituted in opposition to old left tendencies, including Labour, the British New Left took an independent, broadly Marxist, position. Its thinkers thus offered theoretically informed analyses of the party and its role – mainly, as will be seen, in terms of the category *labourism* – that were highly critical. They were preoccupied in particular with the question of whether the Labour Party and movement could be the carrier of socialist ideas and policies, and, for the most part, concluded that it could not. Despite this, New Left activists and thinkers were at various times involved in practical political interventions which were aimed at pushing the party in a leftward direction. At other times (or even simultaneously) New Left intellectuals insisted on the need for the creation of a new political vehicle, leftward of Labour, and in competition with it. Yet attempts to create such a vehicle were only half-heartedly pursued. Overall, then, it must be said at the outset that the New Left displayed a profound ambivalence in its attitude to Labour. Despite the prevalence of analyses which were inclined to view the Labour Party's role as functional for the maintenance of British capitalism, and the Party as in some senses a positive obstacle to change in a leftward direction, the New Left in its various manifestations remained unable to offer any resolution of the strategic political problem posed for socialists by the party's existence and pre-eminence among the organisations of the Left.

What must also be noted from the outset is that, given the ideological trajectory the Labour Party has followed, and the balance of its electoral fortunes during the period in question (from 1956 to the present), New Left interpretations of Labour have been somewhat marginal in political terms. Yet, notwithstanding these caveats, New Left critiques have furnished us with insights which continue to offer a fruitful avenue for explanation and analysis of New Labour and the contemporary British political scene. What is enduringly distinctive and valuable about New Left critiques of Labour and labourism is that they have sought to place analysis of the party, its history and its role within the broadest possible context. Also crucial has been the theoretical context – writers of the New Left have been concerned to apply the gains of a broadened corpus of Marxist theory (especially Gramscism) to their analysis of labour, and this too makes their contribution somewhat distinctive. I argue in this chapter that New Left writers, influenced by a Milibandian perspective but also developing new ones, have made a useful and still relevant contribution to interpretations of labour. I argue also that, notwithstanding this contribution, the New Left has not proved able to offer any solution to the intractable political problem the party poses for socialists – whether to work within or outside it. This apparent conundrum can be understood only in the context of an appreciation of the complex and contradictory nature of the New Left and its legacy, and in particular of its inability to resolve the central question of agency.

The early New Left and Labour

The term 'New Left' is generally used to describe the diffuse and widespread radicalism which developed during the late 1950s and which culminated in the world-wide wave of revolt best exemplified by the May 1968 events in France. As students of the New Left have established, what the multiplicity of movements, initiatives and writers who made up the New Left shared was a profound disillusionment with existing forms of political activity, thought and organisation, whether of Left or Right, and a corresponding desire to occupy a 'new space' in politics. Britain was among the earliest to develop a New Left current (Chun 1993; Kenny 1995). Unlike some of its counterparts elsewhere, here the New Left was predominantly an intellectual tendency, institutionally identified with certain key publishing or academic enterprises, and formed initially by the coming together of two more or less distinct generations of intellectuals. Real differences of emphasis attended the shift from the 'first' to the 'second' New Left, but key questions for both centred around the issue of radical agency, and in particular the relationship of intellectuals to society and the labour movement.

In its early – 'movementist' – phase, the New Left actually *embodied* in its own structure and practices the very questions about agency and the relation of intellectual to political work which it sought to address. For a brief period it attempted to be the organising and intellectual pivot of a genuine New Left movement, which, it was thought, would occupy a new space in politics. This attempt, though brave and valuable, was ultimately unsuccessful, because these crucial questions to which the New Left gave form remained unresolved.

The strategy adopted in relation to the Labour Party by the early New Left's main protagonists was that of 'parallelism'. This necessitated both a separateness from and a dialogue with the party. One the one hand, it was considered vital for the New Left's political project to eschew any organisational links, party controls and discipline, while, on the other, there was a clear recognition of the party's hegemonic status in working-class politics, and of the centrality of its role in left-wing politics. As Hall (1989: 34) has recalled, the first New Left

> remained deeply critical of the Fabian and Labourist cultures of the Labour Party, of its 'statism', its lack of popular roots in the political and cultural life of ordinary people, its bureaucratic suspicion of any independent action or 'movement' outside its limits,

and its profound anti-intellectualism. We opposed the deeply undemocratic procedures of the block vote and the Party's empty 'constitutionalism'. Yet we knew that the
Labour Party represented, whether we liked it or not, the strategic *stake* in British politics, which no one could ignore.

Here, as with its Marxism, the New Left tried to adopt a 'third' position, opposing
both the acceptance of capitalism implied by Gaitskell and Crosland, and the effective refusal by the Labour Left to accept that a new analysis was necessary for the
post-war situation. With its 'one foot in, one foot out' approach, the New Left
spoke of a 'break back' of their ideas into the party, which could lead to a peaceful
revolution. E. P. Thompson (1960: 7) spoke in terms of

> interpenetrating opposites . . . it is not a case of *either* this *or* that . . . It is possible to
> look forward to a peaceful revolution in Britain, not because it will be a semi-revolu-
> tion, nor because capitalism is 'evolving' into socialism, but because the advances of
> 1942–8 *were* real, because the socialist *potential* has been enlarged, and socialist forms,
> however imperfect, have grown up 'within' capitalism.

This dialectical approach was clarified by Saville (1960: 9) when he argued for the
translation of theory into practice, and the embracing of all forms of Left activity:

> Such activities will, inevitably, take new organisational forms, sometimes wholly
> within the Labour Party, sometimes without, sometimes half-in half-out – (i.e. involv-
> ing many Labour Party people and seeking to influence the party, but not restricted to
> or limited by it) . . . At the same time, a genuine forward move involves a) replacement
> of the present leadership of the party, and b) the development of political forms which
> will enable the Left to grow within the Labour movement.

This, then, was the strategy, but how did it work in practice? The unilateralist victory at the 1960 Labour Party Conference provides the clearest example of New
Left influence succeeding in altering party policy (though not for long). For some,
the lesson of this experience was that the New Left should involve itself more
closely with internal Labour Party matters, while by others it was seen as a 'defeat-
in-victory', which illustrated the capacity of the party machine to encompass and
neutralise new positions. For this group, the imperative to maintain independence
from the party and continue to build a base outside it was strengthened by this
experience.

Yet the New Left was reluctant to sponsor initiatives which would place it in
direct competition with the Labour Party. The one real attempt to build an alternative New Left political platform was made by Lawrence Daly's Fife Socialist
League. Daly's astonishing victory as an independent candidate in local elections
in Ballingry in 1958, followed by his decision to contest West Fife in the 1959 general election, raised the possibility of constructing a distinctive New Left political
organisation, in direct competition with traditional parties. After some debate, the
New Reasoner group decided to support Daly, but very significantly *not* as exem-
plifying some general principle of support for Independent New Left electoral
candidates. Its ambivalent attitude and half-hearted support for such initiatives
amounted to a failure of nerve which limited the effectiveness of the 'parallel'

strategy; and, in the context of the conflict at the core of the early New Left – whether it was a journal of ideas or a movement of people – suggested a leaning toward the former. Inability or unwillingness to create a genuine popular base *of its own*, together with the decline of the Campaign for Nuclear Disarmament (CND) and, later, of the New Left clubs, and the gradual shift of emphasis toward accepting the production of a journal as its major responsibility, led in practice towards greater acceptance of the Labour Party as the *only* vehicle for socialist transformation. The need to build both inside and outside the party was repeatedly stated, but there were few practical attempts, or even concrete plans, to do this.

With the decline of CND and the local clubs, the 'movement' phase of the New Left was coming to an end, and its relationship with the Labour Party altered. Parallelism as a strategy was fatally weakened by the demise of the parallel organisations on which it depended. The accession of Harold Wilson to the leadership in 1962 also seemed to create more favourable conditions for the New Left to influence policy formation, and it revived hopes for a change in the direction of the party. For the most part, these hopes were not to be realised. The story of the early New Left's struggle for the 'soul of Labour' was one in which it was continually outmanoeuvred and failed to engage with a clear purpose or a real understanding of the problem confronting it. For Raymond Williams (1979: 365), in retrospect, it seemed that the mistake the New Left made was never to take the Labour Party seriously enough:

> There was a general sense that given its integration into the world of NATO capitalism, it was a negligible organisation: while the marches were so big, and left clubs were springing up all over the country, this outdated institution could be left to expire . . . There was no idea of the strengths of the Labour machine, or of the political skill which the right was able to organise for victory within it.

Critiques of labourism

It was not until after the early New Left had declined that sustained and theoretically informed analyses of the Labour Party and movement began to be offered by New Left thinkers. Ralph Miliband's *Parliamentary Socialism* was published in 1961, Perry Anderson and Tom Nairn's series of essays followed in 1964–65, and other New Left figures including Williams and Saville also wrote regularly on the subject in the pages of the *New Left Review* (*NLR*) or *The Socialist Register*. Though the nuances of interpretation varied among these individuals, the use of the term 'labourism' to denote the limitations placed upon the party by its particular history, ideology and structure, and above all, what Miliband (1972: 13) called its 'devotion to the parliamentary system' was a common feature.

This was not, in itself, a wholly new way of looking at Labour. New Left critiques of labourism in fact represented and continued a strand of Marxist thinking on the party that can be traced back to its inception. John Saville was to acknowledge the particular debt owed in this regard by the New Left to Theodore Rothstein, a Lithuanian Jewish Marxist who spent much of his career as a political journalist and writer in London and whose essays on the subject, written from 1905 onward, were published in 1929 as *From Chartism to Labourism: Historical Sketches of the English Working Class Movement.*

Rothstein's analysis foreshadowed many of the criticisms of the Labour Party that were later to be made by New Left commentators. The major concern of Rothstein, as it was for them also, was with the weakness of revolutionary socialism in Britain. As early as 1898 he had posed the question: 'Why is socialism in England at a discount?', and he concluded that it was the specific character of 'labourism' that had much to answer for (1929: xxi). Encompassed in his analysis was a critique of the reformism and economism of the trade unions, the prevalence of sectionalism within the working class, and also an interpretation of the role of the British State and the bourgeoisie in informing and reinforcing what he saw as the 'non-political, opportunistic and counter-revolutionary' consciousness of the working class (1929: 276). Viewing the native socialist tradition as limited, an offshoot of liberalism rather than a result of revolutionary sentiment among the working class, he blamed the failure of Marxist ideas to take root, in part, on their foreignness to the already established traditions of labourism. Rothstein was also deeply critical of both the Fabian and the Independent Labour Party (ILP) traditions, concluding that even for the latter 'parliamentary activity seemed the highest form of political action' (1929: 279). Of the Labour Party up to the 1920s, he judged that 'its fortunes have most strikingly confirmed the fact that opportunist ideology presented an insurmountable obstacle to the development of a genuine, potentially revolutionary, political class struggle of the proletariat' (1929: 281).

All these themes were later to be taken up and amplified by writers of the New Left, though, as I show, with slight differences of emphasis. The specific contribution of Ralph Miliband is discussed elsewhere in this volume and so will not be treated at length here. The parallels between his work and Rothstein's, however, are clear. The interpretation of labourism offered by Tom Nairn and Perry Anderson in the pages of *NLR* in the mid-1960s had similarities with both Rothstein's and Miliband's, though the two authors referred to neither. Anderson and his collaborators, critical of the early New Left for its populist tone and for sacrificing intellectual and theoretical work in favour of 'a mobilising role which perpetually escaped it' (Anderson 1965a: 17), set out with the bold aim of transforming the intellectual culture of Britain, which they viewed as a pre-requisite of any real socialist advance, by introducing and applying Marxist thought drawn mainly from continental Europe. The Nairn–Anderson theses thus represented an ambitious attempt to pioneer a distinctive analysis of British capitalist development, its state, society and class structure.

Despite a number of shortcomings, some justly identified by E. P. Thompson in his excoriating and famous 1965 attack, what was distinctive and valuable about the Nairn–Anderson project was its attempt to interpret 'the present crisis' diagnosed by Anderson with the historical and structural features of British capitalist development. The theoretical rigour of this enterprise ensured that its interpretation of labourism was something of an advance on previous Left critiques. As is well known, Nairn and Anderson identified various 'peculiarities' or specificities of British history as vital to its subsequent development (Anderson 1964; Nairn

1964a, 1964b and 1964c; for a reassessment see Anderson 1987). These can be summarised into certain key positions having to do with, first, the nature of the British State and establishment, particularly in terms of its class composition, second, the nature of labourism and, third, its intellectual culture.

The major hypothesis advanced was that the nature and development of the British State and its social classes had been crucially conditioned by an historic compromise, or alliance, between agrarian (aristocratic) and mercantile (bourgeois) capitalism. This compromise, which Anderson considered 'the single most important key to modern English history' (1964: 31), was related to certain peculiarities of British history: the absence of any 'true' bourgeois revolution (France was the implicit model); the priority of the industrial revolution; and the experience of empire. From this essentially materialist beginning, Anderson and Nairn went on to emphasise the cultural and ideological consequences, arguing that these historical peculiarities enabled the ruling bloc to impose its own worldview on the rest of society; in Gramscian terms, it was a genuinely hegemonic class. This worldview was characterised as a 'comprehensive conservatism' (Anderson 1964: 40), whose main pillars were empiricism and traditionalism, and which reflected and recreated aristocratic cultural and material values. All this was linked to the idea that the bourgeoisie had never stood in real opposition to the aristocracy, there had never been a full bourgeois revolution and Enlightenment rationalism had never fully replaced the *ancien régime*. The bourgeoisie in England failed to live up to its supposed historical destiny, did not become a fully hegemonic class and so did not develop an 'authentic articulated ideology' (Anderson 1964: 41) to challenge Conservative hegemony.

The history of the Labour Party and movement, for Nairn and Anderson, had to be placed in this context. Developing Anderson's argument (1964: 43) that 'a supine bourgeoisie produced a subordinate proletariat', Nairn identified the high point of working-class struggle with the Chartist movement, a movement which collapsed before *The Communist Manifesto* (Marx and Engels 1848) was written. The lack of availability of socialist theory to the working class, together with its exhaustion after Chartism, and the lack of any experience of a Jacobin alliance with a modernising bourgeoisie, were seen as contributing to a period of quiescence in the nineteenth century, when other working classes in Europe were coming under the influence of Marxist ideas. When working-class activism reconstituted itself, it did so on profoundly moderate and reformist lines.

From that basis, a particular analysis of the Labour Party and movement as a subordinate and corporatist entity was developed. Nairn and Anderson used the term *labourism* to encompass both the Labour Party and the labour movement, influenced by the Gramscian stricture, paraphrased by Nairn (1964c: 39) as 'the history of a party ... cannot fail to be the history of a given social class'. They alleged that labourism was both defined and limited by a number of key characteristics: the pre-eminence of the trade unions; the inherent weakness of indigenous British socialism and the Labour Left; the acceptance of parliamentarism; and the failure of intellectuals to forge a counter-hegemonic ideology. The Labour Party itself was understood as an entity which, while being based on the myth of 'broad church' unity, was actually defined and constituted by the structural subordination of the Left (identified at first with the ILP's ethical socialism) to the Right (identified with the Fabians – pragmatic and competent reformers). Nairn called the Fabians the intellect of the Labour Party and the Left its emotions or subjectivity. The existence of this Left within the party functioned partly to legitimise and reinforce right-wing hegemony within it; the battle in 1960 over Clause 4 was seen as a classic example; with the Left arguing for the maintenance of traditional socialist principles (to which in practice only lip-service had ever been paid) on sentimental grounds. In reality, Nairn argued, the Labour Party was a bundle of disparate forces united by the myth of the possibility of an evolutionary path to socialism.

Although the rift between the first and second New Left groupings meant that dialogue and collaboration between them was patchy, other New Left writers, most notably Williams and Saville, also contributed through the 1960s and 1970s to what we might now regard as a distinctive New Left interpretation of Labour. Saville, like Miliband, treated the party's history predominantly in terms of what he saw as its consistent failure to press for socialist policies. His position, like Miliband's and the *NLR* writers', hardened when it became clear that the 1964–70 Wilson Government was not going to deliver socialist policies nor effect far-reaching alteration to the structures of the Labour Party – such had been the hope, if not the expectation, of prominent New Left theorists upon Wilson's accession to power. For Saville and others, the Labour Party's refusal to take a stand against the American intervention in Vietnam seemed to confirm the (reluctant) conclusion that not only was the party unable to effect radical change, but that its role was actually functional for the maintenance of British capitalism. By the later 1960s Saville (1967: 67) was asserting:

> Labourism has nothing to do with socialism . . . the Labour Party has never been, nor is it capable of becoming, a vehicle for socialist advance, and . . . the destruction of the illusions of Labourism is a necessary step before the emergence of a socialist movement of any size and influence becomes practicable.

Saville's analysis of labourism was similar to Nairn and Anderson's in its emphasis on the importance of the ideological hegemony of the ruling class and the role this played in preventing the development of an independent party of the working class, or a fully developed class consciousness. Thus labourism for him was 'the theory and practice of class collaboration' (1975: 215).

The critics of labourism criticised

By the late 1960s, then, a distinctive interpretation of the history and role of the Labour Party and movement had been offered by New Left writers, around the central organising concept of labourism. Particularly in its Anderson–Nairn variant, this is an interpretation which has been subjected to a number of criticisms, some of them from thinkers associated at one time or another with the New Left itself. Criticism has tended to focus on two main areas. Firstly, critics have alleged an excessive schematism or theoretical abstraction, and a corresponding a-historicism. E. P. Thompson (1965), for instance, famously dismissed the entire Nairn–Anderson enterprise as representative of a reductionist Marxism which eschewed real historical analysis, while two other thinkers also associated with the New Left, Raphael Samuel and Gareth Stedman Jones (1982: 325), were inclined to dismiss the whole category of 'labourism' as offered by Miliband, Anderson and Nairn, arguing:

> What the New Left analysis offered was not a complex location of the history of the Labour Party in specific historical contexts, but rather an eloquent and polemically brilliant phenomenology of a set of 'enduring reflexes', partially embodied in a set of institutions but mainly hovering like a dense mental fog over the low-lying ideological terrain on which the Labour Party operated . . . As a savage and innovatory indictment of the malaise of the Labour Party and labour movement in the late 1950s and 1960s the New Left critique is justly famous. But as a stand in for the history of the Labour Party, it will not do.

A second, and related, charge has been that the New Left analysis of labourism failed to appreciate the importance of indigenous working-class culture, the native roots and variants of radicalism, and, correspondingly, too hastily dismissed the entire Labour tradition as non-socialist. E. P. Thompson, who in his own work *The Making of the English Working Class* (1963) argued that the working class *made itself* as much as it was made, insisted upon the strength and resilience of working-class institutions and took strong exception to Anderson and Nairn's depiction of the working class as irretrievably subordinate and reformist in consciousness. He and others, from a socialist–humanist perspective, argued that Anderson and Nairn (though the same criticism could also to some extent be applied to Miliband and Saville) were implicitly likening the English experience of class and capitalist development to a hidden 'ideal type', and in their implied insistence that socialism had to be Marxist and revolutionary in character were rejecting out of hand indigenous forms of radicalism as both non-socialist and reformist.

Both these strands of criticism somewhat miss their mark if we view (as I argue that we should) the New Left critique of labourism offered by Miliband, the *NLR* writers, Saville and Williams, as a whole – as a developing strand of analysis with a number of contributors. Critics were correct to identify a lack of serious and close historical studies of the Labour Party from a leftist perspective, but, as Samuel and Stedman Jones (1982: 323) themselves noted, this was a result of a bias in Left labour history in general, the prime motivation of which had long been the search for 'an *alternative* non social-democratic tradition'. Thus labour historians had either tended to focus on traditions of dissent and radicalism in opposition to the mainstream, or (like the New Left) been primarily concerned to understand why the Labour Party and movement had not for the most part espoused socialist ideas and policies. True, the New Left critique of Labour would not speak much to those requiring a close historical study of the Labour Party; but neither Miliband nor Anderson–Nairn had ever attempted or claimed to provide such a study. Rather, what they offered was a theoretical framework, more or less derived from Marxism, for understanding its essential nature and the particular role it played in

British capitalist development. There is undoubtedly some truth in Samuel and Stedman Jones's claim that the use of the 'analytical concentrate' *labourism* (1982: 325) can lead to over-simplification of complex historical conjunctures, and, at worst, encourage a circular and self-justificatory logic among those who apply the term. However, these methodological difficulties cannot be said to invalidate entirely the attempt to apply a theory-based interpretation.

The second strand of criticism noted above can also be countered by a close reading of the New Left's work on Labour as it developed over a number of years. Here we must look in particular at the work of Raymond Williams. For while he largely shared the view of labourism offered by his colleagues in the New Left, he, more than they, paid attention to the strengths (as well as the deficiencies) of indigenous working-class culture and socialist thought, as both separate from and contributing to the political and institutional structures of the labour movement. New Left thinkers were broadly agreed that the main ideological component of English working-class radicalism was a tradition of moral critique, having its antecedents more in utopianism (literary as well as political) and religious non-conformity than in Marxism. Whereas Anderson and Nairn were (at first) inclined to dismiss this tradition, however, Williams (along with Thompson) emphasised its value. Williams argued that the potential for this moral tradition to mature and shape the socialism of the labour movement and party had been lost, and he blamed this not only on the Fabians' imposition of a utilitarian outlook but also on the uncompromising economism of the Marxists who opposed them. Thus 'at every level, this was a direct denial of the mainstream of the moral tradition of the British working class movement, with its emphases on local democracy, participation, and the setting of human above economic standards' (1965: 24).

One of the more important and innovative of New Left thinkers, Williams did not sidestep the paradoxes thrown up for the New Left by its study of labourism, but sought to incorporate a concern with culture and humanism into his own reworking of Marxism as 'cultural materialism'. He thus added to the New Left interpretation of labourism a more nuanced and sympathetic element, taking it beyond an orthodox Marxist approach. But though his analysis went further than those of other New Leftists in acknowledging the value of indigenous radical ideas, and the genuine human sources of some Labour Left thinking, Williams nevertheless shared with other New Left writers the view that the dominant traditions and internal structural logic of labourism subordinated and defused these genuinely or potentially socialist elements. By 1967 he, too, was convinced that the Labour Party was no longer 'just an inadequate agency for socialism, it was now an active collaborator in the process of reproducing capitalist society'. He was later to characterise Labour as a 'post social democratic party' essential to British capitalism when economic and social stability demanded a neutralised working class (1979: 373, 377).

Evolution of the New Left critique

Williams's developing perspectives are representative of a broader trend in the evolution of New Left interpretations of Labour, which, though continuing to build on the analytical framework established in the 1960s, subtly altered over time. In general it might be said that the focus shifted from an emphasis on the unique features of the British State, its constitutional, cultural and social order (the early Anderson and Nairn theses) towards an analysis that situated the critique of Labour more firmly in relation to the development of global capitalism and Britain's position within this order. The New Left approach also began to contribute to a broader set of concerns which developed on the Left around the nature of British capitalism, relative economic decline, and the need for far-reaching constitutional change. In this evolution of New Left thinking on Labour, the contribution of Tom Nairn deserves special attention since it both built upon and revised the existing Nairn–Anderson approach, while also reworking it to take account of new political developments and his own changing theoretical preoccupations.

Through the 1970s and 1980s, Nairn reworked the earlier theses, in the process shifting the emphasis towards analysis, not so much of the internal specificities of labourism, but rather of the extent to which the party, in its nature, structures and ideology, was inextricably bound up with the archaism of the British State and the decline of British capitalism: its 'sickness', first diagnosed by Miliband, increasingly viewed as only one symptom of a chronic 'British disease'. One of the fundamental arguments supporting Nairn's diagnosis of this 'British disease' concerned the relationship of the Labour Party with British imperialism and nationalism, now more fully theorised and placed in historical context than it had been in the original theses. Nairn situated the rise of Labour in relation to the heyday of English imperialism and the key tenet that this coincided with an era of exhausted quiescence in the labour movement, and argued that the party had thus from the first confronted 'an epoch of imperialist decline . . . with a philosophy and an organisation rooted in the preceding era of imperial confidence and stability' (1970: 4). He also gave extended consideration to the particular brand of nationalism espoused by the British Labour Party. Advocating entry into what was then termed the European Economic Community (EEC) against the tide of opinion on the Left, he argued that Labour's opposition to the EEC was illustrative of the depth of its commitment to nationalist illusions and of its subordination within the British State formation. It was, Nairn contended (1972: 49–50), constitutionally incapable of putting class before nation in the final test. In sum,

> one may say that while Labour seems . . . to stand for class against nation, it represents in reality the ascendancy of nation and the state over class. In analogous fashion, while at a deeper level the left seems to oppose the right-wing leadership in the name of class socialism, in reality it too sustains that leadership and so, in its own particular way, the nation and the state. The whole structure of the movement represents a complex estrangement of 'class' by 'nation', a process by which a class *both* affirms its own being politically, and consistently loses that being by the very way in which that affirmation is made – via the deep-rooted national-political 'rules' secreted after a long conservative history.

In developing the theme of Britain's 1970s' 'crisis', Nairn returned to the original Nairn–Anderson emphasis on an interpretation of the British situation in its totality. Politically, for Nairn, the best hope for a way out of the impasse that was the 'British disease' was increasingly seen to be some kind of structural break or rupture within one or more of the intertwined elements of Britain's archaic constitutional order. Peripheral nationalism was for a time seen as holding out the possibility for such a 'break up of Britain' (Nairn 1977) and, later, the split in the Labour Party was also viewed in this light. The hope was that the polarisation of the party might presage a disintegration of labourism in its existing form that could enable the Left to break free of its crippling confines.

If this hope proved a vain one, Nairn's work continued to feed into a developing corpus of New Left and Marxist-inspired work which broadened out the analysis beyond labourism and towards a more general critique of British capitalism and the State. Contributing to this were – as well as central figures in the original New Left such as Miliband, Saville, Hall, Anthony Barnett, Nairn and Anderson – a number of other leftists including Andrew Gamble (1974, 1981) and Colin Leys (1983). As chapter 5, by David Coates and Leo Panitch, argues, by the 1980s certain premises of the New Left approach had won general acceptance in much leftist scholarship. The idea of a long-run 'crisis' at the centre of British politics, having to do with the historical specificities of Britain's political and social structures, and conditioning the nature and range of political and economic options, became common currency. So, too, did the idea of the structural weakness of the UK economy as causally linked to the nature of Britain's state institutions and social structures. These were ideas that fed into more mainstream debates about the need for far-reaching constitutional change and electoral reform, and Britain's relative economic decline. Particularly through the journalism of Will Hutton (1996) they have continued to develop in the work of leftist scholars of both the Labour Party and British politics in general.

Strategic orientations

If the New Left's interpretation of labourism has proved influential in an intellectual sense, it has remained somewhat marginal in directly political terms. Despite its articulation of a consistent critique, the New Left was only intermittently involved in directly political initiatives to the Left of Labour, and the central strategic question that its analysis of Labour raised – whether socialists should work within or outside of the party – remained unresolved. The ambivalence of the early New Left towards Labour, as has been seen, undermined its mobilising aspirations and contributed to its disintegration. Though the later New Left eschewed such directly political ambition, and thus avoided a similar fate, it nevertheless remained divided on this intractable issue. Anderson and Blackburn's 1965 volume *Towards Socialism* gave extended consideration to the strategic dilemma posed by the nature and predominance of the Labour Party.

Among the contributions, Perry Anderson's 'Problems of socialist strategy' stands out as one of the most insightful interpretations of the problems and opportunities posed for socialists by Labour that any New Left writer produced, though it had much in common with work produced contemporaneously or subsequently by other New Left writers. Developing the Milibandian critique of Labour's parliamentarism, Anderson went further to argue that in view of the 'statism' of Western social democratic parties, any viable socialist strategy must be based firmly within civil society. The task for socialists, he concluded, was the creation of a truly hegemonic party, proposing a 'coherent, global alternative to the existing social order, and represent[ing] a permanent drive towards it' (Anderson 1965b: 240). Such a party, he stated, should unite the working class and also include technical and white-collar workers, as well as radicalised intellectuals. It needed to direct its activities into cultural and societal fields, as well as the State, and thereby prefigure the new society in its own (democratic) practices.

It was abundantly clear that Labour bore little relationship to Anderson's vision of the hegemonic party; yet, because it was the only working-class party in a nation where the working class comprised 70 per cent of the population, he judged that it could not be ignored. Its position represented a 'permanent chance' for socialism lodged within the British social structure, yet the party itself was constitutionally unable to seize this opportunity. Some of the Left's traditional assumptions regarding the relationship of the Labour Party to the working class were challenged. Anderson pointed out that the supposed 'mass' character of the Labour Party was somewhat overstated: in fact, Labour had relatively few members and activists among the working class, a third of whom actually supported the Conservative Party. And Labour had no strong youth organisation and no dedicated party press. Any claim that it unified the working class was rejected – on the contrary, in its preoccupation with parliamentarism and exclusive dedication to electoralism Labour atomised its support and neglected other forms of political activity.

One of the interesting things about Anderson's essay, in retrospect, is the way it anticipated the contours of later discussion of strategic options on the British Left. His analysis in fact had much in common with that later made by Stuart Hall, whose better-known work on 'Thatcherism' also proceeded from an attempt to apply Gramsci's ideas in an enquiry into the ways and means of hegemonic dominance. Hall's early work on this theme was strikingly similar to Anderson's in its criticism of the Left's fixation with state power and its identification of civil society as the key terrain on which to situate the struggle, and there were also obvious parallels with Raymond Williams's arguments regarding the critical importance of culture and communication. Eric Hobsbawm's influential 1978 Marx Memorial Lecture 'The forward march of Labour halted?' (1981) also made some points similar to Anderson's – some thirteen years later – concerning the relationship of the working class to Labour organisations, beginning a debate which led eventually to the resignation of much of the socialist Left to the 'broad democratic alliance' programme sponsored by *Marxism Today*.

With 'Thatcherism' in full flow in the 1980s the Labour Party under Neil Kinnock, who gave a nod to Hobsbawm's analysis, embarked on a process of 'modernisation' that many characterised as the pursuit of electoral victory at any cost. The dangers of such an approach had been outlined by Anderson in 1965. Discussing the view that the task for Labour was to win over fractions of the Tory vote at each election, he warned that this could only result in a permanent pursuit of the fickle middle-class vote in a way which would damage democracy while doing nothing to advance socialism. However, Anderson simultaneously rejected the traditional Labour Left's alternative of populist appeals to voters' altruism (Bennism, later supported by *NLR*, could be seen in this light). What was proposed instead for socialists and Labour was a *grass-roots* campaign, based in the working class, and aimed at winning 'a permanent sociological majority of the nation'. In sum, the strategy proposed must amount to a systematic effort to 'marry the structure of the socialist movement to the contours of civil society' (1965b: 279). Written at a time when it was becoming clear that Wilsonism, even if pushed to its very limits, held out little promise of embarking upon this kind of transformation, Anderson simultaneously doubted that any other force could emerge outside the Labour Party to mount a realistic challenge. Hence his admission of the 'abstract', or utopian, character of his recommendations in the immediate context: 'An authentic socialist strategy can only be born within the internal dialectic of a mass socialist movement; it has no meaning or possibility outside it' (1965b: 222).

The question of how such a mass socialist movement was to be brought into being troubled *NLR* somewhat less than it had the earlier New Left, Anderson and company having renounced any mobilising role in favour of a project of intellectual transformation. Such a stance enabled *NLR* to escape the fate which had overtaken its predecessor, one which was also to befall the regrouping of some of the early New Left as the *May Day Manifesto* initiative in the late 1960s. Raymond Williams, initially the prime mover in this, was joined by Hall and Thompson, their aim being to produce a new understanding of the changing nature of capitalism and the Labour Party within the context of a non-sectarian organisational initiative. 'Shall we', they asked in the *Manifesto*, 'from the heart of the labour movement, try to create in actuality what has long been imagined in theory, a New Left?' (Williams, Hall and Thompson 1967: 36). The *Manifesto* was launched on 1 May 1967.

Despite the group's desire to take a non-sectarian approach, it was in fact riven, up to the highest level, by serious disagreement on the central strategic question; whether or not it was permissible for socialists to make electoral inteventions to the Left of the Labour Party. Though their disagreement was not made public, Williams was in favour of an extra-parliamentary strategy, while Thompson would not renounce all hope in the PLP. Consequently, no real strategic suggestions were offered during 1967–68. This was part of the reason why the Manifesto movement never really got off the ground as a *political* initiative; the other was that it was simply overtaken by events. By the time its proposed national 'Convention of the Left' was held, in April 1969, and the group finally committed itself to acceptance of the need for 'the formation of a political movement, radical and socialist, primarily extra-parliamentary, but accepting the significance of a national presence', the Paris May and the wave of student activism had left it behind. In some ways its fate recalled that of the 'first' New Left and '*NLR* Mark I': in attempting to move beyond intellectual analysis of the situation to a directly political and mobilising role, it disintegrated. A key sticking point, as before, was a profound ambivalence about the relationship of a New Left to the Labour Party.

By contrast, *NLR*'s increasing orientation towards a revolutionary Marxist politics from the late 1960s hardened its strategic perspective. The Labour Party was increasingly presented in the pages of the journal as a positive obstacle to socialism. An interview with Michael Foot (1968: 28) gave *NLR* the opportunity to warn him that 'young militants ask themselves today whether a struggle against the Labour party as it is might not eventually be an unavoidable form that the struggle for socialism must take at a time when the Labour government is actually the executor of British capitalism'. By the time of the general election in 1970, far from considering it the duty of socialists to try to push Labour in a leftwards direction, *NLR* was able to declare (in its regular editorial introduction 'Themes') that 'its cringing record as a custodian of British capital needs no demonstration here, and poses few problems for Marxists' (*NLR* 1970: 1). Indeed, the sole reason for any continued attention to the party was simply that 'to understand Labourism in its deepest anchorage is a condition of eliminating it in struggle today'. Writing in *Red Mole* shortly before joining the Trotskyist International Marxist Group (IMG), Robin Blackburn (1970: 1) went so far as to declare that the only principled course for socialists would be 'an active campaign to discredit both of Britain's large capitalist parties'.

In 1972 *Parliamentary Socialism* was re-issued, giving Miliband the opportunity to add a postscript in which he argued for 'the dissipation of paralysing illusions about the true purpose and role of the Labour Party' (1972: 377; see also chapter 4 of this book, by Michael Newman). At various points through the 1970s *The Socialist Register* was the locus for a renewed debate on the strategic options available to socialists *vis-à-vis* the party. The nub of the problem was succinctly summed up by Ken Coates, when he said: 'If the Labour Party cannot be turned into a socialist party then the question which confronts us all is, how can we form a socialist party? If we are not ready to answer this question, then we are not ready to dismiss the party that exists' (1973: 155). While in general convinced of the first point, New Left opinion on the rest of Coates's conundrum remained divided. Miliband's exhortation to socialists to 'move on' from Labour and consider how to form 'a socialist party free from the manifold shortcomings of existing organisations' (1976: 140) revived discussion, but little practical progress was made. The terms of the debate were to be altered somewhat by electoral defeat for Labour in 1979. In the ensuing crisis, in particular with regard to the secession of many on the Labour Right to form the Social Democratic Party in 1981 and the advent of Bennism, some of the New Left were to invest renewed hopes in the Labour Left.

This turn back to Labour was motivated by a real hope that Bennism would represent a new formation within the party that would break the confines of labourism and give rise to what Quintin Hoare and Tariq Ali in 1982 called 'a new model Labour party'. The secession of the Right of the party – presaging a possible 'break-up of labourism' – added weight to this view. Some remained sceptical, however. The idea of a rupture in the party creating new opportunities for socialism was not new –indeed it was one of the 'paralysing illusions' that Miliband was keen to dispel. The New Left's own interpretation of labour in many ways gave more grounds for pessimism than optimism about the prospects for Bennism, and the political conclusions that were drawn by some proved, predictably perhaps, to have rested on an overestimation of the possibilities.

The importance attached to 'Bennism' as a force which could break free from Labourist contradictions rested on an underestimation of the extent to which this formation was *itself* a product of those contradictions. In their attempt to displace the moderate leadership of the party the Bennites demonstrated their adherence to the traditional Labour Left belief that leadership 'betrayal' of the socialist 'soul' of the party was the major cause of its failures. Nor did Benn's programme transcend Left labourist confines in other ways. Most crucially, its goals were envisaged as achievable without major change to the Westminster model. Secondly, an implicit assumption of the Bennite project, if it was to be realised, was that not only was there a socialist majority within the labour movement itself but also within the electorate as a whole. In no sense did Bennism really address the problem of how socialist consciousness was to be *created*, both within and outside the party, rather than simply appealed to or mobilised. In immediately political terms, however, the 'socialists in or out debate' must be regarded as somewhat marginal given the scale of Labour's subsequent electoral defeat.

From New Left to New Labour

The lessons drawn by the dominant tendency within the Labour Party from the crushing defeat of 1983 placed it firmly on the course of the 'modernisation' which was eventually to lead to power, but at the cost of accepting much of the social, political, economic and ideological legacy of eighteen years of Conservative rule as unchallengeable. Writers of the New Left during this period offered influential analyses of the New Right, and as ideas of a generalised 'crisis of the Left' took hold, New Left opinion on Labour became increasingly divided between those who tolerated the Kinnockite overhaul of the party as the only way to bring an end to 'Thatcherism' and those who wanted to maintain a 'resolute Left' perspective (for example, Hall 1988; Hall and Jacques 1983). Among the latter we may include Williams, Saville, Miliband and the *NLR* group, several of whom began to view fundamental reform of the structures of the State, and in particular electoral reform, as the best immediate prospect for the Left in decidedly unpropitious circumstances. As it related to the Labour Party, this projection advocated that as much pressure as possible be brought to bear on the party to persuade it to adopt far-reaching constitutional reform measures as part of its programme.

The disinclination of New Labour in power to do more than tinker with the structures of the State has not been viewed with surprise, however, by those who retain a broadly New Left perspective. Recent contributions to the relaunched *NLR* by Nairn (2000) and Anthony Barnett (2000) have catalogued the failings and disappointments of Blair's modernisation agenda, but without being able to suggest any convincing vehicle for advance. This is illustrative of the argument made earlier, that despite having offered insightful, theoretically informed and empirically well-grounded interpretations of Labour over a number of years, New

Left thinkers have been largely unable to help the British Left more widely to over-come the *political* problem of how to transcend or permanently alter Labourism. This in turn should not be viewed as a 'failure' of the New Left. Rather, it is illus-trative of the fact that the New Left since its inception has embodied (the early New left) or in other ways been the pivotal point of (the later New Left) a repre-sentational crisis and a profound uncertainty about the purposes and direction of a socialist project. The legacy of the New Left must be viewed as in key respects an ambivalent, contradictory and problematical one. This is as true of the early New Left as of any later variants.

The arrival of the New Left was a product of a particular conjunction of events – a crisis, for many left intellectuals – which forced them to question traditionally held assumptions and beliefs about the nature of a socialist project and how such a project might be created. From the start the New Left experimented with new ideas about the changing nature of capitalism and the role of class within it. In both its early and late manifestations the New Left has represented a range of approaches to the question of agency and in particular whether sections of society other than the industrial working class might contribute to the creation of a social-ist future. In their endeavours to grapple with such issues the New Left has drawn on novel theoretical influences (finding Gramsci, in particular, an inspiring source). The New Left's nature as an intellectual current obviously has dictated the special attention given to the question of the role that intellectual work and cul-tural transformation can play.

It is easy to caricature the concerns of the New Left (particularly the later New Left) and to fall back too easily on arguments about a retreat into the academy and an exaggerated distance from the concerns of working people. Undoubtedly the New Left does leave us with a generally difficult legacy – it was responsible for a great flowering of Marxist-influenced work in a variety of disciplines and contexts, and yet this work was completed against the political tide.

One might argue also that the New Left's renunciation or questioning of certain of the tenets and assumptions of the traditional Left contributed to a climate of uncertainty and disorientation in which the New Right, rather than the New Left, proved able to seize the initiative. Politically speaking, the New Left must be adjudged to have had only a marginal significance. But one should not conclude from this that its perspectives may be ignored. If the British New Left has proved incapable of influencing political events in anything more than a marginal way, it has nonetheless provided us with perspectives for evaluating and understanding those events which may still prove useful.

This chapter has advanced that argument in relation to one particular aspect of the New Left's work – the interpretation of Labour; and it contends that New Left writers have proved and still prove to be well placed to offer enduringly valuable perspectives on the nature of Labour that help us understand its development and prospects.

References

Unless indicated, the place of publication is London. *New Left Review* is abbreviated to *NLR*.

Anderson, P. (1964) 'Origins of the present crisis', *NLR*, 23

Anderson, P. (1965a) 'The Left in the 50s', *NLR*, 29

Anderson, P. (1965b) 'Problems of socialist strategy', in Anderson, P. and Blackburn, R. (eds) *Towards Socialism*

Anderson, P. (1987) 'The figures of descent', *NLR*, 161

Barnett, A. (2000) 'Corporate populism and partyless democracy', *NLR*, 3

Blackburn, R. (1970) 'Let it bleed: Labour and the general election', *Red Mole*, 15 April

Chun, L. (1993) *The British New Left*, Edinburgh

Coates, D. (1982) 'Space and agency in the transition to socialism', *NLR*, 135

Coates, K. (1973) 'Socialists and the Labour Party', *The Socialist Register 1973*

Foot, M. (1968) (Interview) 'Credo of the Labour Left', *NLR*, 49

Gamble, A. (1974) *The Conservative Nation*

Gamble, A. (1981) *Britain in Decline*

Hall, S. (1988) *The Hard Road to Renewal: Thatcherism and the Crisis of the Left*

Hall, S. (1989) 'The first New Left: life and times', in Archer, R., Bubeck, D., Glock, H., Jacobs, L., Moglen, S., Steinhouse, A. and Weinstock, D. (eds) *Out of Apathy: Voices of the New Left 30 Years On*

Hall, S. and Jacques, M. (eds) (1983) *The Politics of Thatcherism*

Hoare, Q. and Ali, T. (1982) 'Socialists and the crisis of Labourism', *NLR*, 132

Hobsbawm, E. (1981) 'The forward march of Labour halted?', in Mulhern, F. and Jacques, M. (eds) *The Forward March of Labour Halted?*

Hutton, W. (1996) *The State We're In*

Kenny, M. (1995) *The First New Left: British Intellectuals After Stalin*

Leys, C. (1983) *Politics in Britain*

Marx, K, and Engels, F. (1848) *The Communist Manifesto*

Miliband, R. (1972 [1961]) *Parliamentary Socialism*, 2nd edition

Miliband, R. (1976) 'Moving on', *The Socialist Register1976*

Nairn, T. (1964a) 'The British political elite', *NLR*, 23

Nairn, T. (1964b) 'The English working class', *NLR*, 24

Nairn, T. (1964c) 'The nature of the Labour Party I', *NLR*, 27

Nairn, T. (1964d) 'The nature of the Labour Party II', *NLR*, 28

Nairn, T. (1970) 'The fateful meridian', *NLR*, 60

Nairn, T. (1972) 'The Left against Europe', *NLR*, 75

Nairn, T. (1977) *The Break-Up of Britain*

Nairn, T. (2000) 'Ukania under Blair', *NLR*, 1

New Left Review (1970) 'Themes', *NLR*, 60

Rothstein, T. (1929) *From Chartism to Labourism: Historical Sketches of the English Working Class Movement*

Samuel, R. and Stedman Jones, G. (1982) 'The Labour Party and social democracy', in Samuel, R. and Stedman Jones, G. (eds) *Culture, Ideology and Politics*

Saville, J. (1960) 'Apathy into politics', *NLR*, 4

Saville, J. (1967) 'Labourism and the Labour Government', *The Socialist Register 1967*

Saville, J. (1975) 'The ideology of Labourism', in Benewick, R. Berki, R. and Parekh, B. (eds) *Knowledge and Belief in Politics*

Sedgwick, P. (1976) 'The two New Lefts', in Widgery, D. (ed.) *The Left in Britain 1956–68*, Harmondsworth

Thompson, E. P. (1960) 'Revolution', *NLR*, 3

Thompson, E. P. (1963) *The Making of the English Working Class*

Thompson, E. P. (1965) 'The peculiarities of the English', *The Socialist Register 1965*

Williams, R. (1965) 'The British Left', *NLR*, 30

Williams, R. (1979) *Politics and Letters: Interviews with* New Left Review

Williams, R., Hall, S. and Thompson, E. P. (eds) (1967) *The May Day Manifesto*

4

Ralph Miliband and the Labour Party: from *Parliamentary Socialism* to 'Bennism'

Michael Newman

Ralph Miliband completed *Parliamentary Socialism* at the end of 1960 and it was published in October 1961. This proved to be probably the most influential book on the Labour Party written during the post-war era – possibly the most significant of any period. As chapter 5 will confirm, the book helped shape a whole school of left-wing interpretations of the party (Coates 2002; Panitch and Leys 1997) and established an analytical framework that challenged more conventional viewpoints.

Ironically, the argument advanced in *Parliamentary Socialism* was, in the first instance, not entirely obvious, and its impact on many readers was not quite what the author intended. Thus in 1994 Paul Foot of the Trotskyist Socialist Workers' Party (SWP) wrote that no book had 'made more impact on my life'. In 1961 Foot was contemplating a life as a Labour MP: *Parliamentary Socialism*, however, 'put me off that plan for ever, by exposing the awful gap between the aspirations and achievements of parliamentary socialists' (*Guardian*, 6 June 1994). Foot was not alone in deriving this message from the book. Yet, Miliband actually saw his work as an eleventh-hour call for the party to be transformed into an agency for the establishment of socialism, rather than a plea to abandon the party. However, it is hardly surprising that so many could derive the latter message from *Parliamentary Socialism*, as Miliband's attitude to the party in 1960 had been deeply ambivalent. Moreover, by the time the second edition was published, in 1972, his views had changed so much as to require a postscript which maintained that Labour 'will not be transformed into a party seriously concerned with socialist change'. Thus, while the task remained that of preparing the ground for a socialist alternative to capitalism, 'one of the indispensable elements of that process' had now become 'the dissipation of paralysing illusions about the true purpose and role of the Labour Party' (Miliband 1972: 376–7).

In order to help further our understanding of *Parliamentary Socialism*, and situate it firmly in its intended context, this chapter explains the evolution of Miliband's thinking about the Labour Party. It does so by analysing his wider assumptions about political change and the role of parties, and suggests that these were based on an attempt to understand both objective socio-political circumstances and subjective intentions and convictions. In addition, the chapter explains both the continuities and the changes in Miliband's view of the Labour Party between the 1950s and the 1990s.

The argument of Parliamentary Socialism

The opening sentences of *Parliamentary Socialism* effectively summarise Miliband's general outlook. Thus, of those parties 'claiming socialism to be their aim', Labour is characterised as being 'one of the most dogmatic' – not about socialism, but about the parliamentary system. 'Empirical and flexible about all else', Miliband (1972: 13) asserted, 'its leaders have always made devotion to that system their fixed point of reference and the conditioning factor of their political behaviour'. The rest of the book develops this point, providing an interpretation of the party's history and demonstrating that its insistence on parliamentary methods had wasted the potential of those who came to identify with it, and so had thwarted the advance towards socialism.

A significant feature of the book – and of Miliband's overall approach – is the extent to which it differed from both Communist Party (CP) and conventional Labour Left critiques. When CP members wrote about Labour, their argument – implicitly or explicitly – was that only the CP was a truly reliable opponent of capitalism because of its pristine working-class character and acceptance of 'scientific socialism'. Even when advocating unity among all parties on the Left, their underlying proposition was that socialist advance depended on increasing the size of the CP and securing acceptance of its theses. *Parliamentary Socialism* rejected any such notion: its comparatively few comments on CP policies were all negative. According to Miliband, therefore, socialism would not come from a more influential CP.

The *leitmotif* of the Labour Left analysis was, in contrast, the theme of leadership 'betrayal'. The assumption here was that, while Labour as a whole was socialist, its leaders periodically 'sold out' and diluted agreed policies. Miliband certainly shared the Left's insistence on the importance of the party's annual conference in determining policies, arguing it was an obstacle to the 'degradation of the business of politics' (Miliband 1958a: 174). He believed that the Left had two basic purposes, both of which he endorsed: to push the leadership into accepting more radical policies; and to press for more militant attitudes towards Labour's opponents. Moreover, while the leadership 'eagerly' accepted the parliamentary system, the Left adhered to its inhibitions and constrictions 'with a certain degree of unease and at times with acute misgivings' (Miliband 1972: 14–15). Yet, the Left still accepted parliamentarism, something which explained its ultimate failure – from the ILP until it exited the party in 1932, the Socialist League of the 1930s, the Bevanites and Victory for Socialism during the 1950s – to mount a successful challenge to the leadership. Thus, to Miliband, the party as a whole – the leadership as much as the Left – subordinated socialism to the dictates of the parliamentary road.

Miliband's primary argument was that, as a result of this subordination, in practice Labour stood merely for social reform rather than socialism. For whenever there was a possibility of more extensive change through extra-parliamentary action, the party had deliberately dampened it down. The only exceptions to this general rule occurred when such action was thought to be in the 'national interest' rather than for class purposes. Thus when, in 1920, it seemed the Lloyd George Government was about to become involved in war against the Soviet Union, Labour and many trade union leaders were prepared to take direct action to prevent such an outcome. In contrast, when the class element was dominant, the leadership was paralysed. Accordingly, 'it was the class character of the General Strike which made them behave as if they half believed they were guilty men, and which made them seek, with desperate anxiety, to purge themselves of their guilt' (Miliband 1972: 82, 144–5).

Miliband's secondary claim was that, despite Labour never having been socialist in practice, it had always contained socialists within its ranks. Indeed, the 1918 constitution, especially the Clause 4 commitment to extend public ownership, had 'created a basis of agreement between socialists and social reformers'. At the time, however, that which undoubtedly divided these 'two fundamentally different views' of Labour's purpose was 'sufficiently blurred' by the party's 1918 manifesto, *Labour and the New Social Order*, as 'to suggest a common purpose, at least in programmatic terms' (Miliband 1972: 62). In such an arrangement, Miliband argued, the social reformers in the leadership enjoyed hegemony. At the time of writing *Parliamentary Socialism* he nonetheless hoped that 'labourism' – which he defined as the historic coalition of socialists and social reformers – was about to disintegrate. This was because the party's then-leader, Hugh Gaitskell, who apparently wanted Labour to abandon even its notional commitment to socialism, had pitched himself fully against those who sought to fundamentally transform capitalism (Thorpe 2001: 125–44). Miliband appreciated that there would be attempts to sustain labourism and that, in an electoral system which discouraged fission, this would appear a wise course to many socialists. Even so, he considered 'genuine compromise' between Gaitskell and Labour's socialists to be impossible, as any compact that obscured the party's full commitment to socialism would merely allow the leadership to maintain its historic course (Miliband 1972: 345). His conclusion was that Labour should now transcend the orthodoxies of labourism and become a genuinely socialist party. Anything else would mean 'the kind of slow but sure decline which – deservedly – affects parties that have ceased to serve any distinctive political purpose' (Miliband 1972: 345).

Parliamentary Socialism therefore was sustained by a powerful critique of 'labourism', and contemporary reactions, from those whose opinions Miliband most respected, were generally enthusiastic. Yet even they were troubled by the politics of the work (Foot 1961; Hobsbawm 1961; Thompson 1961). This was partly because Miliband concentrated on the negative case against Labour and spent little time exploring alternatives. This unevenness led to the paradox, observed above, that while the author saw his book as a last-minute exhortation for the party's transformation, others viewed it as a call for socialists to abandon Labour. Miliband was undoubtedly guilty of not clarifying his underlying assumptions. The next section explores his obscured purpose in writing the book.

The politics of Parliamentary Socialism

Miliband had been a Marxist since the age at least of 16, when he first arrived in Britain, in May 1940, as a Jewish refugee from Belgium. An understanding of Miliband's Marxism, and especially his distinctive understanding of Marxism's implications, even though not an explicit feature of his analysis, is crucial to any full appreciation of *Parliamentary Socialism.*

As an adolescent, Miliband joined the left-wing Zionist organisation Hashomer Hazair, and it was in that environment where he probably first encountered Marxist thought. Once safely in Britain, he embarked on an analysis of society and politics from an essentially Marxist perspective, but for the first year or so established no formal connection with a political party. Having gained a place at the London School of Economics, which during the war was located in Cambridge, he associated with members of the CP. In June 1943, however, this contact effectively ceased as he entered the Belgian section of the Royal Navy, in which he remained until January 1946. During this period Miliband resumed his largely solitary attempt to make sense of contemporary developments, aided by one of the few copies of *Das Kapital* to find itself on a Royal Navy vessel. Despite this interest in Marxist theory, with the Second World War over he became increasingly critical of Stalin's Soviet Union and the CP over a range of issues – especially Moscow's attempt to bring down the independent communist regime in Yugoslavia and the growing anti-Semitism evident in numerous East European communist parties. As a result, Miliband continued to stay outside the orbit of established communist politics.

Miliband's relatively solitary position on the Left was an important influence on *Parliamentary Socialism* and the key reason for some of its apparent ambiguity. For, it was not the product of a long-time Labour left-winger whose interpretation was forged through the experience of leadership 'betrayal'; nor was it the result of Moscow-imposed orthodoxy. Moreover, Miliband's analysis was set within a broader understanding of the development of socialist politics after 1945 than usually attempted at the time.

One fundamental element in Miliband's wider framework was his vehement condemnation of American international policy. While critical of the Soviet Union, he did not doubt that the USA carried primary responsibility for the Cold War, and that this could be attributed to counter-revolutionary and anti-socialist motives. Furthermore, he was adamant that the USA played a crucial role in upholding West European capitalism. In fact, he argued that the USA had effectively replaced fascism as the established order's guarantor against any threat from the Left – and viewed the North Atlantic Treaty Organisation in this light. As a result, like many on the party's Left, Miliband saw Labour ending its close association with Washington as a pre-requisite for building socialism in Britain.

A second feature of Miliband's broader analysis was his rejection of Gaitskell's 'revisionist' argument – most openly articulated by Anthony Crosland in *The Future of Socialism* (1956) – that post-war capitalism had been transmuted into a less exploitative and more stable 'mixed economy'. In some short, but powerfully argued, pieces written during the late 1950s, Miliband subjected this claim to critical analysis, which foreshadowed his more extensive treatment in *The State in Capitalist Society* (1969). He did not deny that capitalism had changed, but argued that this did not affect its fundamental character. For, in all advanced industrial societies what he termed 'marginal collectivism', based on limited state intervention and welfare provision, had become 'the price which capitalism has learnt it must pay as a condition of its survival as a more or less going economic concern'. In fact, he asserted, no leading capitalist economy could be run efficiently without the kind of welfare state and extensions to public ownership associated with the 1945 Labour Government led by Clement Attlee (Miliband 1958b: 92). Thus, while Miliband thought that some of the reforms associated with marginal collectivism were worthwhile, unlike many in the Labour Party he did not think they marked a step towards socialism.

A third aspect of Miliband's overall argument concerned the role of the major parties of the Left. He believed liberal democracy had re-established itself after 1945 without relying on fascism – as many business leaders had done during the 1920s and 1930s – simply because the Left presented no serious threat. Instead of trying to transform capitalism, they limited their ambition to reconstructing and reforming the existing economic system. This criticism applied as much to communists in France and Italy as to Labour in Britain. Indeed, albeit for different reasons, he doubted that communists or Centre-Left social democratic parties such as Labour would bring about radical change. In the first instance, he believed that 'in every West European society a majority of people . . . would simply not support a Communist-led social revolution, whatever the Communists might say or do' (Miliband 1958c: 43). In contrast, social democrat leaders were everywhere 'primarily engaged in political brokerage' between the trade unions and capitalism – they were not trying to overthrow the latter with the help of the former (Miliband 1958c: 46). Against the Labour Left view that all that was needed was a new leadership, Miliband believed that the integration of parties of the Left into capitalism could not be explained in individualist terms but was the result of deeper structural forces (Miliband 1958c: 43).

The above were central points in the analytical framework behind *Parliamentary Socialism*: on their own they suggest the approach of a detached Marxist. However, like all good Marxists, Miliband wanted not only to interpret the world but to play a part in changing it. This meant he had to become engaged in some form of political activity – albeit of a rather tentative kind.

Miliband never doubted that a political party would be required to achieve socialism, and he was gradually drawn towards Labour, if only because it was supported by most working-class voters, while he was increasingly negative about the CP. The resignation of Aneurin Bevan from Attlee's Cabinet in 1951, after the introduction of prescription charges in the National Health Service, and the subsequent development of the 'Bevanite' movement on the Labour Left, probably finally encouraged him to join. Thus, from 1952 until 1957, the Labour Left was thus the main focus of his political activity. Miliband even participated in the Bevanite 'second eleven', which tried to build up support in the constituencies (Jenkins 1979). In 1955 he also attended the party's annual conference as a delegate for the Hampstead CLP. There he delivered an impassioned, if a fairly conventional leftist, speech on nationalisation and the need for conference to exert its authority over the leadership. He ended by calling for a 'clear and detailed programme to say specifically and clearly that we stand for socialism, that we are a socialist party, and that we shall go on being a socialist party until we have built the socialist commonwealth' (Labour Party 1955: 113).

Even while a Labour activist, however, Miliband never believed he belonged to a truly socialist party; it was, however, the best means of articulating socialism at that time. This position altered slightly with the emergence of the New Left during the late 1950s. The New Left promoted a variety of *avant-garde* endeavours, including cultural politics and the Campaign for Nuclear Disarmament, an intellectual eclecticism encapsulated in the journal *Universities and Left Review*. Miliband found such initiatives encouraging – betokening an ending of the constraining atmosphere of the Cold War – and supported the new movement. However, he attributed greater political importance to the other aspect of the New Left: the exit of many communists following Krushchev's 1956 secret speech, which revealed the true nature of Stalinism, and the Soviet repression of Hungary during the same year. In particular, the resignation of intellectuals, above all, the historians E. P. Thompson and John Saville, was of crucial importance to him. For, it meant that there were finally now Marxists outside the CP with whom he could join. When invited to write for their journal *New Reasoner*, he did so with enthusiasm, and, at the end of 1958, Miliband became the first person never to have been of a member of the CP to join its editorial board.

Despite the rise of the New Left, Miliband remained convinced that socialism needed a political party with strong links to the working class and, in that regard at least, Labour remained crucial. Thus, he continued to be active in the party, during 1958 becoming an executive council member and secretary of the home policy committee of the leftist Victory for Socialism (VFS). Miliband in fact hoped to draw the *New Reasoner* group into an alliance with the Labour Left in the hope that together they would transform Labour into a fully formed socialist organisation. Few others saw merit in his proposal, and, instead, the likes of Thompson joined up with the *Universities and Left Review* to establish the *New Left Review*, a journal which, for all its intellectual merits, never exerted much influence on Labour politics.

Miliband still remained optimistic that Labour would take a decisive turn to the Left as he wrote *Parliamentary Socialism*. It was in 1960 that Gaitskell's attempt to reduce the doctrinal significance of the party's commitment to public ownership suffered a decisive set-back. That year also saw him defeated at conference over unilateral nuclear disarmament. While Gaitskell eventually managed to reassert his position, Miliband's belief in Labour's centrality to any socialist strategy did not alter. He stayed on the VFS executive until the organisation disintegrated in the early 1960s, hoping – probably with diminishing faith – that through a combination of pressure and socialist education, both inside and outside the party, Labour might yet be turned into an body committed to transform capitalism.

There is one final aspect to Miliband's thinking at this time that needs to be highlighted. One of the unanswered questions in *Parliamentary Socialism* concerned the process of transition itself. For it was unclear whether Miliband rejected the possibility of a peaceful road to socialism. In truth, he did not know if violence would be necessary, for that would depend on the balance of forces present at the time of transition. He certainly believed a peaceful transition was the more probable if there was a large majority pressing for socialism, but he was also convinced that the commitment of the political leaders would be crucial. In other words, a party could bring about the transition to socialism only if it was sincere and resolute about its intentions. Thus questions of intention, will, consciousness and conviction were crucial in his attitude to political parties. In 1960 he was sure Labour lacked those qualities, but still held it conceivable that they might be developed through sustained pressure. Given the extent to which *Parliamentary Socialism* reflected Miliband's conditional, tentative and ambiguous support for the party, it is perhaps understandable that so many misunderstood his message.

The search for a socialist party

Unlike many on the New Left, Miliband did not view Harold Wilson's succession to the Labour leadership in 1963 as cause for celebration. Like many he certainly mistrusted Wilson personally. More importantly, however, he was largely alone in preferring that Labour's divisions be further accentuated while the new leader was initially adept at smoothing them over. In contrast to most, Miliband was, moreover, under no illusion about how far the Wilson Government elected in October 1964 was dominated by social reformers. Though it might introduce some valuable changes, there was no prospect of socialism from such a quarter. Nevertheless, during the Government's early days, he was enthusiastic about the possibility of organising seminars for Labour MPs, hoping these might encourage them to press for a more socialist strategy.

As did many others on the Labour Left, Miliband found Wilson's period in office between 1964 and 1970 to be a desperate disappointment. Indeed, it provided the postscript to the second edition of *Parliamentary Socialism* with much material to justify the author's rejection of the party as a vehicle for socialism. Yet Miliband's position had been transformed far earlier than that of most others on the Labour Left who took a similar route. While many activists were frustrated from the start of Wilson's tenure, most gave his government the benefit of the doubt until 1966 – when its wafer-thin Commons majority was, courtesy of the general election of that year, turned into something more substantial. In contrast, Miliband abandoned Labour in May 1965 on the grounds that it would never become a socialist party.

The catalyst for this change of attitude was Wilson's support for the American war in Vietnam. For Miliband, there was no question of compromise here: the Americans were external aggressors upholding a corrupt puppet government in South Vietnam that resisted a popular social revolution and national liberation. Thus, everybody on the Left had to oppose this policy. While many on the Labour Left – especially those associated with the weekly *Tribune* – looked on Vietnam in similar terms, most believed the Wilson Government should be supported given its possible role in reducing inequality and advancing state ownership. For Miliband, however, Vietnam was the decisive issue of the era – the real fault line that divided not only Left from Right, but morality from immorality. Labour under Wilson failed this fundamental test. In some ways Vietnam was merely the straw that broke the camel's back, thus Miliband's final decision might be thought to have been not an especially dramatic one. Even so, given his belief that parties were crucial agencies in the transformation to socialism, it had enormous implications for Miliband who still had no faith in any of the alternatives to Labour. So began his search for an effective substitute, one that would continue for the rest of his life.

As is often the case with converts, Miliband proclaimed his new conviction with an impressive zeal. Indeed, he was so keen to demonstrate that Labour was now an obstacle to socialism that he became wary of any form of association with his old party. Thus, when prominent figures on the Left held a series of meetings leading to the 1967 *May Day Manifesto*, which outlined a strategy to transform Britain into a socialist society, Miliband refused to participate, fearing the project was too preoccupied with his old party. Nor did the events of 1968 help much, although he was naturally heartened by growing opposition to the war in Vietnam and by the mobilisation of students across the West in solidarity with the Vietcong. However, because he was convinced that socialism needed a working class marching in step with an organised socialist party, he never saw the often- anarchic student protest as truly revolutionary. Nor did he have any faith in those Trotskyist and Maoist groups that proliferated in the late 1960s – while the Soviet invasion of Czechoslovakia in 1968 merely confirmed his enmity for communism.

Miliband constantly stressed that democracy and pluralism were integral to socialism, something that should be reflected in all aspects of its theory and practice. If the freedoms associated with capitalist democracy were inadequate, they should never be dismissed as 'bourgeois': socialists should instead aim to increase their scope beyond that allowed by capitalism. Socialist parties, he believed, must have open internal debates with dissenting minorities putting forward their own policies. Furthermore, Miliband argued against the notion of a single party to represent the working class either in capitalist or socialist society (Miliband 1977).

The implication of all this was that a new socialist party had to be established as soon as possible, one that would adhere to both Marxism and pluralism, qualities neither Labour nor its rivals on the Left enjoyed. Miliband had toyed with this idea ever since his break with Labour, but made a more determined attempt to bring it about in the mid-1970s, when professor of politics at the University of Leeds. However, despite various attempts to promote support for an inclusive, democratic, Marxist-oriented party, Miliband was no nearer to establishing such an organisation at the end of the 1970s than he had been at the start. Even so, he played a leading role in a more modest initiative – the Centres of Marxist Education – designed to promote the spread of Marxist ideas in the labour movement. Nonetheless, his aspirations for a party that would propagate socialism to the masses had yet to be fulfilled.

The impact of 'Bennism'

Labour lost the 1979 general election, following what socialists viewed as yet another depressing period in office. Miliband's initial reaction was to criticise socialists who still thought their main goal should be to push the party leftwards. So far as Labour was concerned, Miliband believed the only contribution it could make to socialism was if it split so that its left wing might form the nucleus for a genuinely socialist organisation. Even that he believed to be unlikely. Thus, Miliband was highly sceptical about the merits of the campaign to change the party's constitution, promoted by the likes of the Campaign for Labour Party Democracy to give activists greater control of the leadership. Having participated in the Bevanite campaign of the 1950s, Miliband believed such efforts were mis-conceived, as he was convinced that the social reformers in the leadership would always control policies in practice. Thus, while well intentioned, the attempt to make this hegemony more difficult in constitutional theory seemed to Miliband to be a waste of socialist energy.

During the 1980s Miliband slowly revised his position, due largely to a more positive evaluation of those who sought to take the party in a more socialist direc-tion and especially to his high regard for Tony Benn, their standard-bearer. Miliband was impressed by Benn's refusal to stand for the discredited Shadow Cab-inet after the 1979 defeat, but only got to know him personally in April 1980 after being invited to speak at a day-school in Benn's Bristol constituency. Although Miliband inevitably gave a lecture on why Labour could never become the agency for a socialist transformation of Britain, there were signs of an immediate rapport with Benn, which would develop into a close political and personal relationship. Thus, when Benn, backed by an array of left-wing groups, challenged the incum-bent Denis Healey for Labour's deputy leadership in 1981, Miliband acknowledged the Left's progress within the party. Furthermore, given its acceptance of the need for forms of extra-parliamentary action, this also appeared to be a new kind of 'Left'. He also appreciated the wider political significance of the Left's control of the Greater London Council under Ken Livingstone. Indeed, during the early 1980s the Labour Left appeared to have command of the party for the first time in its his-tory. Not only were many local authorities under its influence but also Labour's basic economic policies now reflected the Left's outlook. Constitutional change had, moreover, reduced the influence of MPs and gave activists a say in the election of both leader and deputy leader. The old left-winger Michael Foot, elected in 1980, was seen as merely a stopgap before Benn could assume the mantle. His campaign to replace Healy as deputy was regarded as a dry run for the leadership itself, and, while bitterly fought, Benn came within less than 1 per cent of winning the post (Seyd 1987).

It was in this context that Miliband became involved in establishing the Social-ist Society, the founding conference of which was held in January 1982. In atten-dance were 1,200 individuals who ranged from members of the Labour Left to those belonging to the SWP and the International Marxist Group. Miliband played an important role in drafting the invitation, which significantly proclaimed that the society aimed to encourage socialist renewal inside the broader labour movement and help those fighting for socialist ideas in the party itself. This did not mean, however, that he was now reconciled to Labour. In fact, he remained worried that the society would become too preoccupied with the party's internal developments and wanted it to keep a critical distance. Nevertheless, this certainly marked a change from his position at the time of the May Day Manifesto, for he was now prepared to work closely with people who were still active in Labour's ranks.

During the early 1980s Miliband's respect for Benn steadily mounted. He viewed Benn as someone who – as a cabinet minister in the Labour governments of the 1960s and 1970s – had seen at first hand how often the party's principles were subordinated to the 'political game', and he learned from the experience. He was also attracted by Benn's energy, constant refusal to accept defeat and conviction that socialism would eventually triumph. Benn was not a theorist, still less a Marxist, but there was a similarity between them in their optimism. It was also relevant that they were almost the same age and so had many of the same formative influences and reference points.

By 1985, however, Benn's star no longer shone as brightly as it had done. He had lost his seat in the 1983 general election – a disastrous defeat for the party nationally for which many blamed the Left's policies. Although returned to the Commons as a result of the Chesterfield by-election a year later, Benn found that the atmosphere inside the party had changed considerably. He had also lost his chance to replace Foot, who had resigned immediately after the end of the 1983 campaign. The main strategy of the new leader, Neil Kinnock, was to push Labour back to the mainstream so as to squeeze out the SDP, formed in 1981 by ex-Labour social reformers who believed the Left had gained permanent control of the party. The SDP almost forced Labour into third place behind the Conservatives in the 1983 election and Kinnock thought Labour's only hope was to abandon most of the positions it had assumed while Bennism was at its peak. In addition, the 1984–85 Miners' Strike which ended in disastrous defeat, and the Thatcher Government's rate-capping of left-wing local authorities further demoralised and divided Labour activists. As a result, many of Benn's sometime supporters re-packaged themselves as the 'soft left' and sought an accommodation with Kinnock.

It was in this inauspicious climate that Miliband made a proposal to Benn when they met in February 1985. Benn's (unpublished) diary records the conversation as follows:

> He [Miliband] said, 'You are a great resource for the movement. Looking back from Keir Hardie, Ramsay MacDonald, George Lansbury, Stafford Cripps, Nye Bevan right through there has never been somebody with your experience of Government who has taken such a radical position on institutional questions – quite exceptional experience and you must use it properly. I would suggest that you keep absolutely away from infighting in the Party which does nothing whatever to assist . . . I don't know if you've read [the] Life of De Gaulle but you are in the position he was at *Colombey les Deux Eglises*, waiting, available, a senior statesman of the left and you should look ahead and address people when you think it right to do so but that is really your function.

'Have you got a think tank – would you like me to help you to get together a few academics who would be prepared to assist?'

I was very flattered. He said, 'You underestimate your role as a leader, we need leaders . . . and I think you should take that role . . .'.

Miliband was not complimenting Benn for the sake of it. After unsuccessfully attempting to convince people that a new party was needed, and finding it so difficult to make progress, he saw Benn as a potential leader, one receptive to socialist ideas. Miliband's recent experience in the Socialist Society had perhaps also persuaded him that such initiatives would always be condemned to marginality unless harnessed to a figure with a national reputation. He therefore thought it important to bolster Benn, to keep alive the kind of socialist commitment he represented, by providing him with an intellectual forum. At the same time Benn's involvement with people from outside the Labour Party might eventually galvanise a wider socialist movement that could lead to the new formation Miliband sought. Moreover, while Miliband realised Benn's importance, this feeling was more than reciprocated and the enduring pattern of their relationship was established.

If Miliband really told Benn he could 'get together a few academics', they were of a very particular kind, for he invited Hilary Wainwright and John Palmer from the Socialist Society, and Perry Anderson, Robin Blackburn and Tariq Ali from the editorial board of *New Left Review*. The group called themselves the Independent Left Corresponding Society (ILCS); and, with a fluctuating membership, the ILCS held monthly meetings for the next few years. Benn and Miliband each derived something from the initiative, but both were aware that they were not entirely united in their aims. While Miliband was trying to draw Benn out from internal Labour politics and make him the rallying point for a new socialist movement, Benn was keen to harness the ILCS to the Labour Left to help it combat the Kinnock leadership.

As time went on, Benn's increasingly marginal role in the Labour Party became ever more evident, as was the position of the Left generally within Margaret Thatcher's Britain. After Labour lost a third successive general election. in June 1987, Miliband persuaded Benn to hold a socialist conference in Chesterfield. Organised by the Socialist Society along with the Bennite Campaign Group of Labour MPs, this was held in October 1987 and drew an attendance of 2,000 people. Miliband was disappointed by the predominance of SWP members and the general focus on Labour politics. Although he remained a member of the organising committee for the second Chesterfield conference, which was held in the following June, and continued to be a friend and supporter of Benn, Miliband probably no longer believed that the socialist breakthrough would occur in the short-term. Indeed, in January 1988, he tried to dissuade Benn from standing for the Labour leadership – this presumably was something De Gaulle would not have attempted. Benn, however, did not take his advice – something he later regretted, for he secured only 11 per cent of the votes in an election that gave Kinnock a much-needed boost. Miliband shared the general view that the second Chesterfield conference was more successful than the first, but he no longer exuded confidence that the Socialist Movement, which emerged from it, was the embryo of a new party. He was well aware that, for the time being at least, the Left was in decline in Britain and that non-aligned socialists of his ilk were highly marginal figures.

If Miliband's role in relation to 'Bennism' is considered in comparison to his earlier attitudes, some striking points emerge about the interaction between the analytical and subjective aspects in his interpretive framework. In 1979, his initial position was to adhere to an analysis based entirely on an understanding of structural factors. From this perspective it seemed clear that Labour would never present a real challenge to the Thatcher Government, and that the Left under Benn could not gain control of it. However, he shifted his position because of an appreciation of the subjective intentions of the Bennites and the character of Benn himself. In the mid-1960s he had written off Labour because the Wilson Government's attitude to the American presence in Vietnam demonstrated its passivity and fundamental lack of morality. In the mid-1980s Miliband was prepared to devote considerable time to Benn for the opposite reason: he believed him capable of providing the right kind of socialist leadership. In other words, Miliband wanted to help Benn because of the latter's convictions and determination. This did not mean his appreciation of the Labour left-winger's personal qualities negated his analytical framework. He was always aware that Benn was unlikely to succeed within the Labour Party and that the tide was turning against the Left in general. Nonetheless, Miliband's allegiances were determined both by his assessment of people's subjective qualities – consciousness, will and ideology – and by his analytical framework. He did not believe, however, that subjective intentions could transcend objective circumstances – as was indicated by another shift in his view of the Labour Party.

After communism

It was argued earlier that Miliband saw developments in the Labour Party from an international perspective: *Parliamentary Socialism* owed much to his understanding of the role of West European social democracy and of an international system dominated by the USA. It is therefore perhaps not surprising that what would be his final position was also based on an analysis of the key changes in the wider world – particularly the collapse of communism.

After 1968 Miliband had regarded the Soviet-backed regimes of Eastern Europe as 'bureaucratic collectivist' systems that had no relation to socialism. However, during the 1980s, when the leader of the Soviet Union, Mikhael Gorbachev, attempted to reform the Soviet regime from within, Miliband become an enthusiast for what was referred to as *perestroika*. With the prospects for the Left generally bleak in the West, he hoped that a successful transformation of the East European system into a form of democratic socialism might revive the prospects for socialism across Europe. If Gorbachev succeeded, the association between the Left and totalitarianism – so powerful a weapon in the armoury of the Right – could finally be broken. Unfortunately, Gorbachev failed and the Soviet Union eventually embraced capitalism rather than pluralist socialism.

Miliband tried to suggest that the downfall of communism was, nonetheless, also advantageous for the Left, given the extent to which the Soviet regimes had long embarrassed Western socialists such as himself. However, he was not entirely convinced by his own argument, and in August 1989, as the East European regimes crumbled, he wrote that, for years to come, 'socialists will be something like a pressure group to the left of orthodox social democracy'. It was social democratic parties such as Labour that 'will for a long time constitute the alternative – such as it is – to conservative governments' (Miliband 1989a: 36). A few weeks later he suggested that the end of communism meant 'socialism has to be reinvented'. 'All anti-socialists', he went on, 'rejoice in what they take to be the death of socialism', and while socialists needed 'to prove them wrong', that 'will require a lot of work' (Miliband 1989b). This was slightly misleading, for he still believed that a Marxist-inspired version of socialism was both valid and possible. Much of the 'reinvention' was therefore also 'reaffirmation', as Miliband was to show in his final (and posthumously published) book *Socialism For a Sceptical Age* (1994). However, acceptance of the fact that social democracy would be the only alternative available to the forces of the Right for a long period had clear implications for his attitude to British politics, for it meant, in effect, acquiescence in Labour's role as the leading party on the Left.

It would nonetheless be wrong to suggest that Miliband had come full circle back to his position of 1960. When completing the first edition of *Parliamentary Socialism* he had also known that the socialist transformation would be 'a long haul' but had thought that the first step should be Labour's conversion to socialist ideas. By 1994 his own commitment remained undiminished, but he knew socialism was not currently on the political agenda. In the meantime Labour could be supported as the alternative – 'such as it is' – to the Right.

Miliband died in May 1994, the same month as Kinnock's successor John Smith, and so did not live to see Tony Blair become leader of what he would refer to as 'New Labour'. It is worth asking what he might have made of events after 1994, had he lived. Miliband would, no doubt, have seen Blair's Labour Party as preferable to the Conservatives. Yet he would probably have regarded it as much further removed from his own convictions than was the Labour Party he had condemned in *Parliamentary Socialism*. He would undoubtedly have been forced to accept that the 'long haul' was now even longer than he had previously believed. Yet he might also have thought it inadequate either simply to denounce 'New Labour' or to give up all hope of socialism. Rather than despairing, he would have analysed Blair's project as part of an international phenomenon and tried to identify the factors likely to produce a more adequate response to the latest phase of capitalism. Most importantly, Miliband would have insisted that – whatever Labour's role in the process might be – it remained both possible and necessary to create a co-operative, democratic and egalitarian society.

References

Unless indicated, the place of publication is London.
Coates, D. (ed.) (2002), *Paving the Third Way: The Critique of Parliamentary Socialism*
Crosland, C. A. R. (1956) *The Future of Socialism*

Foot, M. (1961) 'Review of *Parliamentary Socialism*', *Tribune*, 20 October

Hobsbawm, E. (1961) 'Review of *Parliamentary Socialism*', *New Left Review*, 12

Jenkins, M. (1979) *Bevanism: Labour's High Tide*, Nottingham

Labour Party (1955) *Labour Party Conference Annual Report*

Miliband, R. (1958a) 'Party democracy and parliamentary government', *Political Studies*, 6:2

Miliband, R. (1958b) 'The transition to the transition', *New Reasoner*, 6

Miliband, R. (1958c) 'The politics of contemporary capitalism', *New Reasoner*, 5

Miliband, R. (1969) *The State in Capitalist Society*

Miliband, R. (1972 [1961]) *Parliamentary Socialism: A Study in the Politics of Labour*, 2nd edition

Miliband, R. (1977) *Marxism and Politics*, Oxford

Miliband, R. (1989a) 'Reflections on the crisis of the communist regimes', *New Left Review*, 177

Miliband, R. (1989b) Letter to John Saville, 13 September, held in Miliband's papers

Miliband, R. (1994) *Socialism for a Sceptical Age*

Panitch, L. and Leys, C. (1997) *The End of Parliamentary Socialism: From New Left to New Labour*

Seyd, P. (1987) *The Rise and Fall of the Labour Left*

Thompson, E. P. (1961) 'Review of *Parliamentary Socialism*', *Time and Tide*, 12 October

Thorpe, A. (2001) *A History of the British Labour Party*

5

The continuing relevance of the Milibandian perspective

David Coates and Leo Panitch

> The belief in the effective transformation of the Labour Party into an instrument of socialist politics is the most crippling of illusions to which socialists in Britain have been prone . . . To say that the Labour Party is the party of the working class is . . . important . . . but it affords no answer to the point at issue, namely that a socialist party is needed in Britain, and that the Labour Party is not it, and it will not be turned into it. To say that it is a party of the working class is, on this view, to open the discussion, not to conclude it. It might be otherwise if there was any likelihood that the Labour Party could be turned into a socialist formation; but that is precisely the premise which must, on a realistic view, be precluded. (Miliband 1976: 128, 130)

> Labourism . . . a theory and practice which accepted the possibility of social change within the existing framework of society; which rejected the revolutionary violence and action implicit in Chartist ideas of physical force; and which increasingly recognized the working of political democracy of the parliamentary variety as the practical means of achieving its own aims and objectives. (Saville 1973: 215; see also Saville 1988: 14)

The legacy of Ralph Miliband's writings on the Labour Party has been, and remains, both an important and a controversial one. It is also one that is much caricatured by critics unfamiliar with its central theses. Indeed, too often in collections of essays on New Labour these days, lazy throwaway lines discourage serious readers from exploring its complexity and continuing importance. So, for example, in the essays gathered to mark the Labour Party's centenary (Brivati and Heffernan 2000), the works to be discussed here were dismissed by Ben Pimlott as the 'we wuz robbed' school of party history (Jefferys 2000: 68); and even the more careful Robert Taylor reported that in the work inspired by the writings of Miliband 'trade unions were portrayed as a formidable, defensive barrier to Labour's Socialist advance, supposedly holding back the masses from commitment to a militant socialism' (Taylor 2000: 10). But neither characterisation, though perhaps appropriate to many others, is either accurate or just in respect of Miliband; and, indeed, one reason why this chapter may be of lasting value is that it will demonstrate that impropriety.

For there is a distinctively Milibandian perspective within the historiography of the Labour Party. The content and complexity of that perspective has grown over time, as the early work of Ralph Miliband and his sometime collaborator John Saville has been supplemented by the writings of other scholars persuaded of the importance of their initial formulations. Yet even those initial formulations were not of the 'we wuz robbed' variety. Instead, from the outset, the arguments developed by Miliband and Saville about Labour politics were far more sophisticated and important than that. From its inception, the Milibandian perspective on the Labour Party emphasised the importance of three things. It emphasised, *first*, the centrality of parliamentarianism to the theory and practice of Labour Party politics, and its deleterious consequences for the party's capacity to act as a successfully reformist agency when in office. It stressed, *second*, the functionality of the Labour Party's periodically radical rhetoric to the long-term stability of the British class structure, and its harmful consequences for the creation and consolidation of a radicalised proletariat. *Third*, it emphasised the inability of socialists within the Labour Party to do more than briefly (and episodically) radicalise the rhetoric and policy commitments of the party in opposition, and the deleterious consequences of that inability for the creation of a genuinely potent socialist party in Britain.

It is these three complex propositions that constitute the core of the early-Miliband-inspired scholarship on the Labour Party and its limits; and it is with their establishment and development that this chapter is primarily concerned.

The Labour Party and working-class incorporation

The character of Miliband's early writings on the Labour Party have been documented in the previous chapter, and will not be re-established here. Instead, we begin by observing, lest it be forgotten, that Miliband's later writings were not predominantly focused on the Labour Party, and from 1969 the focus of his work shifted to state theory. This shift – beginning with the publication of *The State in Capitalist Society* (1969) and his famous debate with the Greek socialist theorist Nicos Poulantzas – made him for a while one of the most internationally recognised intellectual figures in political science and sociology in the English-speaking world and beyond. In this change of focus and status, it was not that his original positions on the Labour Party were abandoned so much as generalised.

The thesis in *The State* was the by-now-standard one for the Milibandian 'school' as a whole. This was that democratic politics in advanced capitalist societies operate within powerful class constraints; and that these constraints are structured into the political domain through the conservatism of state bureaucracy, the force of business and financial interests, and the ideological pressure of capitalist values in the mass media. Social democratic parties of the Labour Party variety were not entirely ignored in this analysis; but they appeared there in less prominent roles. They appeared as orchestrators of capitalist legitimation and working-class demobilisation, as part of the political processes that accommodate democratic aspirations to capitalist power structures, and as 'singularly weak agencies of mass education in socialist principles and purposes' (Miliband 1969: 196). What in *Parliamentary Socialism* (1961) had been presented as a vulnerability to parliamentary socialisation now reappeared in *The State in Capitalist Society* as an inadequate capacity for counter-hegemonic politics. Hence the latter book singled out Labour leaders' 'ideological defenses' as being 'generally not . . . of nearly sufficient strength to enable them to resist with any great measure of success conservative pressure, intimidation and enticement' (Miliband 1969: 195).

What was presented in general terms in *The State* also reappeared as very much a United Kingdom phenomenon, in Miliband's *Capitalist Democracy in Britain* (1982). There, the compatibility of capitalism with democracy, now explained in neo-Gramscian terms, was seen as a consequence of 'the hegemony exercised by the dominant class and its conservative forces' (1982: 15). The capacity of that hegemony to survive unscathed was, in considerable measure, still seen as a product of past Labour Party policy. Miliband was clear on this when critiquing the arguments of his mentor Harold Laski:

> The whole political scene would indeed have been transformed had the Labour Party in the inter-war years been the socialist party which he wanted it to be, or at least believed that it must soon become. But one of the most significant facts about the British political scene was precisely that the Labour Party was not then, and was not on the way to becoming, such a party. This gave Laski's argument a certain air of unreality, which the passage of time has made even more pronounced. This is a great pity because the argument itself is right: the political system would be fundamentally affected if the Labour Party (or any other party) did become a major force for socialist change; even more so if it was able to form a government and sought to implement a programme of socialist policies. But the fact is that the political system has never had to face such a situation. This of course is something which itself requires explanation. (Miliband 1982: 16)

Key to that explanation for Miliband, in 1982 as much as in 1961, was the Labour Party's own exposure to (and enthusiasm for) the rules and institutions of parliamentarism as these were generally understood among the British political class. 'Nothing', he wrote,

> has weighed more heavily upon labour politics in Britain than the existence of a strong framework of representation: however inadequate and undemocratic it might be, there did exist, it was believed, a solid proven structure that could be made more adequate and democratic, that had already undergone reform, and that in due course could be used to serve whatever purpose a majority might desire, including the creation of a socialist order. (Miliband 1982: 27)

Parliamentarism of this kind worked, according to Miliband, by co-option and incorporation. 'It simultaneously [enshrined] the principle of popular *inclusion* and that of popular *exclusion*' (Miliband 1982: 38): co-opting and incorporating the working class as an electorate, their more radical parliamentary representatives, and their trade union leaderships. The British parliamentary State sustained the private rule of capital in the UK by drawing all these potentially oppositional social forces and political institutions into a form of democratic politics that left elected governments subject to the constraints of a conservative state apparatus and a well-entrenched business and financial class, and left their electorate subject to heavy ideological pressure from schools, churches and the media. The Labour

Party leadership, Miliband argued, had long been an active player in that process of political socialisation and incorporation: training early generations in the rules of parliamentary politics (especially in the illegitimacy of the use by Labour of industrial power for political ends); and repressing (until challenged by the Bennite internal party reforms of the early 1980s) internal party democracy, so that MPs could remain free of effective pressure from constituency activists and Labour Cabinets could remain free of party control (Miliband 1982: 68–76).

The question of 'betrayal'

Quite contrary to what their less than careful critics often assert, neither Miliband nor Saville subscribed to some 'sell-out' theory of British labour, some notion that the British working class was inherently socialist but was persistently betrayed by its moderate political leadership. The Milibandian understanding of the relationship between Labour as a political party, the working class as a social force and socialism as a body of ideas was always far more complex than that. As Marxists Miliband and Saville always believed that the contradictory relationship between capital and labour in a capitalist society precludes an effective long-term realisation of working-class interests without a major resetting of property relationships. They did not apologise for perpetually raising the socialist question, seeing it still a legitimate issue to discuss when exploring left-wing political formations. But their critique of British Labour was *not* that an already existing socialist working class required better political leadership. Such a claim constituted, in Miliband's view, a 'gross overestimation of the strength of the socialist forces in the Labour Party and in the labour movement at large' and, as such, 'obvious nonsense' (Miliband 1977a: 47). He later wrote:

> There is no point pretending that there exists a ready-made majority in the country for a socialist programme. How could there be? One of the fruits of the long predominance of labourism is precisely that the party of the working class has never carried out any sustained campaign of education and propaganda on behalf of a socialist programme; and that Labour leaders have frequently turned themselves into fierce propagandists against the socialist proposal of their critics inside the Labour Party and out, and have bent their best efforts to the task of defeating all attempts to have the Labour Party adopt such proposals. Moreover, a vast array of conservative forces, of the most diverse kind, are always at hand to dissuade the working class from even thinking about . . . socialist ideas . . . a ceaseless battle for the 'hearts and minds' of the people is waged by the forces of conservatism, against which have only been mobilized immeasurably smaller socialist forces. (Miliband 1983a: 304–5)

The Milibandian thesis was never that an inherently socialist working class was periodically betrayed by Labour Party moderation. It was rather that the possibility of creating such a radicalised class has been blocked by, among other things, the presence of a party committed to Labourism rather than socialism, and the periodic leftwards shift in rhetoric made by the Labour Party whenever working-class militancy intensified. The Milibandian argument was always that the emergence of such a working class was, with the Labour Party in the way, extraordinarily difficult to trigger; but it was also that the creation of mass support for socialist programmes was both possible and necessary. The whole thrust of the Milibandian argument on the working class and socialism was that the fusion between the two was one that had to be *created*, and that such a creation required clear and unambiguous political leadership of a kind that the Labour Party systematically declined to offer. As Miliband and Marcel Liebman (1986: 481) put it:

> The notion that very large parts of 'the electorate', and notably the working class, is bound to reject radical programmes is a convenient alibi, but little else. The real point, which is crucial, is that such programmes and policies need to be defended and propagated with the utmost determination and vigour by leaders totally convinced of the justice of their cause. It is *this* which is always lacking: infirmity of purpose and the fear of radical measures lies not with the working class but with the social democratic leaders themselves.

Careless critics have therefore moved too quickly to condemn those who take this perspective for misunderstanding the Labour Party's project as something other (and more radical) than it was. Not so. They always understood that project – in all its moderation and episodic radicalism – well enough. They simply found it wanting both when measured against its own promises and when set on the wider map of European and global working-class politics.

The Miliband legacy

To dwell, as we have thus far, on Ralph Miliband's contribution to the study of the Labour Party minimises the great effect of the broader role he played in founding a creative new current of Marxist political analysis. The remit of his *Marxism and Politics* (1977b: 14), arguably his greatest book, was the need to show clearly

> what a Marxist political theory specifically involves; and to indicate how far it may serve to illuminate any particular aspect of historical or contemporary reality. For this pupose, the developments in Marxist political thinking in recent years have obviously been of great value, not least because the constricting 'triumphalism' of an earlier period has been strongly challenged and the challenge has produced a much greater awareness among Marxists that Marxism, in this as much as in other realms, is full of questions to be asked and – no less important – of answers to be questioned. Many hitherto neglected or underestimated problems have attracted greater attention; and many old problems have been perceived in better light. As a result, the beginnings have been made of a political theorization in the Marxist mode. But these are only beginning.

It was this broader perspective, this invitation to go beyond the old Marxist paradigm and create a new and richer one, that excited the new generation of intellectuals and scholars that emerged in the 1960s and 1970s, the two of us among them. Unconnected with each other in any way, we took up many of the themes that Miliband (and Saville) had already sounded in their studies of Labourism, seeking not only to extend their account of the contemporary party's history but also to develop further the conceptual apparatus for doing so. Like Miliband, we also sought to go beyond the Labour Party in this respect and to contribute to the development of Marxist political theory in general. Unlike him, however (he once privately admitted to being bored by economics), we also sought to engage on this basis with the new Marxist political economy. Thus in our accounts of the Labour Party from the 1960s to the 1990s we both built on what he had established and yet departed from him in various ways. This meant telling the history of policy and intra-party conflict in more detail than he did, and concentrating much more on economic policy and political economy.

Miliband was therefore not alone in turning from the focused analysis of one political party to a more general political sociology of social democracy and the State. By the mid-1970s Leo Panitch had already intervened significantly in the emerging international debate on corporatism (Panitch 1977a, 1980a, 1981), and had made his initial contributions to the new Marxist work on the State (Panitch 1976, 1980b, 1986b, 1986c). After *Labour in Power?* (Coates 1980), Coates's own Gramscian turn then produced *The Context of British Politics* (1984a) and *Running the Country* (1995 [1990]), both of which sit alongside Colin Leys's *Politics in Britain* (1983) as major attempts to produce a general assessment of the parameters of Labour politics in the manner of Miliband's writings on the State. Such initiatives then extended into intellectual territory that Miliband did not explore – rounding out this Marxist political sociology with a series of studies in international and comparative political economy. Panitch encouraged (and developed himself) a new approach to democratic state administration (Albo, Langille and Panich 1993) and a distinctive *Socialist Register* position on the relationship of globalisation to the State (Panitch 1994); and Coates produced, first, a detailed survey of British economic under-performance (Coates 1994) and then a comparative study of models of capitalism (1999a, 2000a). This set of later publications produced new frameworks for analysing developments in Labour politics: not only by exploring the limits of Old Labour politics through a discussion of 'corporatism', but by examining the limits of New Labour through notions of 'progressive competitiveness'. In this way, a Milibandian perspective was eventually brought to the analysis of New Labour, one that was armed with a range of concepts and arguments that went beyond those available to it in the first phase of its work on the Labour Party.

The issue of 'corporatism'

The first moves in these new directions came in response to the experience of Labour in power between 1974 and 1979. Through his intervention in the famous profits squeeze debate of the 1970s, Panitch stressed the centrality of class conflict to understanding the crisis of the British economy (Panitch 1977b). In a study initially designed as an update of *The Labour Party and the Struggle for Socialism*, Coates developed what was an early attempt at Milibandian political economy to explain Labour's dismal performance in office. In *Labour in Power?* (1980) Coates argued that, though vital as a first step, it was no longer enough merely to list the range of powerful interests constraining Labour governments, because to do only that was to imply that those interests were in control of their world even if Labour was not in control of its. What was needed instead was the recognition that 'neither private elites nor public figures either understood or were in complete control of the main processes which shaped the world economy over which they presided', and that it was the *capitalist* nature of that world economy that ultimately held the key to the failure of this Labour Government and to the growing estrangement of trade unionists from it. 'To understand the events of the 1970s', Coates (1980: 160–1) argued, 'to assess the true impact of elite constraints, to place the power of British trade unionism, and to discuss the future of the Left in Britain, the question of capitalism had to be faced, and its impact on British politics fully understood.'

The question was how best to do that. One answer came from a systematic examination of the class constraints then eroding the viability of corporatism. In a widely cited article written against the background of the second Wilson Government, Panitch (1977a: 66) defined corporatism as 'a political structure within advanced capitalism which integrates organized socio-economic producer groups through a system of representation and co-operative mutual interaction at the leadership level and of mobilization and social control at the mass level', emphasising its inherent instability with the presence of strong social democratic labour movements. The class parameters surrounding even the corporatist version of the capitalist state, Panitch argued, and the resulting policy outputs reflecting 'capitalist class dominance' had eventually to draw the unions out of corporatist structures, or had at least to oblige them 'to abstain from accommodative behaviour if they were not to be repudiated by their rank and file membership' (Panitch 1977a: 138). This explanation of the propensity of Labour governments to succumb to winters of discontent of the 1978–79 variety also figured in David Coates's later writings on this last example of Old Labour in power. What Labour then understood to be socialism, he wrote,

> was more properly understood as a mild form of corporatism, the sharing of political power with bureaucratized trade union leadership and corporate capital. Yet . . . this power sharing was itself a major barrier to capital accumulation, and so proved destructive of the very economic growth that Labour governments sought to extract from the mixed economy . . . For even on such favourable political and industrial terrain corporatism proved to be extraordinarily brittle. Anaesthetizing rather than removing the basic cleavage of interest between capital and labour, by pushing that tension down to lower levels of decision-making, corporatist structures . . . in the end fell victim to the contradictions they were supposed to suppress. (Coates 1984a: 258; see also Coates 1984b: 131)

The political economy of 'New Labour'

This repositioning of the study of the Labour Party on the wider canvas of state theory and corporatist political practice moved the centre of gravity of such studies away from the detail of Labour Party political developments into a more general analysis of capitalism and the contemporary state. That move was accentuated through the course of the 1980s and 1990s by further emphasis on questions of political economy. The long years of Thatcherism imposed their own imperative here. David Coates probed the adequacy of Thatcherite claims about the adverse *economic* consequences of a strong labour movement, and argued against the low-wage, low-welfare, growth strategy that the Conservatives were then pursuing. Panitch followed his colleague Greg Albo in theorising that strategy as one of 'competitive austerity', contrasted it to the emerging Centre–Left enthusiasm for strategies of 'progressive competitiveness', and developed arguments about the inadequacies of each (Albo 1994, 1997). As New Labour repositioned the party's economic policies – from both the radical statism of both the Bennite alternative economic strategy and Old Labour corporatism – Panitch saw parallels between Labour's growing enthusiasm for reskilling as the key to industrial modernisation and 'Clintonomics', and warned the Left about both.

> The two centuries-old search for a cross-class 'producer' alliance between labour and national capital as an alternative to class struggle has taken shape in recent years in the form of the progressive competitiveness strategy, but its weaknesses have been very quickly revealed in the context of the globalization of capital. (Panitch 1994: 87)

Similar arguments were by then appearing sequentially in Coates's writings on the British economy. These came first in the form of a critique of Thatcherite low wage-growth strategies (Coates 1994), and later as critiques of New Labour's emerging political economy and of contemporary social democratic growth strategies of the Swedish or Clinton–Reich variety (Coates 1999a, 1999b, 2000a). By the time *Models of Capitalism* was published, towards the end of New Labour's first term, those following a Milibandian perspective had equipped themselves with a set of *political economy* theses that both illuminated central weaknesses in New Labour's economic strategy and rounded out what had hitherto been an approach to the politics of Labour more narrowly anchored on the terrain of history and sociology.

Limits to Labour Party radicalism

Between the 1980s' writings on the limits of Old Labour's corporatism and the 1990s' writings on the dangers of New Labour's enthusiasm for 'progressive competitiveness' – came a further refining and deepening of some of the older strands of the Milibandian approach to Labour politics. This focused particularly on the inability of the party to transform itself into an effective counter-hegemonic force, and the inability of the Labour Left, however well endowed, to transform Labour into a socialist organisation. The argument on the link between Labour's electoral politics and its weakness as a hegemonic force occurs in a number of places in Coates's work (Coates 1983: 98; 1986: 423; 1989: 102–3; 1996a: 63–4). On each occasion Labour's electoral fragility was linked to its inability or refusal to forge more than an episodic and limited electoral relationship with its mass base. In 1996, Coates noted the high 'degree of assistance from external events and forces the Labour Party has always needed to create an electoral bloc sufficiently substantial to give it parliamentary power', and its long-established failure to establish any of the institutions –'newspapers, clubs, communities' – of a fully functioning Labour movement. Restricting itself to a vote-getting relationship with its work-ing-class base, so the argument went, and mobilising even that relationship only episodically, Labour left the formulation of mass opinion to more conservative sources of values and policy in the privately owned media. This left Labour marooned as a largely 'passive recipient of electoral swings', with its politics never normally in possession of 'sufficient magnetic force to redraw the shape of elec-toral Britain by the power of its own programme and possibilities alone'. No wonder, then, Coates (1996a: 63–4) argued, that majorities so gratuitously won were easily lost, or that 'Labour majorities when they come tend to be accidental rather than created, and invariably prove to be as tenuous as they are fortuitous'.

Although most of those inspired by Miliband moved away from Labour Party studies to produce more general work that engaged with political sociology and political economy, those adopting a Milibandian view were not silent on the detail of developments within the party during its long years of opposition after 1979. In fact, they played a full part in the debates triggered by the 1983 electoral defeat. They argued in particular against the 'move to the right' logic of Eric Hobsbawm's *The Forward March of Labour Halted?* (Mulhern and Jacques 1981; see Coates 1983; Panitch 1986a) while also chronicling and commenting on the party's policy trajectory after 1983 (Coates 1996a). Panitch and Leys's *The End of Parliamentary Socialism* (2001 [1997]), dedicated as it was to Miliband's memory, directly spoke to the continuing relevance and importance of the approach he pioneered to the understanding of the detailed internal development of the Labour Party. Ever since *Parliamentary Socialism,* the argument for socialist politics had engaged with suc-cessive generations of the Labour Left; but not until *The End of Parliamentary Socialism* had any of the academics closely associated with Miliband addressed themselves in a detailed, focused and sympathetic way to Left Labour politics. That omission was now addressed, with the post-1970 Labour Left treated as a *new* Left sensitive to the weaknesses of its predecessors. *The End of Parliamentary Socialism* offered a detailed guide to the conflict within the party from 1970 to 1983. It explored the radical democratic character, as well as the weaknesses, of Bennism, the Campaign for Labour Party Democracy and the alternative economic strategy. It documented the role the union leadership and the Old Left played in their ulti-mate defeat; and then analysed the process of policy reformulation and the disem-powerment of activism within the Labour Party up to the end of the century.

The end result of this intellectual journey has been the creation of a distinctively Milibandian voice in the current set of debates on the nature and potential of New Labour. The Milibandian voice in the burgeoning literature triggered by the 1997 victory has been distinctive in at least three ways. Though as concerned as other scholars and commentators to isolate what is new is New Labour's 'Third Way' (Panitch and Leys 2001: 237–61; see Coates 2000b), it has been distinctive partly through its propensity to combine its recognition of novelty with an emphasis on continuities in the politics of New Labour: underlying continuities (with Old Labour) in the party's continuing enthusiasm for a co-operative relationship with the business community; continuities with Gaitskellite revisionism from the 1950s; and continuities (between New Labour and the Major Government which preceded it) in basic industrial and employment policy (Coates 2000c). In this writing on New Labour, therefore, there is still more than an echo of Miliband's propensity to see Labour leaderships of whatever stripe as a political force which acts 'as a safe alternative government for the British establishment' (Panitch and Leys 1997: 218).

The school's scholarship remains distinctive, too, in the persistence of its focus on New Labour's economic and social policy. Unlike many other analyses of New Labour, it has not set much store by the Blairites' constitutional agenda, preferring instead to address the policy (and ultimately electoral) consequences of New Labour's enthusiasm for the 'new growth theory'. This focus definitely reflects the school's post-1980 shift away from Labour Party studies mentioned earlier, a shift that ironically and by a quite circuitous route left those influenced by Miliband well positioned to explain the constraints on New Labour when the revamped Labour Party returned to power. For by moving the focus of our work into international and comparative political economy, those of us who earlier had been so persuaded by Miliband's work on the Labour Party found that, when we came back to writing about New Labour, we were better situated to write about the Blairite *economic* project than were many of the scholars whose work had remained sharply focused on party politics and party issues alone, as ours, broadly speaking, had not.

A third distinctive feature of our work on New Labour in power has been its propensity still to measure New Labour's performance – as once we measured Old Labour's – against various kinds of socialist yardsticks. By those tests, the party led by Tony Blair is far less a party of social reform even than was that led by Harold Wilson; and of course the Blair-led Government is light years away from the reformist party long sought by the Labour Left – the one briefly brought into view again by Bennite pressure between 1970 and 1983 before being 'modernnied' away by Kinnock and Blair. As Colin Leys (who joined Panitch as co-editor of *The Socialist Register* in 1997) argued well before New Labour came to power, to criticise such policy realignments was not to deny that policy modernisation was necessary to win victory after nearly two decades in opposition. What did concern him, however, even before they came to office, was whether, as New Labour deployed 'the buzzword of "modernization" to good short-term electoral effect . . . any serious project for social change, let alone one that can seriously be called socialist, can be constructed on such a foundation' (Leys 1996: 26). In keeping with the Milibandian perspective as a whole, he proved correct in thinking that the answer to that concern would soon be given with a resounding 'No'.

The development of such arguments since 1979 means that additions now need to be made to the three core elements of the Milibandian perspective on the Labour Party laid out at the start of this chapter. To those can be added, *fourth*, the centrality of corporatism to the politics of Old Labour, and the particular inappropriateness of that form of politics to parties of social reform in an economy with so weak a manufacturing base and so globally focused a set of financial institutions. *Fifth,* the peculiarly electoralist nature of the Labour Party's relationship with its potential mass base, and the particularly inappropriate nature of that relationship for a party requiring to consolidate a counter-hegemonic presence. *Sixth* the attractiveness of the Bennite attempt to reset Labour Party politics, and the necessary limits of that attempt. *Seventh,* there should be added the centrality to the New Labour project of strategies of 'progressive competitiveness', and the particular inappropriateness of those strategies for a party seeking both a prolonged period of majority electoral support and a strengthened industrial base from which to finance social provision.

The continuing relevance of the Milibandian perspective

Complex and extensive bodies of argument require careful reading, and such readings take time – time that many critics of the Milibandian perspective have not always afforded it. As we noted at the start of this chapter, too often the whole corpus has been dismissed as merely criticising the Labour Party for not being a socialist party when in truth it had never set out to be one; as though that was the argument being offered in *Parliamentary Socialism* and in the scholarship inspired by it. But that was never the Milbandian view of the Labour Party. The Labour Party has always been understood from within this perspective – even at moments of the party's greatest radicalism – as at most a *reformist party.* It has always been understood, moreover, as more normally at best a *party of social reform,* one within which Centre-Left and Centre-Right social democrats battled for dominance (with the latter invariably in the ascendant). The whole focus has been not on the politics of Labour as a party that betrays its own socialist goals and its already socialist working-class constituency, but on the politics of labourism and its consequences. The whole focus has been on a party that was moderate in its fundamental aims, even when these were articulated in some form of socialist discourse. Such scholarship has always understood the Labour Party as one which, through its particularly 'narrow interpretation of parliamentary democracy' (Panitch 1988: 349), locked itself very early in its career onto a trajectory of increasing conservatism, a trajectory which arguably has now repositioned the party to the Right of any programmatic position that could be described as even progressive, let alone socialist, in intent. The Milibandian perspective has always conceded the presence within the Labour Party of individuals and programmes of a socialist or progressive kind; but it has always insisted too that socialists within the party have never enjoyed more than a minority and subordinate presence.

The frustration which more moderate commentators on Labour matters down the years have expressed with Milibandian writings seems to have been created in part by the fact that the concept of 'socialism', used as a yardstick against which to judge New, as well as Old, Labour appears insufficiently defined. In defence we would simply say that this frustration ignores those writings in the Milibandian genre that do offer varying degrees of specification of what may be meant by 'socialism' today. There have been many such (Albo 1994; Albo, Langille and Panitch 1993; Burden, Breitenbach and Coates 1990; Leys 1999; Miliband 1977, 1994b;

Panitch 1980b, 2001; Panitch and Gindin 1999; Wainwright 1994). It is not that there is a single Miliband-inspired definition of an alternative order. Such a specification would have an arbitrariness that would render it valueless. It is rather that we can point to various moves to specify part of what that socialism might be, to put some flesh on what Panitch and Leys's 2000 *Socialist Register* termed 'necessary utopias', to engage in what Gindin and Panitch in that volume called 'rekindling the socialist imagination'. If Labour Party scholars do not read this work, it says something significant – and sad – about their lack of interest in answering the question: what is socialism? In that sense, the frustration of those who criticise Milibandians for their lack of clarity is matched by our frustration with their apparent total lack of interest in the issue of alternatives to the status quo.

The Milibandian argument has always been, in that sense, an argument addressed only to part of the audience interested in the Labour Party. It has been (and it remains) an argument – a set of theses about Labour and its possibilities – addressed primarily to the concerns of socialists – those inside the Labour Party itself and those beyond. *Is activity within the party a precursor of the creation of a mass base for socialist politics, or a debilitating distraction from that creation?* This is the central Miliband question. Those who take that perspective have always been keen to ally with the Labour Left and to support its growth (Panitch and Leys 1997: 268). Ultimately, however, they have also been, as Hilary Wainwright once called herself, 'obstinate refusniks' (Wainwright 1987: 6) on the question of taking membership of the Labour Party for socialist purposes. And they have always recognised that the creation of a socialist working class in Britain was a task that would take a long time, which is one reason why they have argued that the Labour Party's short-term electoral concerns so obviously predisposed the party against any attempt to undertake it.

A final word on the importance of Ralph Miliband himself. Because time is passing since his death, and because his major writings of the late 1960s were not directly focused on the Labour Party, there is a danger that new generations of Labour Party scholars will discount his importance. That would be a great loss to left-wing scholarship in Britain. We have separately recorded our own personal debts to him and his work (Coates 1996b; Panitch 1995); but the debt (and the importance of his work) runs wider than that. Ralph Miliband was a member of that generation of socialist intellectual giants who, by the sheer force of their personalities, the charisma of their teaching and the quality of their scholarship created a huge (and more or less safe) intellectual space within which radical students could pursue radical research. Before them, the range of the tolerable (and the tolerated) in the study of British Labour was narrow and arcane. We have the freedom to react to them now, to decide how much to take from their work as our own, because they won for us a width and a quality of scholarship missing in their youth. This intellectual space has been much eroded of late by the enthusiastic absorption of neo-liberal orthodoxies by the vast majority of Centre-Left parties; which is one of the reasons why we believe that intellectuals of their stature are needed again: to stem and to reverse that tide.

References

Unless indicated, the place of publication is London.

Albo, G. (1994) 'Competitive austerity and the impasse of capitalist employment policy', in Miliband, R. and Panitch, L. (eds) *The Socialist Register 1994*

Albo, G. (1997) 'A world market of opportunities? Capitalist obstacles and Left economic policy', in Panitch, L. (ed.) *The Socialist Register 1997*

Albo, G. Langille, D and Panitch, L. (eds) (1993) *A Different Kind of State: Popular Power and Democratic Administration*, Toronto

Brivati, B. and Heffernan, R. (eds) (2000) *The Labour Party: A Centenary History*

Burden, T., Breitenbach, H. and Coates, D. (1990) *Features of a Viable Socialism*

Coates, D. (1975) *The Labour Party and the Struggle for Socialism*, Cambridge

Coates, D. (1980) *Labour in Power? A Study of the Labour Government 1974–79*

Coates, D. (1981) 'The Labour Left and the transition to socialism', *New Left Review*, 129

Coates, D. (1982) 'The limits of the Labour Left: space and agency in the transition to socialism', *New Left Review*, 135

Coates, D. (1983) 'The Labour Party and the future of the Left', in Miliband, R. and Saville, J. (eds) *The Socialist Register 1983*

Coates, D. (1984a) *The Context of British Politics*

Coates, D. (1984b) 'Corporatism and the State in theory and practice', in Harrison, M. (ed.) *Corporatism and the Welfare State*, Aldershot

Coates, D. (1986) 'Social democracy and the logic of political traditions', *Economy and Society*, 15:3

Coates, D. (1989) *The Crisis of Labour*, Oxford

Coates, D. (1994) *The Question of UK Decline*

Coates, D. (1995 [1990]) *Running the Country*

Coates, D. (1996a) 'Labour governments: old constraints and new parameters', *New Left Review*, 219

Coates, D. (1996b) 'The view at half-time: politics and UK economic under-performance', *University of Leeds Review*, 38

Coates, D. (1996c) 'Roger Scruton and the New Left', in Kirk, N. (ed.) *Social Class and Marxism*, Aldershot

Coates, D. (1999a) 'Models of capitalism in the new world order: the British case', *Political Studies*, 47:4

Coates, D. (1999b) 'Labour power and international competitiveness: a critique of ruling orthodoxies', in Panitch, L. and Leys, C. (eds) *The Socialist Register 1999*

Coates, D. (1999c) 'Placing New Labour', in Jones, B. (ed.) *Political Issues in Britain Today*, 5th edition, Manchester

Coates, D. (1999d) "The novelty of New Labour: the view at half-time', paper to the American Political Science Association's Annual Conference, Atlanta, GA

Coates, D. (2000a) *Models of Capitalism: Growth and Stagnation in the Contemporary Era*, Cambridge

Coates, D. (2000b) 'The character of New Labour', in Coates, D. and Lawler, P. (eds) *New Labour in Power*, Manchester

Coates, D. (2000c) 'New Labour's industrial and employment policy', in Coates, D. and Lawler, P. (eds) *New Labour in Power*, Manchester

Hobsbawm, E. (1978) 'The forward march of Labour halted?', reprinted in Mulhern, F. and Jacques, M. (eds) (1981) *The Forward March of Labour Halted?* and Hobsbawm, E. (1989) *Politics for a Rational Left*

Jefferys, K. (2000) 'The Attlee years', in Brivati, B. and Heffernan, R. (eds) *The Labour Party: A Centenary History*

Leys, C. (1983) *Politics in Britain*, Toronto

Leys, C. (1996) 'The British Labour Party's transition from socialism to capitalism', in Panitch, L. (ed.) *The Socialist Register 1996*

Leys, C. (1999) 'The public sphere and the media', in Panitch, L. and Leys, C. (eds) *The Socialist Register 1999*

Miliband, R. (1961) *Parliamentary Socialism*

Miliband, R. (1965) 'What does the Left want?', in Miliband, R. and Saville, J. (eds) *The Socialist Register 1965*

Miliband, R. (1969) *The State in Capitalist Society*

Miliband, R. (1972) *Parliamentary Socialism*, 2nd edition

Miliband, R. (1976) 'Moving on', in Miliband, R. and Saville, J. (eds) *The Socialist Register 1976*

Miliband, R. (1977a) 'The future of socialism in England', in Miliband, R. and Saville, J. (eds) *The Socialist Register 1977*

Miliband, R. (1977b) *Marxism and Politics*, Oxford

Miliband, R. (1978) 'A state of de-subordination', *British Journal of Sociology*, 29:4

Miliband, R. (1982) *Capitalist Democracy in Britain*, Oxford

Miliband, R. (1983a) *Class Power and State Power*

Miliband, R. (1983b) 'Socialist advance in Britain', in Miliband, R. and Saville, J. (eds) *The Socialist Register 1983*

Miliband, R. (1989) *Divided Societies: Class Struggle in Contemporary Capitalism*, Oxford

Miliband, R. (1994a) 'Thirty years of "The Socialist Register"', in Miliband, R. and Panitch, L. (eds) *The Socialist Register 1994*

Miliband, R. (1994b) *Socialism for a Sceptical Age*, Cambridge

Miliband, R. and Liebman, M. (1986) 'Beyond social democracy', in Miliband, R., Saville, J., Liebman, M. and Panitch, L. (eds) *The Socialist Register 1985–86*

Miliband, R. and Saville, J. (1964) 'Labour policy and the Labour Left', in Miliband, R. and Saville, J. (eds) *The Socialist Register 1964*

Panitch, L. (1971) 'Ideology and integration: the case of the British Labour Party', *Political Studies*, 19:2

Panitch, L. (1976) *Social Democracy and Industrial Militancy: The Labour Party, the Trade Unions and Incomes Policy 1945–1974*, Cambridge

Panitch, L. (1977a) 'The development of corporatism in liberal democracies', *Comparative Political Studies*, 10:1

Panitch, L. (1977b) 'Profits and politics: Labour and the crisis of British capitalism', *Politics and Society*, 7:4

Panitch, L. (ed.) (1977c) *The Canadian State: Political Economy and Political Power*, Toronto

Panitch, L. (1979) 'Socialists and the Labour Party: a reappraisal', in Miliband, R. and Saville, J. (eds) *The Socialist Register 1979*

Panitch, L. (1980a) 'Recent theorizations of corporatism: reflections on a growth industry', *British Journal of Sociology*, 31:2

Panitch, L. (1980b) 'The State and the future of socialism', *Capital and Class*, 11

Panitch, L. (1981) 'The limits of corporatism: trade unions and the capitalist State', *New Left Review*, 125

Panitch, L. (1986a) 'The impasse of social democratic politics', in Miliband, R., Saville, J., Liebman, M. and Panitch, L. (eds) *The Socialist Register 1985–86*

Panitch, L. (1986b) *Working Class Politics in Crisis: Essays on Labour and the State*

Panitch, L. (1986c) 'The tripartite experience', in Banting, K. (ed.) *The State and Economic Interests*, vol. 32, Toronto

Panitch, L. (1988) 'Socialist renewal and the Labour Party', in Miliband, R., Panitch, L. and Saville, J. (eds) *The Socialist Register 1988*

Panitch, L. (1994) 'Globalisation and the State', in Miliband, R. and Panitch, L. (eds) *The Socialist Register 1994*

Panitch, L. (1995) 'Ralph Miliband: socialist intellectual 1924–1994', in Panitch, L. (ed.) *The Socialist Register 1995*

Panitch, L. (2001) *Renewing Socialism: Democracy, Strategy and Imagination*, Boulder, CO, and Oxford

Panitch, L. and Gindin, S. (1999) 'Transcending pessimism: rekindling socialist imagination', in Panitch, L. and Leys, C. (eds) *The Socialist Register 2000*

Panitch, L. and Leys, C. (2001 [1997]) *The End of Parliamentary Socialism: From New Left to New Labour*

Panitch, L. and Leys, C. (eds) (2000) *The Socialist Register 2000*

Saville, J. (1967) 'Labourism and the Labour Government', in Miliband, R. and Saville, J. (eds) *The Socialist Register 1967*

Saville, J. (1970) 'Britain: prospect for the seventies', in Miliband, R. and Saville, R. (eds) *The Socialist Register 1970*

Saville, J. (1973) 'The ideology of Labourism', in Benewick, R., Berki, R. N. and Parekh, B. (eds) *Knowledge and Belief in Politics*

Saville, J. (1988) *The Labour Movement in Britain*

Saville, J. (1995) 'Parliamentary socialism revisited', in Panitch, L. (ed.) *The Socialist Register 1995*

Taylor, R. (2000) 'The trade unions and the formation of the Labour Party', in Brivati, B.and Heffernan, R. (eds) *The Labour Party: A Centenary History*

Wainwright, H. (1987) *Labour: A Tale of Two Parties*

Wainwright, H. (1994) *Arguments for a New Left*

Wainwright, H. (1995) 'Once more moving on: social movements, political representation and the Left', in Panitch, L. (ed.) *The Socialist Register 1995*

6

An exceptional comrade?
The Nairn–Anderson interpretation

Mark Wickham-Jones

Since the early 1960s, in a series of articles and books, Tom Nairn has articulated a distinct and challenging interpretation of Labour Party politics. Many of these publications formed part of a wider project, one closely associated with the work of Perry Anderson which examined the trajectory of British political development over the last 300 years.

While there was much overlap with Anderson's concerns, Nairn's central – and initial – contribution to this undertaking focused on a particular account of the character of British reformism. Two of Nairn's publications stand out as especially relevant in this regard. First, in 'The nature of the Labour Party', a paper in two parts originally published in *New Left Review* during 1964 and subsequently merged as a chapter of Anderson and Blackburn's *Towards Socialism* (1965), he gave a coruscating overview of the party's failures during the first sixty years of its history. In passing, the reader should note that although these publications are cited by their original titles as papers, where applicable, they are quoted from the volumes in which Nairn and Anderson later republished them. Second, in *The Left Against Europe* (Nairn 1973), a short book originally published as a special issue of *New Left Review*, Nairn assessed what he considered to be the British Left's inadequate response to the Conservative Government's application for membership of the Common Market.

Aspects of Nairn's critique of the Labour Party are not original, echoing those associated with other condemnations of 'Labourism'. Taken together, however, his work has provided a distinctive explanation of the difficulties encountered by the party, the failures it has generated and the many disappointments it has induced. His analysis is, moreover, unusual in the emphasis it placed on the need to examine Labour's record within the context of European social democracy. Interestingly, many of Nairn's points echoed those made by Egon Wertheimer, a German social democrat and journalist, one of the first to compare Labour to its continental counterparts. Wertheimer's 1930 *Portrait of the Labour Party* was, however, a largely descriptive and fairly positive account, whereas Nairn's analysis of Labour politics is a blunt and often scornful evaluation of its weaknesses.

Nairn's emphasis on the exceptional character of British reformism provides the basis for a discussion of a feature of Labour's politics that has been often over-looked by academics: the party's insularity. To be sure, commentators have noted the party's isolation – in terms of ideological contacts and organisational commu-nications – from other parties of the Left. Rarely, however, have they assigned causal significance to that remoteness in defining Labour's character. It is worth noting that at the time Nairn's 'The nature of the Labour Party' was published, some commentators and scholars concluded that Labour was finally starting to look towards European social democracy for inspiration. A frequent claim made during the early 1960s (and since, for that matter) was that Labour's right-wing revisionist leadership wanted to mimic the outlook adopted by continental reformist parties. Before fully setting down his thought on the subject, even Ander-son thought that the party's right-wing intellectuals, in particular Anthony Crosland, saw Sweden as 'an exemplary model of an existing socialist society, and one from which we have much to learn' (Anderson 1961a: 4; see also Anderson 1961b as well as Elliott 1993: x and 1998: 2–3).

While this chapter examines mainly Nairn's interpretation of Labour politics, Anderson's work is referred to when relevant. It focuses on a distinct aspect of their joint endeavour, the contrast between British social democrats and their European counterparts. It does not, however, address the wider context within which Nairn located his account – the 'Nairn–Anderson theses' which, in the latter's words, drew up 'a general map of English class society' and constructed a 'framework for understanding the national crisis of British capitalism' (1992d: 2). That is some-thing more completely covered in chapter 3, by Madeleine Davis.

I first outline the central features of Nairn's argument, leaning heavily on his original two-part article and assessing where it fits with the work not only of his collaborator Anderson but that of other leading figures on the New Left, especially Ralph Miliband. As one way of examining the veracity of Nairn's substantive points, Wertheimer's earlier and friendlier analysis is also cited. The chapter then addresses the extent to which Nairn's approach can be reconciled with the often-made claim that Labour sought to learn from Swedish social democrats during the 1950s and 1960s. Finally, the strands of the chapter are drawn together in assessing what Nairn's work contributes to our understanding of the party.

An anatomy of 'Labourism'

For the purposes of this chapter, there are three inter-related parts to Nairn's expla-nation of Labour's supposed bankruptcy as a reformist party. First, he considers that the party exhibited a 'well known antipathy to theory' (Nairn 1965: 159); second, that Labour was dominated by its trade union affiliates; and, third, that the party persistently demonstrated a defensive and subordinate outlook. Together these determined the character of British reformism, which Nairn describes as 'Labourism', a term first articulated in debates at the start of the twentieth century (for a general discussion see Fielding 2000). In the early 1960s, members of the

New Left, including most notably Ralph Miliband, redeployed the term. While there were differences in the meaning Miliband and Nairn respectively attached to the concept, aspects of the former's account nonetheless resonate with the latter's analysis.

The first element that makes up Nairn's appreciation of Labour's failure to develop into a fully fledged reformist party was its atheoretical and empirical stance. This meant it did not draw on Marxist or, for that matter, any other ideas; it assigned intellectuals no substantive internal role; and it was unable to outline a coherent theoretical design of what might be involved in a socialist transition (Nairn 1965: 165–6; see also Chun 1993: 80). Labour's 'empirical and flexible' outlook was also a central feature of Miliband's seminal text *Parliamentary Socialism* (1972: 1). Wertheimer (1930: 46, 195 and 202) similarly contended, and with considerable emphasis, that there was a 'mistrust of theory and systematic thought' within the wider labour movement. In *The Future of Socialism* Crosland, in 1956 out of the House of Commons, developed a related premiss: Labour 'was not founded on any body of doctrine at all, and has always preserved a marked anti-doctrinal and anti-theoretical bias' (1956: 80).

Hence Anderson could lament 'the failure of any significant body of intellectuals to join the cause of the proletariat until the very end of the nineteenth century' (1992a: 34). Yet, even that inflow was characterised as comprising pseudo-intellectuals and essentially bogus socialists, whose most important constituent was Fabianism, which was committed to merely piecemeal and practical reforms enacted through the parliamentary system. Anderson defines it to be a 'leaden legacy' (1992a: 35); while for Nairn (1965: 167) the Fabians were, if nothing else, 'the technicians of reform – perhaps the most able reformers of this kind produced by socialism in any country'. Moreover, from Labour's first days, overtly socialist groups were marginalised, while other left-wing elements, most obviously the ILP, were as weak as the Fabians in taking up and deploying ideas. Lacking coherence, the ILP was characterised by a strong moral outlook, one inspired by Christianity (Nairn 1973: 56). These groups 'accepted – the Fabians by conviction, the ILP socialists for want of an alternative – the *evolutionary* character of socialism' (Nairn 1965: 166; his emphasis). The failure of the party to offer intellectuals a meaningful part in its strategy had significant consequences, resulting in 'the lack of the catalyst element a socialist movement requires to be itself' (Nairn 1965: 174; see Anderson 1992a: 35). Wertheimer was less contemptuous of Labour's emphasis on practical measures at the expense of theoretical commitment. He even considered the party's vagueness about ultimate goals to have helped in recruiting the unions (1930: 49), while its consequently 'elastic methods' ensured that it became – at the time of writing – 'the most powerful among the Labour parties of the world' (1930: 204).

The second element to Nairn's overall analysis is the fact that in organisational terms, from the party's foundation, Labour was dominated by the trade unions. This meant, as Anderson notes, that at its origins 'there was to be no mention of socialism' (Anderson 1992b: 160). It also meant that when, in 1918, the party adopted a new constitution, including an ideological position, Clause 4, which apparently defined Labour's commitment to public ownership, it had little practical force. Despite appearances, Nairn (1965: 184) argues, this did not signify a conversion to socialism; it rather assigned the latter 'to its proper place, the constitution, where it could be admired occasionally and referred to in moments of emotion'.

Of more practical significance than Clause 4 was the party's structure, outlined in the 1918 constitution (and not substantively revised until 1997), which ensured continued union ascendancy. Most obviously, union block votes cast at its annual conference, for Nairn (using an often repeated phrase) 'the dead souls of labourism', elected most of the seats on the ruling National Executive Committee and determined the fate of proposals submitted to conference (Nairn 1965: 180). This is because, for most of the party's history, block votes constituting the affiliated members of trade unions massively outweighed the party's individual membership. In similar vein, Wertheimer likened some of the block vote to 'dead souls', those whose levies were paid by union officials despite their memberships having lapsed (1930: 23). Writing years later, Anderson also took up the metaphor: 'Over time, it [the block vote] raised up a Leviathan of dead souls, whose mythical millions enabled party leaderships to crush rebellions and to finance elections' (1992c: 349). It was these unions that constituted 'the real basis of labourism' (Nairn 1965: 208).

The union ascendancy made the development of a mass party much harder than it would otherwise have been, as apolitical affiliated members undermined the financial and electoral need to expand Labour's active base. 'The lack of any intensive local party life and the slender threads that bound trade unionists to the party', Wertheimer stated (1930: 22), 'tended to work against the formation of a strong individual socialist consciousness.' Sharing a commitment to piecemeal measures, the Fabians and the trade unions formed an enduring alliance (Nairn 1965: 180–1). Compelled by a deep-seated loyalty and acutely aware of its own weaknesses, the party's Left was however unable to challenge this bond. At times the link between the unions and the PLP nonetheless endured what appeared to be an unbearable tension. Wertheimer puzzled over its persistence in the face of manifest incompatibilities over policy, in what Lewis Minkin (1991) characterised as 'Wertheimer's paradox'. Nevertheless it is an attachment that has been sustained in one form or another to the present day.

The third part to Nairn's analysis is the apparently defensive nature of Labour's outlook. From its earliest days, the overriding concern of the unions was not socialism but the protection of workers' living standards. They decided to establish and foster their own political party in response to several factors, including: the economic crises of the late nineteenth century; frustration over lack of support from the Liberals; and legal judgments against them. In fact, Nairn concludes (1965: 162), 'trade union leaders were only convinced of the necessity for working class politics when such action became necessary to safeguard trade-unionism itself'.

The party's defensive orientation led to a concern with parliamentarianism and – in order to win votes – 'respectability': this alignment explains Labour's support for and belief in the 'nation'. Paradoxically therefore Labour became both a party of class (the working class) and a party of the nation and 'Labourism is really the history of this ambiguity' (Nairn 1973: 49). Wertheimer noted that Labour's transformation from pressure group to governing party was comparatively relatively easy (Wertheimer 1930: 46; see also 75–7). This is because, unlike other continental parties, it had never been illegal; did not see the state as repressive; and had no record of opposition to existing political arrangements. Thus the labour movement quickly became 'an integral part of the British nation'. Reflecting its unique status, from promoting gains by the working class, Labour frequently served to defuse pressure for more far-reaching reforms to promote national unity. Hence the measures brought about by the 1945–51 Labour Government were meant not to bring victory to the proletariat but 'to integrate the working class more adequately into national life' (Nairn 1973: 71). The effect of Labour's hostility to the European Common Market after 1970 served likewise to calm more radical demands as it switched attention away from the class conflict that threatened to engulf Heath's Conservative administration (Nairn 1973: 80–3).

As already noted, Nairn's denunciation of Labour's defensive outlook echoed that of Miliband. The latter also argued Labour played an integrative role in capitalist society similar to the subordination highlighted by Nairn (Miliband 1958: 46). Later, in his postscript to *Parliamentary Socialism*, Miliband argued (1972: 376) that capitalism 'badly needs' Labour 'since it plays a major role in the management of discontent and helps to keep it within safe bounds'. In his study of incomes policy, Leo Panitch (1976) also took up the integrative role of the Labour Party in a sustained and persuasive analysis. David Coates and Leo Panitch further develop some of these themes in chapter 5 of the present volume. In a detailed analysis of Anderson's account, Robert Looker (1988: 17) notes the similarities of his approach to that of many other critics of Labourism, concluding it to be distinguished from them only by its essentially 'relentlessly dismissive' tone.

Nairn (1965: 179, 208) saw these three features, taken together, as creating a party characterised by 'subordination and defeat' as well as by a 'sclerotic conservatism'. Anderson similarly emphasised the corporately defensive nature of Labour's configuration: the party, he believed, made no sustained attempt to be a hegemonic transforming force in British politics (Anderson 1992a: 33). In the early 1960s several features of Labour's subordination stood out: one-third of working-class voters supported the Conservatives; the party lacked activists (in fact more workers were members of the Conservative Party); it had a weak youth movement; and did not have the support of a partisan press (Anderson 1965: 251–5).

Both Nairn and Anderson allude somewhat elliptically to the form which a successful reformist party might have taken in the context of British politics. Given that their original argument was much influenced by Gramscian analysis (see Forgacs 1989: 74–6), it is unsurprising that one significant feature of such a party would be its hegemonic aspirations: for 'a hegemonic class seeks to transform society in its own image, inventing afresh its economic system, its political institutions, its cultural values, its "mode of insertion" into the world' (Anderson 1992a: 33). The implication of their argument is that such a party required a coherent theoretical understanding of a socialist transformation (Chun 1993: 80). Thus, 'armed with a more systematic vision, [Labour] would no doubt still have been defeated, but its struggles would have entered an enduring tradition, capable of informing the future' (Anderson 1992a: 33). For a brief period, in the early 1960s, *New Left Review*'s position, under Anderson's editorship, indicated a hope that Harold Wilson's leadership of the party might just transform it into such a hegemonic party. Anderson believed that Labour had some potential, provided it was prepared 'to transform the structure of British society' (*The Times*, 7 June 1965). It was a position *New Left Review* soon abandoned (for a sympathetic account see Elliott, 1998: 18–32; for critical comment see Birchall 1980–81 and Sassoon 1981).

The exceptional nature of British reformism

The notion of British exceptionalism is central to the Nairn–Anderson theses. They maintain that exceptionalism permeated class forms and relations in Britain (notably the form taken by the dominant land-owning class), the character of capitalist development, and the proletariat's defensive and subordinate ethos that shaped labourism. Repeatedly Nairn emphasised the different historical path taken by reformists in the United Kingdom, a trajectory that led directly to the exceptional form of labourism as a peculiarly British phenomenon. Although lacking Nairn's historical perspective, Wertheimer's discussion of Labour politics also accords a fundamental significance to exceptionalism. His central contrast was with the German Sozialdemokratische Partei Deutschlands (SPD) but he also drew more general parallels between Britain and Europe. The opening sentence of his book is blunt: 'The foreign socialist undertaking a study of the British Labour party is met by the surprising fact that its organisation completely departs in every way from all that he has hitherto thought desirable and necessary' (Wertheimer 1930: 1).

In particular, Nairn (1973: 71), in the first place, regards continental reformists as much more open to ideas in the construction of a socialist programme, asserting: 'Above all, [British Labour] has much less in common than appears with the traditions of Marxist internationalism which constitute the most precious inheritance of the European working class.' Wertheimer (1930: 45) similarly notes the differing status given to theoretical programmes: 'In contrast to the continental parties, whose every stage of development was accompanied by a corresponding programme, the British Labour party from its hour of birth to the last years of the war had been quite content with the annual resolutions of the party conference.' Of Labour's 1918 programme, he thought that as 'an example of theoretical insight and knowledge' it was 'far inferior to the most elementary of continental socialist programmes' (1930: 60). In a discussion recorded with a trade union official during his trip to study Swedish social democracy, Anderson (1961b: 41) reports: 'We in Britain are more empirical – we don't have this ideological approach you continentals have.'

Second, Nairn believes the unions have not dominated European social democratic parties in the way they have governed Labour (1965: 168). Anderson

(1992b: 161) contrasts Labour's structure with those found on the continent: 'Its new [1918] constitution formally ratified the absolute dominance of the unions inside the party with a voting structure unlike that of any European social democracy, which effectively neutralized the admission of individual members'. For Wertheimer, the relationship between Labour and the union was 'utterly different' from that on the continent (1930: 49).

Third, Nairn contends that Labour's European equivalents were less defensive and subordinate in their outlook. Although many looked towards parliamentary tactics, they did not demonstrate the kind of utter devotion to this path characteristic of Labour. This accords with Miliband's view: 'Parliamentarism in the British Labour movement was only unique in that it was so much more explicit, confident and uninhibited than its continental counterparts, and that it met with so much less resistance' (1972: 1–2). In distinguishing Labour's attitude from that of European parties, Anderson is scathing:

> In Britain, the working class has developed over one hundred and fifty years an adamantine social consciousness, but never a commensurate political will. The very name of its traditional political party underlines this truth. Alone of major European working class formations, it is neither a Social Democratic nor a Socialist nor a Communist Party; it is the Labour Party – a name which designates not an ideal society, as do the others, but an existent interest. (1992a: 37; see also Fanti 1964: 31–2)

Despite a large working-class base and heavy industrialisation, political labour was slow to organise in Britain, in marked contrast with most of Europe (Anderson 1992b: 159). Anderson judges that, 'In consciousness and combativity, the English working class has been overtaken by almost all its continental opposites' (1992a: 26). He has repeated the point: 'The political subordination of the British Labour stood out in any comparative perspective' including, for that matter, the United States (Anderson 1992b: 161). Likewise Wertheimer (1930: 212) noted: 'Membership [as a union affiliate] is therefore most frequently only an attribute of loyalty to the union, and by no means the result of personal inner conviction as on the continent'.

Wertheimer (1930: 87–8) reported additional significant differences between Labour and its European counterparts. For he judges Labour's ultimate policy aims were focused on public ownership while continental parties wanted to transform the nature of work. European parties also adopted cultural aims, for example regarding the relationship between Church and State. Labour in contrast was judged to be more embedded in the prevailing dominant culture than its Left–reformist counterparts were within their own polities (1930: 89–93). He also remarked on the related ease with which Labour's parliamentary leadership controlled the party, for this was a product of the structure of union affiliations which contrasted with the continental experience of party machine domination (1930: 216).

Labour's 1945 general election victory meant that, for a fleeting moment at least, '[t]he national "British way" appeared vindicated' (Nairn 1973: 72). In the event, though full employment was temporarily achieved, the basic configuration of capitalism was not challenged and the City of London, Britain's financial sector, recovered its dominant position within the economy (Anderson 1992b: 166). After 1948, the Fabian notion of inevitable progress according to which reform led to further reform was discredited as the Labour Government struggled to sustain the pace it had established during its first years in office: 'in reality, the Labour party's loss of confidence was the dominating fact' (Nairn 1965: 195). The relative prosperity that followed this reassertion of capitalist power also disoriented Labour: 'For about ten years after the defeat of 1951, Labourism seemed to drift at the mercy of events, feebly trying to discover a new formula' (Nairn 1965: 199).

Labour's singularity is therefore central to the explanation that Nairn and Anderson offer of its ultimate failure. In his re-evaluation of their work, Anderson (1992b: 190) summarises the correlates that defined British reformism, 'a pervasive and deep-rooted union implantation' with 'a traditional lack of central authority and obdurate resistance to rationalization of the factors of production'. He asserts that this combination precluded the construction of 'a Swedish or Austrian path in the post-war UK'. From this claim, it can be inferred that Anderson considers – in a way similar to later analysts – that union structures have ruled out the construction of corporatist-type arrangements in which short-term costs might be traded for longer term gains (for a discussion of which see Garrett 1998). Interestingly, at the time of his support for Wilson's Labour, Anderson had indicated (1964: 25) tentative support for incomes policies as a path by which socialist objectives might be advanced.

Anderson and Nairn's stress on the exceptional character of British political development as an explanation of the many disappointments undergone by the labour movement has attracted considerable academic attention. In his polemical response, E. P. Thompson (1965: 312) was bitterly critical of their notion that other countries did things 'in every respect better'. Thompson (1965: 337–9) criticised the lack of empirical detail in Nairn's account, a deficiency which he thought led the latter, on the one hand, to exaggerate the role played by Fabianism and, on the other, to neglect the contribution made by the more radical socialists. More friendly critics like Raphael Samuel and Gareth Stedman Jones (1982: 325) charged Nairn and Anderson with using particular episodes to construct a misleading 'ideal-type' of labourism which they then used as a framework through which to view the party's history. In response to Thompson, Anderson conceded that his original analysis was overly cultural and neglected the contribution of the Communist Party to the labour movement (1992b: 168; 1966: 24). Nonetheless, George Lichtheim praised both Thompson and Anderson–Nairn with equanimity. Noting the emergence of an 'Anglo-Marxism', he concluded that 'Thompson is right: the British development fits the Marxian categories as much as does the French' while stating that Anderson and Nairn's 'brilliant' and 'fruitful' conceptual approach 'looks like a remarkably successful naturalisation of Gramsci's neo-Marxism' (Lichtheim 1965: 14–15).

Labour and Sweden in the 1950s

In their analysis, Nairn and Anderson say less about the insular outlook of British reformism than about its exceptional nature. Implicit in their approach, however, is the conviction that not only does Labour differ by comparison with other social democratic parties but that it is *isolated* from them, with detrimental consequences for the reformist project in the UK. Thus, in his discussion of Swedish social democracy, Anderson contended that the British Left 'has usually tended to be insular' and had 'much to learn from Sweden and other countries' (1961a: 4–5). With regard to ideas, Nairn (1965: 164) argued: 'The leaders of labourism thought that, however appropriate Marxism might be in foreign countries, it just had no reference to Britain.' He went on to quote G. D. H. Cole's reference to Ben Tillett, a union militant, who declared in 1893 that 'he would sooner have the solid, progressive, matter-of-fact fighting trade unionism of England than all the harebrained challenges and magpies of continental revolutionists' (Nairn 1965: 171). A general belief in insularity also figures prominently in Wertheimer's account. He observed (1930: 53) that when, in 1918, Labour did finally adopt a policy document – *Labour and the New Social Order* – which outlined a set of aims, it had little impact abroad, which Wertheimer took to be a reflection of the party's isolation from other reformists.

A significant criticism of the notion that Labour has been from the outset an insular exceptionalist–reformist party, however, is to be found in the argument that, during the 1950s and early 1960s, some of its senior figures – namely revisionists on the party's Right – looked towards their European neighbours in a systematic and determined fashion. This need not, however, be seen as contradicting Nairn and Anderson's case, as it may simply mean that the likes of Gaitskell and Crosland reached similar conclusions at about the same time and decided to tackle the party's historical isolation. Notes from a talk given by Crosland certainly demonstrate some sympathy for the Nairn–Anderson interpretation including such headings as 'Britain: what's wrong' or 'Continuous under-estimate of Eur. Mov.', 'Nostalgia for Little England', and 'No foreign invasion or defeat'. Crosland appeared to echo Anderson's historical analysis in writing: 'Class structure not abolished: aristocracy peacefully embraced new classes' (Crosland nd). Anderson's pieces on Swedish politics were in fact based on his belief that Labour was beginning to open itself up by looking at social democratic achievements elsewhere – although he soon abandoned that position. Nairn (1964: 65) does not appear to have ever adopted such a view, for he characterised revisionism as a recasting of Fabianism and saw Gaitskell as the 'chosen vehicle' for the 'continuation of the alliance between Fabian intellectualism and trade union bureaucracy'. His scepticism on this point is confirmed by a later comment that, the revisionists constituted a generation of 'liberal thinkers' who 'invented "social democratic" forces for the Labour party, based upon *largely spurious parallels* with continental socialist reformism' (Nairn 1981: 51; my emphasis).

In contrast to this, a number of academics have asserted that Labour's revisionists did look towards Swedish social democracy with genuine interest. David

Howell (1980: 193) argued that, in the 1950s, the revisionists 'proclaimed Sweden as a worthy example for British Labour to emulate, regarding it as a society where social democracy had adapted itself successfully to material affluence in such a way as to appear the natural governing party'. Howell (1980: 201) claimed vindication in positions found in Crosland's *The Future of Socialism* (1956) and especially in his 1963 *The Conservative Enemy*. Further support is offered by Stefan Berger's claim (2000: 322) that Crosland 'like many in the Labour Party remained in touch with mainland European reformism, in particular in the Scandinavian countries'.

Just how significant an influence was Swedish social democracy on Crosland is debatable. The question is, however, important as Crosland enjoys considerable status as perhaps the pre-eminent post-war social democratic theorist. Moreover, while he opened *The Future of Socialism* with the statement 'This book is about socialism in Britain', he continued parenthetically that it 'draws freely on the experiences of other countries, notably Sweden and the United States'(1956: 12). Anderson (1961a: 4) considered Crosland to draw heavily on the former's experience and, while he noted that the latter received an equal number of mentions, 'of the two [Crosland] gives the palm to Sweden as coming nearest to "the socialist's ideal of the 'good' society"'. In fact, the Index to the book lists over 80 references to the United States but only around 30 to Sweden, a pattern repeated in *The Conservative Enemy* where there are 13 references to Sweden and a further 4 to Scandinavia, but nearly 40 to the United States. Moreover, in both volumes, Crosland's references to Sweden focus descriptively on particular aspects of its political economy and society: few make normative points about Swedish social democracy and what it might imply for Labour's programme.

At points Crosland is in fact keen to distance himself from the Scandinavian model, suggesting in particular that joint enterprise councils and incomes policies should not be applied in Britain because they were inappropriate to the national context (1956: 342, 458). Hence, although impressed by the Swedish social democrats' electoral success, Crosland believed the programme that underpinned it held little relevance to Britain. Hence the absence of a detailed critical engagement with Swedish politics is unsurprising because central aspects of the Swedish model were far removed from the one that Crosland lays out. In his discussion of wages, for example, Crosland (1956: 451) cites the 1953 translation of a Swedish trades union confederation – the *Landorganisationen* (LO) – report. This document laid out in detail what was to become the Rehn–Meidner model, which functioned in the period of full employment to facilitate labour mobility and wage restraint while promoting a measure of egalitarianism in the determination of wages. Although Crosland described this as containing an 'excellent discussion' of wages policy, he disagreed with its substantive argument. High profits, Crosland argued, would inevitably undermine wage restraint, which in such circumstances would have to be abandoned. The LO's position, in contrast, was to tackle rising profits accruing to employers during a period of full employment through a fiscal squeeze while maintaining some form of wage restraint. Perhaps indicative of Crosland's work's insularity, Sassoon (1996: 244) considers that, while deemed to be of so much influence in Britain, *The Future of Socialism* had very little impact elsewhere in Europe.

If Crosland was not interested in looking closely at the Swedish experience, neither were other members of the British labour movement (see Wickham-Jones 2001). Between 1951 and 1964 only one Labour Party delegation and one Trades Union Congress (TUC) group visited Sweden to investigate how their counterparts went about matters. The 1951 Labour Party visit was of little consequence and accorded only the briefest of references in the party's annual report. The TUC visit in October 1962 was of more moment as it was interested in discovering the basis for union centralisation, the reasons for Sweden's calmer industrial relations and how the national interest could be reconciled to that of individual unions. It concluded, however, that '[c]lear and precise answers were not obtained to each of these questions' (TUC 1962: 1). Members of the TUC Economics Committee were also quick to argue that 'great care' should be taken in drawing conclusions about the extent to which aspects of the Swedish system were applicable in Britain: it was always unwise, and could be dangerous, to assume that what worked satisfactorily in one country could be imitated in another' (TUC Economics Committee 1963: 24).

The most common reasons given at that time by British social democrats and trade unionists as to why the Swedish approach was inappropriate concerned structural differences between the two polities. Given Labour's advocacy of an incomes policy, and the support offered for a time by the TUC to the party on this matter, however, the structural argument is not persuasive. Other critics of the Swedish model focused on its goals to conclude that the British movement should not adopt such policies because they were undesirable. This is because the Swedish road included collaboration between organised labour and employers, something which many British union leaders feared would erode their independence and ability to advance their members' interests. The TUC's 1962 trip was nonetheless a serious initiative in looking at social democratic arrangements, but little came of it. When corporatist-style policies were adopted in the UK in the mid-1960s, they were very different (and much less successful) than those adopted in Sweden.

Further evidence of Labour's insularity is to be found in its economic policy-making process of this time. Few policy documents looked at the experience of social democratic parties abroad. In the case of Sweden, only one internal document, a report of a Socialist International experts' conference, held in 1955, discussed features of its model. And this did not feed into the party's policy-making machinery. Although on some issues the party did look at arrangements abroad, for example concerning planning, when Labour returned to the question of incomes policy in the early 1960s it did not address either the Swedish experience or those of social democratic parties elsewhere. The overall impression is therefore of an insular and internalised policy-making process (Wickham-Jones 2001).

Two significant points emerge from this discussion of Labour's supposed attempt to learn from the Swedish experience. First, the claim that Labour looked towards Sweden is exaggerated. Second, Nairn's argument about the defensive and subordinate outlook of British trade unionism is only partly confirmed. In some ways, the TUC was more open than was the party, although the reasons why it eventually rejected the Swedish model are redolent of the labourism that Nairn claimed was so influential in shaping Labour politics.

Conclusions

This chapter has outlined Tom Nairn and Perry Anderson's account of Labour Party politics. It has proved to be immensely influential over the last forty years. Their polemical dismissal of the party has become an important part of the discourse by which Labour's failings as a reformist project are frequently and critically evaluated. To give just one example, in his best-selling *The State We're In*, Will Hutton (1995: 46–8) laments the 'poverty' of Labour's strategic thinking and the domination of the party by economistic unions, the party's constitution being 'disfigured' by block votes.

Nairn and Anderson emphasise the force of historical development: how much their characterisation of British reformism depends upon this particular trajectory is, however, uncertain. One can accept their conclusions about Labour's atheoretical outlook, subordination to the trade unions and defensive outlook without endorsing their analysis of British history. Nairn and Anderson nonetheless make a series of powerful points about the possible origins of Labour's failure to more fully transform capitalism.

It is arguable that some of their reasoning is exaggerated due to the polemical idiom in which they were expressed. At times the party may not have been as hostile to theoretical influence as Nairn suggests: the work of G. D. H. Cole, Evan Durbin and R. H. Tawney is pertinent here, as is Crosland's own contribution (for a useful survey on these issues see Thompson 1996). A lack of regard for Marxism did not necessarily mean the party was uninterested in ideas. There have also been constraints on the unions' domination of the party: the leadership has been able to extract resources and money as well as acquiescence over certain policy issues in exchange for meeting union demands. At times these exchanges, a central theme of the work of Lewis Minkin, which is highlighted by Eric Shaw in chapter 11 of this collection, have been far less one-sided than Nairn indicates. Indeed, from Nairn's standpoint, Wertheimer's paradox – the policy disparity between economically-minded union leaders and politically driven parliamentarians – is inexplicable. As a series of exchanges, both rational and norm-driven, the relationship makes more sense. Finally, Labour has not always been as defensive and subordinate in outlook as Nairn claims: radical programmes have been designed that go beyond the kind of practical reformism associated with Fabianism. In practice, however, the impact of such programmes has often been disappointing while the party's experience in office has often been, to say the least, disappointing.

The notion of exceptionalism is a powerful one. From its foundation in 1900, there were significant differences of outlook, policy, organisation and ethos between Labour and other European reformist parties. In a recent work, Fielding (2000) argues persuasively that the distinctions between Labour and some mythical norm of what constituted European social democracy have been exaggerated. Yet, while defining any 'European model' is problematical, it is evident that many continental social democratic parties have shared a range of features, especially in terms of their programmes. The German Wertheimer certainly believed they enjoyed a common identity, discourse and programme, and that Labour did not.

Take the contrast between Labour and the Swedish social democrats in the 1950s: they had different organisational structures (including distinct relationships between the party and the unions) and varied policy commitments which in turn reflected diverse conceptions as to what should be the goal of social democratic parties. There was a clear hostility in the United Kingdom, noted above, towards a mimicking of Swedish arrangements. Other European parties looked towards each other and learned from each other; in contrast, Labour did not. When Swedish labour economists sought to discuss their programme with the TUC their advances were rebuffed (Wickham-Jones 2001).

Labour's exceptionalism, in turn, has been related to its insularity. The concept of insularity exposed by Anderson and Nairn is an important one: it provides an explanation, in part at any rate, for the particular character of British reformism and for the kinds of policies that the party has articulated. For much of its history Labour has been reluctant to discuss, let alone learn from, experiences elsewhere. The disparities between Labour and Europe were well illustrated in the debate over British membership of the Common Market. In 1971, the left-wing MP Eric Heffer told the special Labour Party Conference that debated British membership of the Common Market: 'We must have confidence in our ability to build a socialist Britain, and not to look for some panacea outside' (Labour Party 1971: 339). A decade later, in 1981, Tony Benn complained about a draft policy paper because it was 'a real bureaucrats' paper – let's copy France and Japan. There was nothing about social justice or socialism' (Benn 1992: 150). These statements are redolent of a prevalent insularity that has defined much of the Labour Party's history – one evident on both the party's Right and its Left.

Whether the party remains as insular as it once was is another matter. During the 1980s, partly in response to a general Europeanisation of British politics, Labour looked overtly to the European social democrats, although Anderson doubted the extent of this development (see 1992c: 328). During the 1990s, the party under Tony Blair's leadership became more eclectic, looking to the experience of the Democrats in the United States but also the Australian Labour Party (see King and Wickham-Jones 1999). Arguably, however, these developments came too late to revive the reformist project within the UK. Indeed, by the 1990s, it could be argued, Labours' leaders looked abroad to find ways of finally killing off the hope that the party would ever be the means by which capitalism would be radically transformed.

References

Unless indicated, the place of publication is London.

Anderson, P. (1961a) 'Sweden: Mr Crosland's dreamland', *New Left Review*, 7

Anderson, P. (1961b) 'Sweden II: study in social democracy, *New Left Review*, 9

Anderson, P. (1964) 'Critique of Wilsonism', *New Left Review*, 27.

Anderson, P. (1965) 'Problems of socialist strategy', in Anderson, P. and Blackburn, R. (eds) *Towards Socialism*

Anderson, P. (1966) 'Socialism and pseudo-empiricism', *New Left Review*, 35

Anderson, P. (1992a [1964]) 'Origins of the present crisis', in Anderson, P., *English Questions*

Anderson, P. (1992b [1987]) 'Figures of descent', in Anderson, P., *English Questions*

Anderson, P. (1992c) 'The light of Europe', in Anderson, P., *English Questions*

Anderson, P. (1992d) *English Questions*

Benn, T. (1992) *The End of an Era*

Berger, S. (2000) 'Labour in comparative perspective', in Tanner, D., Thane, P. and Tiratsoo, N. (eds) *Labour's First Century*, Cambridge

Birchall, I. (1980–81) 'The autonomy of theory: a short history of *New Left Review*', *International Socialism*, 10

Chun, L. (1993) *The British New Left*, Edinburgh

Crosland, C. A. R. (1956) *The Future of Socialism*

Crosland, C. A. R. (1963) *The Conservative Enemy*

Crosland, C. A. R. (nd) 'Britain', unpublished notes, Crosland Papers, 4/8, London School of Economics.

Elliott, G. (1993) *Labourism and the English Genius*

Elliott, G. (1998) *Perry Anderson: The Merciless Laboratory of History*, Minneapolis, MN

Fanti, G. (1964) 'The resurgence of the Labour Party', *New Left Review*, 30

Fielding, S. (2000) 'Labourism and the British Labour Party', *Les Familles politiques en europe occidentale au XX siécle*, Rome

Forgacs, D. (1989) 'Gramsci and Marxism in Britain', *New Left Review*, 176

Garrett, G. (1998) *Partisan Politics in the Global Economy*, Cambridge

Howell, D. (1980) *British Social Democracy*

Hutton, W. (1995) *The State We're In*

King, D. and Wickham-Jones, M. (1999) 'From Clinton to Blair', *Political Quarterly*, 70:1

Labour Party (1971) *Report of the Annual Conference*

Lichtheim, G. (1965) 'Review', *New Statesman*, 2 July

Looker, R. (1988) 'Shifting tradjectories: Perry Anderson's changing account of the pattern of English historical development', in Barker, C. and Nicholls, D. (eds) *The Development of British Capitalist Society: A Marxist Debate*, Manchester

Miliband, R. (1958) 'The politics of contemporary capitalism', *New Reasoner*, 5

Miliband, R. (1972) *Parliamentary Socialism*

Minkin, L. *The Contentious Alliance*, Edinburgh

Nairn, T. (1964) 'Hugh Gaitskell', *New Left Review*, 25

Nairn, T. (1965 [1964]) 'The nature of the Labour Party', in Anderson, P. and Blackburn, R. (eds) *Towards Socialism*

Nairn, T. (1973 [1972]) *The Left Against Europe*, Harmondsworth

Nairn, T. (1981) *The Break-Up of Britain*

Panitch, L. (1976) *Social Democracy and Industrial Militancy*, Cambridge

Samuel, R. and Stedman Jones, G. (1982) 'The Labour Party and social democracy', in R. Samuel and G. Stedman Jones (eds) *Culture, Ideology and Politics*

Sassoon, D. (1981) 'The silences of *New Left Review*', *Politics and Power*, 3

Sassoon, D. (1996) *One Hundred Years of Socialism*

Thompson, E. P. (1965) 'The peculiarities of the English', *The Socialist Register 1965*

Thompson, N. (1996) *Political Economy and the Labour Party*

Trades Union Congress (1962) 'Draft report of visit to Sweden', Economics Committee, 3/1, TUC Papers, MSS 292B/560.1/5, Modern Records Centre, University of Warwick

TUC Economics Committee (1963) Minutes, 9 January 1963, Modern Records Centre, University of Warwick

Wertheimer, E. (1930) *Portrait of the Labour Party*

Wickham-Jones, M. (2001) 'Missed opportunities: British social democracy and the Rehn model, 1951–64', in Milner, H. and Wadensjo, E. (eds) *Gosta Rehn, the Swedish Model and Labour Market Policies*, Aldershot

7
Class and politics in the work of Henry Pelling

Alastair J. Reid

In the ranks of that distinguished generation of post-war British academics who established labour history on a professional footing, Henry Pelling is generally regarded as worthy but rather dull. For he did not share the more colourful far-left political affiliations of figures such as Eric Hobsbawm and Edward Thompson. Indeed, when these Marxists were at the height of their influence in the late 1960s and 1970s, Pelling's careful history of the British Communist Party was frequently dismissed as Cold War propaganda. At that time his contributions to the history of the Labour Party were commonly pigeon-holed as scholarly but narrow, for they were seen as mere political history with no obvious wider implications for the analysis of society as a whole. As Jay Winter (1983: x) put it, albeit respectfully, in the Introduction to a collection of essays in Pelling's honour:

> In place of what may be called the 'sixty years' march syndrome' of labour history, Pelling quietly and authoritatively provided . . . a rigorous and accurate account of the evolution of the institutions of the modern labour movement . . . In a sense, his political histories have helped to fulfil the classic aim of historical scholarship: the replacement of mythology or vague memory by painstakingly-researched and documented historical analysis.

At the same time, many modern British political historians, increasingly interested in Labour's replacement of the Liberals as the main party of progress, were associating Henry Pelling's name with an interpretation of the rise of Labour based on broader social trends. Thus, in one popular survey, Paul Adelman (1972: 87) outlined the work of a school of historians who emphasised the extent to which the Liberals' political base had decayed before the outbreak of the First World War:

> Pelling, for example, has emphasized repeatedly the enormous importance of increasing trade union affiliations for future Labour development . . . Moreover, he stresses the importance of those more general social and economic factors – growing difficulties in basic industries like coal, for example, coupled with increasing geographical unity on the one hand but deeper class divisions on the other – which were bound eventually to play into the hands of the Labour Party.

Indeed, Winter claimed that Pelling had been able to bridge the divide between the approach associated with an older generation of historians, who emphasised activism and struggle, and that of a younger generation, more concerned with popular Conservatism and apathy. In that sense he considered that Pelling had made an influential contribution to 'a better understanding of the multiple political and social meanings of the experience of class in modern Britain' (Winter 1983: xi).

Early career

Clearly there are some threads to be disentangled here, and it may be helpful to begin with some biographical information. Like most of the other members of the founding generation of labour historians, Pelling's early life was dominated by a combination of studying history at Cambridge University and serving in the armed forces during the Second World War (Winter 1983: viii). Indeed, he came from a conventional upper-middle-class family and started out with classics, so it was the interruption of his studies by the experience of military service which turned him towards more progressive politics and more recent history. Perhaps because this shift in his interests coincided with the Labour Party's landslide election victory of 1945 and the urgent tasks of post-war reconstruction which it then faced in government, Pelling was never attracted to the Communist Party. On the contrary, his role as secretary of his university Labour Party and Fabian Society allowed him to meet such memorable celebrities as the Cabinet Minister Hugh Dalton. Meanwhile, one of the more significant influences among his teachers was the economic historian Michael Postan, an outspokenly anti-Marxist East European emigré, close to figures on Labour's right wing such as Hugh Gaitskell. Moreover, Pelling's subsequent doctoral research on the early history of the ILP brought him into personal contact with many of the by-then-elderly pioneers of British Labour politics, and he struck up particularly warm relationships with such ethical socialists as Kathleen Bruce Glasier.

As already indicated, when this research began to appear in published form it had something of a paradoxical character. For, on the one hand, Pelling paid a great deal of attention to the detail of political events. In his own words at the beginning of his first major work, *The Origins of the Labour Party*: 'This book is an attempt to describe how the Labour Party came into existence. It is primarily a study in the development of new political structure' (Pelling 1954a: v). He looked in particular at the leadership, the ideas and the interaction between such small groups as the Social Democratic Federation (SDF), the Socialist League, the Fabian Society and the ILP. And his sources were largely institutional ones: the newspapers, pamphlets and minute books of these organisations, supplemented where possible by correspondence between their leaders, which he had frequently collected himself from those directly involved. On the other hand, however, Pelling also sometimes accounted for long-term political trajectories in much broader social terms. Thus he concluded his 'Introduction' by discounting the influence of political thought on the emergence of the Labour Party, emphasising instead 'the continually increasing importance of the "labour interest" in a country which, with a maturing capitalist economy and a well-established class system, was now verging on political democracy' (Pelling 1954a: 12).

Given the political and intellectual context in which his own basic approach had been formed, it would have been surprising had there been no comments of this sort in Pelling's work. For Labour's triumph in the general election of 1945, and the creation of the National Health Service and the nationalisation of leading industries that followed, were widely seen as the fulfilment of earlier socialist predictions about the evolution of modern industrial societies. There may have been some brief setbacks on the way, but history seemed to be on their side and to have turned in their direction gratifyingly quickly, indeed within the space of one lifetime. It was, after all, only forty-five years since the foundation of the Labour Party, and only sixty years since the emergence of the earliest modern socialist groups.

Perhaps that was all there was to it: Pelling had intended to write only narrow political history, but had been swept along by the surrounding atmosphere into making unguarded comments reflecting the times he lived in rather than his own considered judgements. His contribution to the history of the Labour Party would therefore best be appreciated by discarding the dated chaff of his more general remarks in order to preserve the fertile seed of his detailed institutional analysis. And his reputation would remain worthy but still dull.

The remainder of this chapter suggests, however, that to do so would be a misunderstanding of the way he opened up the serious historical study of the Labour Party, and that it would risk leaving out the core of his own interest and motivation. The first two sections look more closely at Pelling's early work on the origins of the Labour Party and show how it was based on a coherent, if theoretically understated, conception of class and politics in modern Britain. The third section examines some of Pelling's unpublished papers to explore the influences on his thinking of a distinctive and, for an allegedly dull historian, perhaps surprisingly continental strand of socialist thought. More broadly, this chapter hopefully demonstrates that a position sympathetic to the moderate mainstream of the Labour Party, rather than to the Communist Party or the New Left, does not need to be intellectually uninteresting.

The Origins of the Labour Party

The apparent paradox in Pelling's work was already evident at the start of his first major book. For *The Origins of the Labour Party* (1954a) begins by accounting for organised labour's adherence to the Liberal Party in the 1860s and 1870s in specifically political terms, as a result of the restricted franchise and limited financial resources, alongside the appeal of William Gladstone's progressive policies. But it then goes on to introduce the changes of subsequent decades with the broader social claim that 'large-scale industry developed a class solidarity among the workers which in the end facilitated effective political action in the interest of labour as a whole' (1954a: 4). More careful consideration, however, reveals aspects of this claim that otherwise may not be immediately obvious.

Firstly, the conception of 'class solidarity among the workers' was not framed in orthodox Marxist terms as a reduction of distinctive positions to a lowest common denominator of economic deprivation, leading eventually to a bitter political revolt. Rather it was seen in quietly revisionist terms as an increase in material well-being and organisational strength, leading to a growing capacity for constructive political reform. Thus Pelling followed the passage cited above with a description of the establishment of the Trades Union Congress (TUC) in the late 1860s, its success in improving the legal status of trade unions, the rising expectations of the craft bodies and the first signs of organisation among less-skilled workers in the early 1870s.

This period of progress was soon followed by a long economic depression which, contrary to orthodox Marxist predictions, 'so far from encouraging Socialism and the break-up of the Liberal Party, actually discouraged working-class militancy and destroyed the "advanced" elements then in existence' (1954a: 6). However, the more positive dynamic was reasserting itself by the late 1880s, for 'throughout the last half of the century the effective political strength of labour was almost constantly increasing: the growth of industry, the improvement of real wages and conditions, and the extension of educational facilities all combined to maintain this long-term trend' (1954a: 7). Even in discussing the widespread feeling of insecurity in the trade union world following the defeat of the engineers by an aggressive employers' lockout in 1897, Pelling was still at pains to highlight the distinctive conditions affecting each organisation. Thus long-term unemployment in metalworking, new technology in shoemaking and printing, and poor working conditions on the railways were neither reduced to one underlying trend nor seen as leading to any kind of revolt against the system: 'the attitude of the bulk of the unions now favouring independent labour representation was dictated more by fear for the security of their existing position than by the hope of any millennium' (1954a: 211). Moreover, it was just as important that they had been able to build up the financial reserves to allow them to do something about it.

Secondly, the nature of 'effective action in the interest of labour as a whole' would be fundamentally shaped by the political terrain to be traversed. In the British case this meant above all that any attempt to turn it in a revolutionary direction would lead to a dead end. Thus, in reviewing the trajectories of different socialist groups in the Conclusion to *The Origins of the Labour Party*, Pelling remarked that 'the British working class as a whole had no use for the conception of violent revolution. Any leader who failed to recognise this could not expect to win widespread support' (1954a: 231). Indeed the leader of the SDF, H. M. Hyndman, had already been dismissed in a way which was humourously appropriate both in itself and in its application to later generations of would-be revolutionaries:

> Hyndman saw himself as the Chairman of the Committee of Public Safety, installed in office by an untutored but enthusiastic mob aroused to violence by the bitterness of capitalistic crisis. It was an entertaining if somewhat unreal expectation that he, the City man, complete with the frock-coat and top-hat which were his customary dress, should be borne to power as the workers' choice in order to inaugurate the dictator-

ship of the proletariat. History has seen many ironies, but this was one which it was not to tolerate. (1954a: 49)

In addition to the revolutionaries' underestimation of the intelligence of ordinary people and misunderstanding of the impact of economic circumstances, this was also due, in Pelling's view, to the extension of political democracy in late nineteenth-century Britain. For working men were increasingly able to express their views peacefully through the doubling of the national electorate by the 1884 Reform Act, accompanied by less dramatic but equally important legislation of 1882–83 removing the property qualifications for candidates in borough elections and preventing most methods of bribing voters. Moreover, the wider background to such appeal as socialism did have in the British context was strongly coloured by radical land reformers like Henry George and backward-looking cultural critics like Thomas Carlyle and John Ruskin. Thus among the early socialist groups it was the Fabian Society's decision to adopt constitutional reformism and evolutionary gradualism that provided an appropriate application of Marxist social theory to British political conditions as well as synthesising it with indigenous intellectual traditions.

Thirdly a grasp of the correct overall strategy would, however, rarely be enough, for political success also depended on being able to choose the right tactics. Thus, while Fabianism provided an accurate analysis of trends in British society and politics, it made little contribution to the foundation of the Labour Party because its leading figures, based as they were in London, became too bound up in futile attempts to permeate the existing Liberal and Conservative Parties. By contrast, other reformist socialists committed themselves to building up independent labour representation by following the example of the Irish Nationalists, who had obtained concessions by securing the election of a group of MPs large enough to hold the balance of power in the House of Commons. The most prominent among this type was Keir Hardie, from the west of Scotland, who combined this parliamentary ambition with the struggle to build an alliance between his ILP and the TUC in order to tap the latter's financial resources, eventually leading to the foundation of the Labour Representation Committee (LRC) in 1900. Although Hardie had begun as an enthusiastic Gladstonian Liberal, his personal experience of the brutal conditions of the coalmining industry led him to advocate a break with both existing parties from surprisingly early in his political career:

Labour questions, thought Hardie, should take precedence over all other questions, and working men irrespective of party should combine to effect this. Nor was this, he considered, an impossible task: for even without further constitutional reform, working men could exert a decisive influence at Westminster. But it could only be done if those who were sent to Parliament to represent labour were bound to a definite labour programme. (1954a: 75)

Fourthly, the effectiveness of the tactics chosen would be vitally dependent on the responses of significant political opponents and rivals. Thus the sharp growth in trade union affiliations to the LRC after 1901 was a result of the latest manifestation of hostile judge-made law in the Taff Vale ruling. This stipulated that, although individual leaders were now safe from being sued through the courts for criminal conspiracy for their actions during industrial disputes, the unions as organisations could be sued for civil conspiracy and the amounts involved in payments of damages to employers could be very substantial. Even more vitally, the growing momentum of the LRC within the overall 'progressive alliance' between organised labour and middle-class liberalism was the result of the stubborn resistance of the local Liberal Parties to the adoption of trade union candidates, despite consistent pressure in that direction from their national organisers:

> All along, there is little doubt that most of the non-Socialist trade-union leaders would have been happy to stay in the Liberal Party – which most of them had belonged to in the past – if the Liberals had made arrangements for a larger representation of the working class among their Parliamentary candidates . . . Even Keir Hardie's revolt at Mid-Lanark in 1888 had been directed, not against the policy of Gladstone, but against the system by which the local association chose its candidate. (1954a: 235–6)

Yet the Liberal leadership itself was not exempt from criticism for its handling of the new political currents, for it proved to be surprisingly slow in pressing seriously for the state payment of MPs' salaries and of returning officers' fees, both reforms which might have helped to retain the loyalties at least of the smaller trade unions.

Fifthly, and finally, a complete historical account of effective political mobilisation would require not only an evaluation of the intellectual analysis available but also an appreciation of the level of emotional commitment involved. Here, as Pelling made clear in reviewing a collection of essays on Sidney and Beatrice Webb, was another major weakness of the Fabians:

> The paradox of the Webbs was that, fundamentally, they did not understand politics . . . They knew how institutions worked, and within certain limits they could work them; but they could not measure the forces that transmuted and transcended these institutions – the elemental forces of political power. 'Marriage', said Beatrice, 'is the wastepaper basket of the emotions'. She did not realize that the same could be said of politics or indeed of almost every field of human endeavour. (Pelling 1950: 507)

By contrast, the success of the early ILP was bound up with its quasi-religious outlook and the powerful motivating force of its members' passionate faith in the ultimate victory of their cause. Indeed, a strictly accurate estimate of resources and prospects was not always advisable:

> It does not matter if the faith feeds on illusions, for it is capable of conquering reality . . . It was this crusading zeal which drew attention to the Socialists in the eighties, and enabled them . . . to have an influence in politics far beyond what their numbers justified. (Pelling 1954a: 229–30)

Drawing on the deep traditions of popular religious nonconformity was probably inevitable, given the family backgrounds of most of those involved, and this bedrock of emotional attitudes was fundamental to the ILP activists' sense of purpose and enthusiasm. It was also fundamental in shaping their public performances, especially in the case of Hardie and Philip Snowden, both of whom delivered speeches consciously based on the sermonising techniques of evangelical revivalism.

Labour and politics

For Pelling, then, class was intimately bound up with politics. In so far as there were important 'pre-political' elements of 'class solidarity among the workers', providing an underlying foundation, they were not confined to material forces. For they included not only such economic trends as larger workplaces and higher wages, but such social trends as increasing education and literacy, and such cultural and religious traditions as literary Romanticism and popular nonconformity. But class, for Pelling, was not something which impinged on politics from the outside; rather it was to a very large extent the *result* of political processes. The choice of strategy and tactics, the response of rivals and the mobilising of emotion among potential supporters were all vital elements in facilitating 'effective political action in the interest of labour as a whole'. Indeed, he was later to comment of the ILP leaders that 'by their constant emphasis on the importance of "labour representation" they had done much to foster the growth of class solidarity' (Bealey and Pelling 1958: 283). Thus *The Origins of the Labour Party* concluded with a passage which begins by celebrating the formation of a permanent party, moves on to highlight its dependence on human agency and ends on what might be read, in the increasingly faction-ridden 1950s, as a note of warning:

> [T]he unity of the party, once established, remained substantially intact, and in the first half-century of its life, every General Election but two that it fought resulted in an increase of the aggregate Labour poll. The association of Socialist faith and trade-union interest, of hope for an ideal future and fear for an endangered present, seemed on the point of disruption at times: yet it survived, for a variety of reasons which lie outside the compass of this book, but also because in the years before the party's birth there had been men and women who believed that the unity of the working-class movement, both in industry and politics, was an object to be striven for, just as now most of their successors regard it as an achievement to be maintained. (1954a: 241)

Pelling, then, was clearly not an orthodox Marxist; nor, despite his close attention to institutions, was he a straightforward Fabian. *The Origins of the Labour Party*, as its very title suggests, did contain significant teleological elements, for it identified those chains of events which led to the end-point of the foundation conference in 1900. However, his immersion in the study of the late nineteenth century was deep enough for Pelling to have detached himself from the inevitable evolution assumed by most of his left-wing contemporaries. Instead he was able to pay attention to the ways in which the two older parties had also been able to reconstruct genuine appeals, even under a more democratic franchise. For the Liberals had been able to draw on the traditions of nonconformity and temperance, and under Gladstone become associated with highly emotional struggles for the extension of the franchise and a democratic foreign policy. Meanwhile, the Conservatives, partly defined in opposition as the party of the established Church and the brewing trade, had actively associated themselves with such equally emotive issues as paternalistic social reform and hostility towards immigrants. A Labour Party had undoubtedly emerged, but there had been nothing inevitable about it and, though active in a rapidly changing social context, the party was to remain deeply influenced by the political background out of which it had stepped:

> Its principal leaders were all ex-Liberals, many of them Liberals still in all but name; and the object of its policy in its first thirty years of life seemed to be not so much to win the confidence of the whole working class as to supplant the Liberal party. In this aim it succeeded, and by the nineteen-twenties it had become the party of the Celts and the nonconformists, of the teetotallers and the pacifists. The process of adaptation to make it a national party and to redress its bias of old Liberalism seems to be still in progress, not having gone all the way when the party attained power for the first time in 1945. (Pelling 1953: 238)

It should now be clear that for Pelling political agency and the legacies of previous political actions were the decisive factors in understanding the origins and nature of the Labour Party. Social trends did provide important material for politicians to work with, and on the whole those in Britain favoured increasingly effective democratic reformism. However, there was no concession to any notion of a unified working class as the basis for explanations of political behaviour. On this issue there is a clear line to be drawn between Henry Pelling's approach and those not only of contemporary orthodox Marxists such as Eric Hobsbawm, but of younger post-Marxists such as Gareth Stedman Jones and Ross McKibbin. For all of these other historians assumed the economic formation of a homogeneous working class in late nineteenth-century Britain and consequently saw the main task as being to explain its lack of interest in socialism, let alone revolution (Hobsbawm 1984; McKibbin 1990; Stedman Jones 1983; and for further discussion of these issues see Reid 1995). In some contrast it is striking that in his second major work, *Labour and Politics, 1900–1906*, written jointly with Frank Bealey, Pelling went out of his way in his introductory chapter to emphasise that, even after the formation of the Labour Party, popular attitudes remained highly fragmented along regional lines. This was a development of his long-standing interest in the very different characteristics of labour politics in the south and the north, partly already explained as a result of the more open and more radical nature of London Liberalism, but now increasingly also seen as a result of deeper cultural traditions. To some extent these might be understood in terms of the relationship between each region and the central State. For example, on the issue of the Boer War, which was just coming to an end at the time of Labour's foundational conference, the adoption of political positions 'was largely determined by traditional sectional loyalties which in some cases had been maturing since the Middle Ages. The Welsh, the Irish, and to some extent the Scots, with the aid of the English religious dissenters, stood against the tide of Imperialism' (Bealey and Pelling 1958: 2).

As that statement itself indicates, however, Pelling was increasingly concerned with the impact of religious affiliations. Characteristically, this was to be understood less in terms of the intellectual or moral teachings of the churches and more in terms of such pragmatic influences as family environment and denominational schooling. Thus, having charted the local levels of attendance at Church of England schools and shown their striking correlation with levels of support for the

Conservative Party in the same areas, Pelling concluded that 'this classification provides a much better index of political feeling for provincial England than any that is simply based on class differentiation or degree of industrialisation' (Bealey and Pelling 1958: 5). Most of the urban industrial regions showed a characteristic combination of nonconformity and popular Liberalism, and the major exceptions could now be understood in religious terms. In particular, the regional strength of Anglicanism helped to account for the Conservative bias of Lancashire, while the weakness of all denominations in the much more mobile context of the metropolis helped to account for the more secular and materialist tone of politics in London. Indeed the influence of religious affiliation was seen as part of the explanation for regional variations in the appeal of the newer socialist bodies themselves, with the rationalist and anti-clerical Fabians and SDF making more headway in Lancashire and London, while the idealist and evangelical ILP had a greater appeal in nonconformist areas, especially in the north.

Nor was this tendency towards the regional fragmentation of politics seen as being counteracted by the growth of trade unionism. For, despite its intimate connection with economic inequality, that too remained marked by weakness and sectionalism. The degree of unionisation varied markedly across occupations, with agricultural labourers still being the largest single group but barely organised, while the centres of manufacturing industry were still, as often as not, characterised by small firms, out-work and non-unionism:

> Industrialisation, always a catalyst of change, transformed the social structure sufficiently to bring new political forces into play: but since the new industries grew up in a piecemeal, localised fashion, the national pattern was hardly less variegated than before. (Bealey and Pelling 1958: 284)

Thus even those occupations that did have a significant union presence still tended to be found in particular industrial districts and were merged into regional political traditions. Cotton-workers were mainly concentrated in Lancashire, strongly influenced by local Conservatism and therefore less motivated towards direct labour representation. Coalminers were dispersed in a number of county unions, usually in nonconformist districts, so, while able and willing to elect significant numbers of their own officials as MPs, still found a congenial home within the Liberal Party. Meanwhile, those groups like the metalworking craftsmen who did have more of a national presence were usually spread too thinly to be able to influence political outcomes in particular constituencies.

Direct labour representation had taken a new form with the LRC in 1900 and worked up enough momentum in the general election of 1906 to adopt the grander title of the Labour Party. But Pelling was underlining the factors which meant that for most of the century to come Labour would experience enormous difficulties in constructing a governing majority:

> Both in Parliament and out, the stresses and strains of the party structure revealed themselves, as they had done earlier, in controversy, in recrimination, even in secession. In these events we can see the very essence of British politics – the social, industrial, and religious differences, the peculiarities of local situations, the interplay of

environment, of personality, and even of sheer accident. Nor is this surprising. The story of a great political party contains within itself the history of a nation. (Bealey and Pelling 1958: 288)

Note again that ending: the history of a *nation*, not the history of a *class*. For the lasting value of Henry Pelling's work is not just to be found in his commitment to accurate archival research, pioneering though that was in its day, but above all in his determination to locate the history of labour within the history of the country as a whole. This is a challenge which still needs to be taken up more widely if labour history is to find its rightful place once again at the centre of our understanding of the recent past.

Socialism and democracy

Thus far, this account has been based on a close reading of Pelling's published work, and elements of it may therefore be quite familiar. At least it should have demonstrated that he was an unusually intelligent historical observer, but it may still appear that he was only stumbling on insights in the course of narrow, empirically defined research projects. However, a number of unpublished papers delivered to a variety of university audiences in the late 1940s present a very different picture. For here we find Pelling involved in a series of rigorous encounters with socialist thought and prepared to make broad generalisations. Initially surprising in relation to his later public reputation, this is less so when we consider their original context. For both the author and many of those in his audiences had just been de-mobbed from a costly war against German Nazism only to be confronted with the intensification of a Cold War against Russian communism. Much has been made of this highly charged ideological context in relation to the distinguished group of Marxists who emerged from the discussions of the Communist Party Historians' Group. From what follows it should be clear that this appreciation needs to be broadened to include the more moderate mainstream of the university Left of that period (for some aspects of the intellectual environment in Cambridge University at the time see Taylor 1997; for the unusual German ethical-socialist influences on Allan Flanders, a parallel figure in the field of industrial relations, see Black 1999 and Kelly 1999).

Already in what seems to be the earliest of these papers, probably given to an informal audience of research students while he was working on his doctoral dissertation on the early history of the ILP completed in 1950, Pelling made it quite clear that his motivation was to produce work that was 'relevant to contemporary problems and future action' (Pelling nd a: 1). Moreover, he explained that his initial institutional focus was meant only as a point of entry to a much larger field:

> Its formal structure is a foundation for one's studies, which will then be able to extend and broaden until one can appreciate the wider historical perspectives, and if desired, comprehend the philosophical and political thought of the period and its general social attitudes. (Pelling nd a: 5)

Such wider perspectives were indeed explored in the most revealing of those unpublished talks, 'Socialism and democracy', given on the centenary of *The Communist Manifesto* in 1948. For on that occasion Pelling was prepared to make a clear distinction between the principles of Marxist social theory and the variety of political strategies which could legitimately be derived from them. He quoted at length from Engels on the broad theory of historical materialism and underlined its prophetic anticipation of the emergence of independent working-class politics. However, he also argued that Marx and Engels themselves had deliberately left some room for manoeuvre in particular national circumstances and it had only been Lenin who had insisted on the necessity of the violent overthrow of the bourgeois state. In contrast, Western European reformists, especially in France and Germany, had argued that 'in certain countries the tradition of democratic government had developed sufficiently for the class struggle to be modified into constitutional channels' (Pelling 1948: 6). Thus it would seem as if Pelling's understated historical observations on the improvement of economic conditions and the extension of the franchise in late nineteenth-century Britain were not just chance insights, but rather were connected to a familiarity with the emergence of revisionist trends within Western European Marxism. In other circumstances the public presentation of his work might have taken a different form, but the intensity of the Cold War at the time hemmed him in on both sides. For the label 'Marxist' was largely restricted to the Soviet-aligned communist parties, while any innovative references to historical materialism were likely to attract only Stalinist rebukes:

> [O]ne might say that what distinguishes Marx from earlier thinkers is simply his application of scientific method to history and his discovery of the central importance of economic motivation. Any political thinker who follows in the path of Marx and who develops his doctrine still further and in so doing modifies his conclusions or introduces new complications into an apparently simple picture at once lays himself open to accusations from what I might call the theological Marxists, the patristic commentators, of deviating from the true 'line' of Marxist thought. In so far as I deal with developments in the twentieth century I shall therefore attempt to avoid confusing meanings by [not] introducing the word Marxist in any sense at all. (Pelling 1948: 4)

Pelling, then, was familiar with Marxist theory and prepared to locate himself in relation to it, but even without the Cold War he would probably have found that tradition too constraining. For in the context of the debates on strategy within the Second International, it was the eclectic ethical socialism of Jean Jaures that he found particularly attractive. The reference to Jaures is to his interventions at the 1903 Bordeaux Congress of the French Socialist Party, during which he was attempting to find a middle way between reformists and revolutionaries, increasingly divided on the issue of joining a coalition government. Pelling probably came across this speech in R. C. K. Ensor's *Modern Socialism* (1904: 163–86), which was part of his own private collection of books, and which contained a wide selection of British, French and German socialist texts. The middle way of Jaures gave Pelling a more general framework for understanding that parliamentary politicians were likely to be tempted to join coalition governments and make too many compromises, and for concluding that this could be avoided only if reformist parties remained firmly based on the extra-parliamentary movements of the working class, 'that is, upon those who have suffered most from the inequalities of the present social system' (Pelling 1948: 16; for the reception of Jaures in Britain in the 1900s, see Tanner 1991). This seems to have been particularly appealing as an antidote to the traumatic memory of Labour's former leader Ramsay MacDonald's formation of the National Government in 1931, its subsequent imposition of a cut in the level of unemployment benefit in the face of strong opposition from the TUC, and a near-fatal split in the Labour Party:

> The Socialist party [Jaures argues] must defend democratic liberties; it must be mindful of the national culture; yet it must bear in mind the possibility of violent capitalist reaction using the State machinery against the proletarian class, and therefore it must safeguard its hold upon the sympathies of the workers and retain its defensive organisation of their interests. (Pelling 1948: 8)

This would suggest, therefore, that Pelling's appreciation of the ILP's tactics of independent labour representation was not just the result of a pragmatic evaluation of their important contribution to the foundation of the Labour Party, but reflected a deeper sense of the ethical basis of political action and the moral responsibilities of democratic politicians.

Familiarity with these general principles in continental socialist thought also led him to a number of broad conclusions about the peculiar nature of British historical development, with a special focus on the ways in which it had further intensified existing Western European trends towards parliamentary reformism. Relative geographical isolation had protected the country from much of the political upheaval accompanying periodic waves of military aggression in the rest of Europe, and it had consequently been able to develop as a more continuous unified state with a stronger parliamentary tradition. The former had contributed to a widespread sense of the complexity of national affairs and the inappropriateness of dealing with them through such channels of direct democracy as popular assemblies, the election of delegates and the use of referenda. The latter had evolved as a combination of an electoral system which gave the strongest party in the country a majority of seats in the House of Commons and a custom of forming governments which then gave that majority a complete monopoly of cabinet offices. Socialist activists in Britain took this so much for granted that they rarely reflected on its peculiar propriety to their own political project:

> a system which, in spite of being undemocratic, or rather perhaps because of it, is admirably suited to express in constitutional form not only the idea of the class struggle, but also the concept, apparently so unconstitutional, of the dictatorship of the proletariat. The agency of this dictatorship would be the cabinet, which is both the central authority of initiative in legislation and the final arbiter of executive policy. (Pelling 1948: 12)

It was characteristic of Pelling's approach both that the peculiarities of British development should thus have been seen in terms of political rather than economic or social structures, and that these broad outlines should have been followed immediately by an account of specific political actions. For against this background there had still been a lively debate on the British Left involving Marxist and syndicalist rejection of the parliamentary road, and ultra-radical calls for a major overhaul of the constitution. Although in the end Pelling judged that MacDonald had gone too far in the direction of parliamentary reformism, it had been his consistent political intelligence and effective leadership that had kept the early Labour Party on a peaceful and gradualist path more appropriate to British conditions:

> What a contrast there is between this and Leninism! The Bolshevik theory has been defined as Socialism while you wait, or rather Socialism while you won't wait; and for some countries, unfortunately, it may be the only approach to Socialism that is possible. But this country, which has already benefited by peaceful transfers of power from older to newer aristocracies in earlier centuries, will permit the internal transformation of institutions while retaining the outward forms of those institutions comparatively unchanged. (Pelling 1948: 14. For the importance of MacDonald's contribution see also Pelling nd a: 16, and Pelling nd b: 1–2, 9–10)

These reflections on British history by a Labour moderate in the late 1940s strikingly anticipated the more open-minded and imaginative debate which became possible among Marxists after the splits in the communist world over the Soviet acknowledgment of Stalinist excesses in 1956. Indeed, Pelling's emphasis on the impact on Labour reformism of the survival of aristocratic power and traditional institutions in Britain was remarkably close to the position later taken by such leading figures among the younger generation of the New Left as Perry Anderson and Tom Nairn, though of course in their case the analysis was inflected with tones of bitter regret (Chun 1993: 69–76; Reid 1978).

Given the overall framework of Pelling's 'Socialism and democracy' talk as a reflection on one of the foundation texts of Marxism, it is not surprising that he referred frequently to 'the working class', and in his more specific comments on the British Labour Party clearly underlined the centrality to its constitution of 'working class organisations', most notably in the case of the trade unions which controlled a majority of votes at its annual conference. In his broader conclusions about the peculiarities of British development, however, he also emphasised that it was the country's relatively peaceful history and its high level of individual liberty which had allowed the open formation of a large range of voluntary associations, including dissenting churches and co-operative societies, and also the trade unions themselves. As a result, these

> organisations, while often of working class origin, tend to cut across the direct distinctions of class conflict as defined by Marx; moreover, by exerting their strength in political action they have obtained important concessions from the State, concessions which associate them, if not with capitalism itself, at any rate with the so-called capitalist State. This accounts for a strong tendency in Britain to distrust Marx's theory of economic classes as a misleading abstraction from the complex structure of society. (Pelling 1948: 9; see also Pelling nd b: 1)

Here, then, anticipating the trail of his later historical work, we can see how Pelling's encounter with socialist thought involved, first, a careful revision of many of its implications and applications and, then, a turning back again to undermine some of its key presuppositions. For, having emphasised amelioration, constitutionalism, political traditions and political agency, he went on to question the whole notion of *class* itself, at least in its application to the British context (for his very early interest in regional differences see Pelling nd a: 8–12).

Still worthy, but dull?

Henry Pelling's work on the early Labour Party was undoubtedly informed by the empirical method, with all that implies for the careful collection and open-minded consideration of the relevant evidence. However, the insights he produced were not the result of a blinkered stumbling about in the archives, but rather of a conscious interaction with key issues in Western European socialist thought. As already mentioned, the Cold War environment was one reason he did not make this more explicit, but another was his aversion to becoming trapped in an excessively rigid intellectual framework (though some broader thinking was indicated, in a muted way, in Pelling 1954b: 1–16). It seems likely that in this respect he consciously modelled himself on what he saw as a further distinctive strength of British Labour strategy:

> The theory is there, but it is worked out empirically and is seldom coherently expressed. Like the British constitution, it has never been precisely formulated and committed to writing. The party has had its prophets and its visionaries; it has had its active apostles of its gospel, tireless and innumerable; but it has no summary creed and no constraining intellectual discipline. Perhaps this is an advantage, for future developments may require subtle modifications which would be difficult to make if everything had been set down once and for all on paper. (Pelling 1948: 18)

Perhaps, then, it has been a mistake to attempt to explain and clarify the ideas underpinning Pelling's work. But that may still be redeemed if we are able to keep them at the back of our minds as a kind of sounding board, rather than relying on them as a set of rules to be followed, which would only get in the way of a clear reconstruction of the peculiarities of historical processes as they are recorded in the complexities of historical evidence.

References

Unless indicated, the place of publication is London.
Adelman, P. (1972) *The Rise of the Labour Party, 1880–1945*
Bealey, F. and Pelling, H. (1958) *Labour and Politics, 1900–1906. A History of the Labour Representation Committee*
Black, L. (1999) 'Social democracy as a way of life: fellowship and the Socialist Union, 1951–9', *Twentieth Century British History*, 10:4
Chun, L. (1993) *The British New Left*, Edinburgh

Ensor, R. C. K. (ed.) (1904) *Modern Socialism. As Set Forth by Socialists in Their Speeches, Writings and Programmes*

Hobsbawm, E. J. (1984) *Worlds of Labour. Further Studies in the History of Labour*

Kelly, J. (1999) 'Social democracy and anti-communism: Allan Flanders and British industrial relations in the early post-war period', in Campbell, A. McIlroy, J. and Fishman, N. (eds) *British Trade Unions and Industrial Politics*, vol. 1: *The Post-War Compromise, 1945–64*, Aldershot

McKibbin, R. (1990) *The Ideologies of Class. Social Relations in Britain, 1880–1950*, Oxford

Pelling, H. (nd a) 'The history of the Independent Labour Party', unpublished paper, currently in the author's possession

Pelling, H. (nd b) 'Socialism in British politics – up to 1914', unpublished paper, currently in the author's possession

Pelling, H. (1948) 'Socialism and democracy', unpublished paper, currently in the author's possession

Pelling, H. (1950) 'Review of M. Cole (ed.) *The Webbs and Their Work*', *Cambridge Journal*, 3:8

Pelling, H. (1953) 'H. H. Champion: pioneer of labour representation', *Cambridge Journal*, 6:4

Pelling, H. (1954a) *The Origins of the Labour Party, 1880–1900*

Pelling, H. (ed.) (1954b) *The Challenge of Socialism*

Reid, A. (1978) 'Politics and economics in the formation of the British working class. A response to H. F. Moorhouse', *Social History*, 3:3

Reid, A. J. (1995) *Social Classes and Social Relations in Britain, 1850–1914*, Cambridge

Stedman Jones, G. (1983) *Languages of Class. Studies in English Working Class History, 1832–1982*, Cambridge

Tanner, D. (1991) 'Ideological debate in Edwardian Labour politics: radicalism, revisionism and socialism', in Biagini, E. F. and Reid, A. J. (eds) *Currents of Radicalism. Popular Radicalism, Organised Labour and Party Politics in Britain, 1850–1914*, Cambridge

Taylor, M. (1997) 'The beginnings of modern British social history?' *History Workshop Journal*, 43

Winter, J. (1983) 'Introduction: labour history and labour historians', in J. Winter (ed.) *The Working Class in Modern British History. Essays in Honour of Henry Pelling*, Cambridge

8

Ross McKibbin: class cultures, the trade unions and the Labour Party

John Callaghan

The work of the historian is always a complex and heterogeneous aggregate of theories, narrative, interpretation and analysis. Such originality as it possesses lies more often than not in the distinctive pattern which the historian gives to the components of his or her work, rather than the components themselves, many of which may be found elsewhere. The three books by Ross McKibbin which form the focus of this chapter raise interesting questions for the study of the Labour Party largely because of this type of originality in which familiar elements are given novel interpretation and arrangement. These studies are linked but they do not represent a systematic investigation of my subject matter; there are too many discontinuities for that in McKibbin's lines of enquiry: questions raised in relation to the years 1880–1914, for example, are simply dropped for the period 1918–50. Nevertheless a more or less coherent picture emerges of Labour's history in the first half of the twentieth century.

It is an account of the Labour Party that is intimately related to the social history of the working class. The main explanation of Labour's politics, achievements and limitations which emerges from McKibbin's work is grounded in the culture of its principal constituency – the British working class – rather than the party's leadership, organisation and programme. Though the first of his studies – *The Evolution of the Labour Party* (1974) – is an institutional history of the party, McKibbin was already persuaded that political action is the result of social and cultural attitudes which are not primarily political. Politics itself is said to play only a subordinate and inarticulate part in people's lives. The general thesis of this book – an implicit theory of British society – attributes both the rise of the Labour Party in the years up to 1924 and the slow attrition on the part of the Liberal Party to the growth of 'an acutely developed working class consciousness'. But it is a class consciousness which obstructed the spread of socialism and excluded Labour from many areas of working-class life. Though the Labour Party remained ideologically vague until at least the end of its third decade, according to McKibbin, it was unable to become the sort of catch-all 'people's party' which some of its leaders desired. It remained a class party.

The growth of 'an acutely developed working class consciousness' thus involves a paradox: Labour's rise both depended on and was restricted by it. *The Ideologies of Class* (1990) promises to make this paradoxical thesis more explicit by pursuing answers to the question: 'What was the social character of the British working class in the period we conventionally think it to be most mature, that is from the 1880s to the early 1950s?' At this point the range of the investigation is broadened. McKibbin now wants to examine the relations of the working class to the rest of society as well as its relations to the Labour Party. *Classes and Cultures* (1998) takes this a stage further, and though the Labour Party itself virtually disappears in the process McKibbin tells us that his biggest study to date is 'a political book ... probably more a book about the social and ideological foundations of English politics than anything else'.

I begin by considering McKibbin's account of the working class in the period of Labour's birth, broadly the years 1880–1914, a time when Britain had proportionately the largest working class in the world. The working class represented about 75 per cent of the population and was largely free of the ethnic, linguistic, national and sectarian divisions which obstructed class solidarity elsewhere. Class divisions were both conspicuous and acute. Class segregation, according to McKibbin, even intensified in the years between 1918 and 1951, as the classes became more isolated, occupationally and residentially, each from the others. The future that had been predicted in the 1880s was that of a social explosion resulting from class conflict. But it was a future that failed to materialise. Britain alone of the major European states produced no mass Marxist party in the years up to 1914. While Werner Sombart famously puzzled over the question 'Why is there no socialism in the United States?' McKibbin considered that the question of 'exceptionalism' might be asked more fruitfully of Britain which was similar enough to continental Europe to make the difference more intriguing.

'Why was there no Marxism in Britain?' To answer that question, and to examine the larger anomaly of British exceptionalism, McKibbin advances four subsidiary questions:

- How far did the structure of the workforce promote collectivism?
- To what extent did the associational culture of the working class accelerate or impede the transmission of rejectionist ideologies?
- How far did the working class feel excluded from civil society? and
- To what degree did it possess a leadership capable of articulating and directing a specifically socialist working-class politics?

McKibbin proceeds to account for the special path taken by the British working class, though he does so without the aid of comparative analysis and in such a way that it is difficult for the reader to find a structured answer in the mass of independent variables which he brings to bear on the problem. His answer has significance, however, for a number of reasons. First it uses arguments which clearly inform his discussion of the nature of the Labour Party. It lays bare some of the interpretive issues which McKibbin's empirical histories conceal or leave implicit.

Second, McKibbin draws from a common pool of arguments about the 'peculiarities' of the British working class which have found favour with a number of influential historians of quite different ideological persuasions. Those arguments and theories have become almost received wisdom. They are overdue for a reappraisal.

McKibbin begins by drawing attention to the weakness of the collectivist elements affecting the working class. The trade unions reached only 15 per cent of the employed workforce in 1901 and an even smaller proportion of working-class women. Much of the workforce was seasonal labour, fragmented and unstable; the service sector was 'the most rapidly growing part of the Edwardian economy'; then there was 'that vast and unnumbered race who worked for themselves or others on a catch-as-catch-can basis' (McKibbin 1990a: 3). While shop-assistants and clerks were deprived of the social intercourse which facilitated organisation, and other workers were subjected to conditions which left them economically insecure and isolated, there were some workers – such as the penny capitalists of the London streets – who positively rejoiced in 'a jaunty and attractive individualism [that] was essential to life' (1990a). Other features of the economy served to localise industrial relations and encourage paternalism. During the Edwardian period only 100 firms employed more than 3,000 people, accounting for at most 700,000 workers. Small-scale enterprise dominated and relations with employers were either close or mediated by sub-employers. The sexual division of labour also militated against a communitarian solidarity by excluding women from politics as well as the workplace, while providing men with an occupational rather than a neighbourhood loyalty.

McKibbin assumes that the rich associational life of the working class stood in the way of both a rejectionist ideology and the development of a party successfully integrating these interests under its own roof, as the Social Democratic Party is said to have done in Wilhelmine Germany. Wage levels in Britain also permitted 'more or less everything that made up late nineteenth-century working class pastimes' and 'gave the working class a certain autonomy . . . not available to any other European work-force'. Thus any working-class party 'had to compete with an existing working-class culture which was stable and relatively sophisticated' (1990a: 13). Though McKibbin is also of the view that poverty and the daily struggle for survival did not conduce to a collectivist political commitment, the main thrust of his argument is that working-class leisure activities presented opportunities for an active engagement in society outside of politics: inclusion rather than social exclusion, then, but both beyond the reach of national politics. Political ambitions existed – indeed the working class was 'intensely political' according to McKibbin (1990: 296) – but these interests were 'scattered and localised' among a profusion of associations. Was this because there was no overwhelming sense of grievance which could have united the working class against civil society? McKibbin certainly considers this to be part of the argument. Walter Bagehot was right, on this view, to identify deference as a factor in political stability. But he supplied only half the explanation.

McKibbin points to the increasing ideological hegemony of Crown and Parliament in the last quarter of the nineteenth century, the acceptability of both to the working class and the security of the existing status order, institutional structure and class system which derived from it. How was this possible? The Crown evolved, he says, as an 'even-handed guarantor of the class-neutrality of Parliament'. Parliament itself was the focus for working-class political aspirations. Action outside of the political system, narrowly conceived, was widely accepted as illegitimate. In part this perception was informed by the observation that the upper classes themselves adhered to the rules of the political game. Patriotism – both cause and effect of crown worship – reinforced the sense that Crown and Parliament belonged to and represented the nation. But in McKibbin's view the working class was far from being the dupe of these arrangements:

> it is entirely arguable that the traditions, catch-phrases, and ideological fragments that shaped working-class politics also helped to shape the politics of all other social classes . . . that the freedom of the middle and upper classes to *choose* one political strategy as against another was thereby limited by these historical imperatives, while, equally, the ability of the working classes to modify the social and economic relationships they inherited was proportionately enlarged. (1990a: 26)

The rules were thus binding on both sides. Coercion was ruled out to a greater degree in the UK than on the continent. The State was more or less compelled to keep out of industrial relations, and the unions by 1875 had a freedom of action 'unique' in Europe. A 'bloody-minded and ill-disciplined workforce' (1990a) had to be tolerated as part of this equation. The working class was subject to neither incorporation nor coercion, and was able to extract these benefits in return for its deference to the class and institutional status quo. It created its own institutions within that framework and produced its own leaders, rather than having to adopt them from among an alienated intelligentsia, as on the continent. The Labour Party was, of course, one of these institutions led by working-class men. But for Labour to establish itself with the craft-divided organised working class, whose interest in the party was 'only intermittent', it had to tread cautiously and embrace only those commitments which did not disturb any particular working-class interest. An anodyne ethical socialist rhetoric was acceptable on this basis, but so too was much of the liberal ideology. The career of Arthur Henderson (who was party secretary during 1911–34, foreign secretary in 1929–31 and, briefly, leader in 1931–32) illustrates all of these points.

For McKibbin, Henderson was by 1931 as representative of the rank and file 'as any individual could be' (1990b: 63). He was also a 'type' – one recognised by Lenin, Weber and Michels – for whom politics was both a vocation and a system of party patronage – a system which he had a hand in creating. Henderson was a leading Wesleyan Methodist, temperance reformer and an 'advanced radical' all his life. He was rooted in trade unionism and advanced his parliamentary career, with the help of Liberal patrons at every turn, through the Friendly Society of Ironfounders, as a candidate of the union's Liberal wing. Yet he was one of those who came to realise that his parliamentary career could not depend on the Liberals and it was this realisation which redirected him to the cause of independent labour representation, as it did for many similar men.

This turn did not involve an ideological shift from liberalism. Henderson's maiden speech was in favour of free trade. He supported the First World War in common with the vast majority of his fellow-trade unionists, though strongly sympathising with much for which the dissident and pacifist-leaning Union of Democratic Control stood. He also believed in harmonious class relationships, favoured the conciliation and arbitration of industrial disputes, and was openly class-collaborationist, as dictated by his social Christianity. He wanted Labour to represent the community, to become a 'national people's party'.

Here, however, he ran up against the 'industrial sectionalism' of the unions and the realisation that he was leader only on sufferance, unable to impose on the unions ideologies which adversely affected their interests. For McKibbin Henderson's career discloses what Labour was and what Labour could not become. Henderson was ideologically representative of a generation of Labour leaders who began by seeking parliamentary careers as Liberals and ended up being catapulted by the First World War into the leading place in British politics because of structural rather than ideological changes in the political system. The extension of the franchise and the enlarged role of the unions brought about by the war made this possible. But Henderson's leadership was always organisational and rhetorical, and its limits were set by the unions in which he had his roots.

The Evolution of the Labour Party (1974)

Up to 1924 the Labour Party was at all levels, according to McKibbin, a working-class organization . . . a truly proletarian party' (1974: xiii). Labour emerged from the war in 1918 even more 'an agent of the unions' than it had been in 1914, the war having probably strengthened the right-wing of the party rather than the left-wing. Though McKibbin says he is concerned primarily with the 'mass organization', rather than the parliamentary leadership, of the Labour Party for these reasons – arguing that its centre of gravity, at least until 1922, was extra-parliamentary – there are some curious omissions in his history. He has almost nothing to say about the political impact of the massive growth of the unions and the industrial conflict of the years 1910–14. On methodological grounds he does not consider the impact of the First World War on Labour and trade union politics, years in which the unions continued to grow, especially in heavy industry. The immediate post-war years, up to the severe slump of 1921, complete the cycle of events which saw trades union membership peak at 8.25 million. But in largely ignoring the industrial conflict, political ferment and structural changes of those years, McKibbin has eliminated much from his narrative that bears on class consciousness and socialism – Labour's dominant rhetoric by 1931 – and robs his narrative of a dynamic that helps to explain this otherwise unlikely ideological development.

McKibbin has two further objectives, beyond explaining the character of the Labour Party through an analysis of its mass organisation; first, to suggest reasons why it replaced the Liberal Party as the principal party of the Left; second, to explain why the Labour leadership was unable to emulate the German SPD and create a *global* working-class movement. Henderson's career has already provided the reader with relevant evidence. More generally McKibbin sees a social gulf separating the leaders of the craft unions from the Liberal Party when the Labour Representation Committee was set up in 1900. The issues that divided organised labour from the Liberal Party were less of policy and more of class understood in this way: ideologically there was little difference between the two parties (1974: 54), as can be seen throughout the Edwardian years when Labour's electoral fortunes depended largely on avoiding contests with Liberal candidates and it was difficult to disentangle the Liberal and Labour elections campaigns. Thus at the elite level – as in the Gladstone–MacDonald electoral deal of 1903 – Labour depended on an agreement with the Liberals. But at the grass-roots level local Labour Parties depended on the unions: the local parties worked effectively when the unions gave their support. Labour organisation made no impression in constituencies held by candidates of the Miners' Federation, for example, until the union changed sides from Liberal to Labour – a process not yet completed in the localities by the outbreak of war. The grip of the unions on Labour by 1910 is also illustrated by the 11 trade unionists who sat on the 16-man National Executive Committee (NEC) of the party and the fact that all but 35,377 of the 1,430,539 members were trade unionists (over half a million of whom were miners). But it is illustrated also in the fact that until 1918 the characteristic local organ of the Labour Party was the trades council (1974: 33).

The self-restraint that made the understanding between the parliamentary Liberal and Labour Parties work began to break down at the local level between 1910 and 1914 as initiatives were undertaken locally to contest elections, whether the Liberals liked it or not. McKibbin resists the idea that this had much to do with growing ideological differences, or because of objectionable policies associated with the Liberal Government. He allows that the industrial militancy of 1911–13 may have contributed but says that this is difficult to prove. Instead he attributes the change to a growing 'feeling' that the Liberals were not working class while Labour was (1974: 70–1). This, it might be noted, is also difficult to prove, but McKibbin allows the discussion up to 1914 to end on that note. In fact he later suggests that the industrial unrest may have made local parties more militant and that the attraction of many union members, from among the growing number of trade unionists, to the Labour Party contributed to this change of mood. For at least some of those people the conversion to Labour may have had more to do with the industrial conflict than Labour's political activities (1974: 86).

That, however, is not the main thrust of his argument. Half the working class is still voteless, of course, but by 1914 Labour is stronger organisationally at local level, the trades councils are performing their political functions more effectively, and the Liberals reply in kind to the greater combativity of the local Labour organisations. The evidence, McKibbin suggests, is that, but for the outbreak of war between 150 and 170 Labour candidates would have contested a 1915 general election, including single-member constituencies, without regard for electoral pacts of the sort brokered and still favoured by Ramsay MacDonald. By-elections and municipal elections after 1910 suggest Labour was getting stronger (1974: 84–5).

McKibbin denies that there was any significant move to the Left during the war. The same people were in control of the party in 1918 as in 1914. The unions supported the war while the Left was defensive and divided. Opposition to socialism within the unions 'was inflamed by the war' (1974: 90) and the unions forced a change in the method of electing the NEC, in 1917, which further concentrated power in their hands. In that year a new political formation of trade unionists and co-operators was mooted – to be called the 'People's Party' – and though nothing came of it McKibbin offers it as evidence of the alienation of many trade unionists from the socialists. These were still largely to be found in the small ILP, which was excluded from the Reorganisation Committee which was put together to draft a new constitution for the Labour Party. Discussion of doctrine is absent from the record of the committee's deliberations. Henderson refrained from mentioning socialism during his tour of the districts to sell the new constitution. The real issue, from the unions' standpoint, was who would dominate the NEC (1974: 98 and 102). The 1918 TUC showed that there was still considerable support for a separate 'Trades Union Labour Party' even though the unions got their way on the substance of the new constitution. The Parliamentary Committee elected at this TUC was as patriotic as any elected before it, and, according to McKibbin, 'the membership of this committee was a more important determinant of the Labour Party's development than the break-up of the Liberal Party, the Russian Revolution, the work of the Webbs, or even what Henderson thought he was doing in 1917' (1974: 103).

The Russian Revolution, McKibbin allows, had taught Henderson 'that a powerful parliamentary alternative to Bolshevism was immediately required', and this also informed the new constitution (1974: 92). Clause 4 was vague enough to be acceptable in that context. The unions supported the sort of wartime collectivism that they had just experienced and they were 'more anxious' than they had been that the forms of collectivism they had always supported – such as selective nationalisations – should find their way into legislation. This was the point of overlap where the socialist minority and the trade unions could find common ground. But 'in Britain alone the left wing of the working class movement did not emerge from the war in some way stronger than it entered it . . . the war did not necessarily mean the defeat of socialism in Britain, it did mean the defeat of the socialists' (1974: 105–6). The strength of the Left in Scotland, particularly of the ILP, is allowed as an exception to this pattern, though McKibbin is quick to link it with the weakness of the Scottish unions outside Glasgow (1974: 163).

In 1924 *Labour Organiser* could find only two strong local Labour Parties based on individual membership – Ardwick and Woolwich. Local parties were still very reliant on union branches. Most funds were supplied locally, most candidates were chosen by the unions, not by head office. No further consideration was given to an electoral pact with the Liberals after 1918, and Labour contested as many seats as it could in the belief that it was competing for the same electorate as the Liberals. It consciously aimed to forestall a Liberal revival (1974: 120). The ease with which individual Liberals moved into the Labour Party, however, 'is evidence that the political differences between Liberal radicals and the Labour movement were by no means unbridgeable', despite Labour's commitment to nationalisation. Differences in policy were less important, according to McKibbin, than 'social and psychological resentments which powerfully directed Labour's actions towards the Liberal Party' (1974: 121). This argument, the reader will note, has already been employed to explain the divergent paths of the two parties by 1914. McKibbin now informs us that the Liberals were 'bourgeois in a particular way' – 'self-consciously superior', patronising and condescending, they rubbed up the Labour leaders with their 'scarcely concealed snobbery' in entirely the wrong way. The minority Labour Government of 1924 was a 'propaganda exercise' designed to show that Labour could do without them.

Leading figures in the Labour Party were impressed by the organisational feats of the German SPD. Herbert Morrison did his best to emulate its methods in London, but his attempts to create a network of Labour associations constituting a genuine Labour community failed (1974: 171). McKibbin attributes this to the evident lack of unity of purpose of the British working class which was also revealed in the abortive attempts to institutionalize relations with the Co-operative Union in 1921. He alludes to the cultural enmeshing of the working class into the national culture – a point on which he is less sure in *Classes and Cultures* – partly because 'sport as a working-class pastime was so much more important in Britain than anywhere else in Europe' (1974: 234). Morrison's efforts succeeded, however, in frightening head office which was deeply suspicious of anything beyond its control. The party's relations with the Labour Research Department and the *Daily Herald* further illustrate its centralising tendencies and its concern about 'troublemakers', especially communist troublemakers. Trade union pressure 'is the most insistent theme' in these episodes, though one which complemented the centralising instincts of party leaders such as MacDonald. But what about the spectacular collapse of trade union membership from 1920, the defeat of the General Strike and the reprisals which followed it? Was Labour's apparent dependence on the unions undisturbed by these developments? Did its growing strength in local government fail to supply a different dynamic? McKibbin has no answers to these questions. Indeed they do not arise, – even in his later discussions of the inter-war years.

At this point it is instructive to turn to McKibbin's explanation for Labour's success in eclipsing the post-war Liberals (for an alternative view, see Tanner 1990: 1–16). For McKibbin the Representation of the People Act of 1918 'was of the first importance' in Labour's eclipse of the Liberals (McKibbin, Matthew and Kay 1990: 82). The 1916 split in the Liberal Party is downplayed as a causal factor. McKibbin argues that the Labour splits of 1914, August–September 1917 and November 1918, which received as much contemporary publicity as had the Liberal split, suggest that there were other reasons for the decline of the Liberals than the splits themselves. Nor does he accept that the Liberals were somehow more averse to wartime collectivism than the Tories. The war itself, in this view, is overrated as the cause of Labour's success and the Liberal's decline (1974: 240). Everything, according to McKibbin, points to 'Labour's enduring *ante-bellum* character'. It simply continued to reap the benefits of 'an already existing industrial class consciousness'.

Because 'it had no life apart from the unions it gained electorally from their growth'. Meanwhile the Liberals suffered from their inability to claim the loyalties of any class. But the union-based class consciousness which benefited Labour also set limits on what it could achieve. The working class 'did not lead their social lives within the confines of their Party, nor did they regard Party allegiances as the judge of their cultural values' (1974: 245). Politics had to compete with 'too many other things'; the working class had not suffered the active persecution visited upon their German counterparts; and the unions had more limited objectives than the Hendersons and Morrisons and held the power to get their way. In McKibbin's view Labour inevitably failed, in a nation 'profoundly divided by class', to break out of its electoral dependence on the unions, despite a propaganda appeal that was designed to be classless. He concludes with a remark that might have been intended as a riposte to Miliband: 'If it is objected that it has not served the cause of socialism or even the "true" interests of the working class the answer is that it was never designed to do so' (1974: 247).

Class relations

McKibbin confronts the paradox of a working-class party that was unable to attract the votes of most of the working class – despite the growth of class consciousness – when he turns to the inter-war years and the Conservative electoral hegemony which followed the introduction of universal suffrage. He is clear that by 1918 'society's relations with the working class had at last become the central question' (1990c: 259), and yet a reasonable estimate suggests that by 1931 around 55 per cent of the working class voted for the Conservative-dominated national candidates while 50 per cent did so in 1935. The Conservative hegemony rested on this 'exceptionally high working-class vote and the tenacious social unity of the non-working-classes'. From 1920 Britain lived under a deflationary regime which tolerated mass unemployment in the interests of holders of money. Finance was put before manufacturing, 'the anxieties of one social class over those of all others' (1990c: 267). It was the middle class which benefited most from these arrangements and the working class which suffered. The middle class flocked into the Conservative Party in the early 1920s. Its individual membership was double that of Labour's by 1925. The social composition of the parliamentary party was increasingly middle class. The links seem clear. But the real strength of the Tories was their ability to articulate the fears, prejudices and aspirations of 'the public'. Labour's weakness was its identification with the organised working class, a sectional interest. 'The public' was everyone else. The Conservative preponderance among women is explicable in these terms. 'The social world of the organized working class was sectional, collectivist and masculine'. But 'the public' was a status category to which women could belong, as could the unorganised workers, the seemingly unorganisable workers, and the anti-union workers. When representatives of 'the public' spoke of the working class they meant 'manual workers in well organized trades with aggressive unions' (1990c: 271). In doing so they drew on a reservoir of 'ideologically determined class stereotypes and conventional wisdoms' which helped to mobilise nearly all those who were not working class and then much of the working class as well.

In the excellent essay 'The "social psychology" of unemployment in inter-war Britain' (1990d) McKibbin explores this issue in relation to the State's management of unemployment. The grim and shabby Labour Exchanges, he tells us, were regarded by the unemployed as 'enemy territory'. The staff were primed to find abuse. A 'permanently interrogatory air' accompanied the hunt for scroungers as the unemployed were subjected 'to a futile and sometimes brutal ritual in which few believed'. After 1931 the 'means test' intruded humiliatingly into working-class privacy.

> Thus one of the purposes, and certainly one of the consequences of unemployment insurance legislation was to marginalize the unemployed, to divide them by newer and ever more refined discriminations and, by a public pursuit of the scrounger, to confirm politically necessary stereotypes. (1990d: 252)

The stereotypes included workers who were prone to endless industrial dispute as well as the unemployed who would not work and the scroungers who, though they might also have jobs, made high taxes necessary by their scrounging and cheating (1990c: 273). The dole was the preferred method for treating the unemployed because it enabled the Conservatives to maintain a dependent workforce and keep these stereotypes alive, while diverting the political energies of the unemployed into the dole bureaucracy in pursuit of fair payment – localising and rendering them harmless in the process. It was one of the ways in which the State, even though it might not have created working-class Conservatism, helped to entrench it.

McKibbin identifies three ways in which the State did this. First, by identifying the Labour Party exclusively with its unionised base and identifying 'the political idea' of the working class exclusively with a necessarily sectional Labour Party. Second, by ensuring that everyone outside this sectional working class would define themselves in opposition to it. Third, by trying to weaken and then marginalise the old unionised working class. The deflationary financial regime adopted in 1920 had assisted this process, as had the provocation and defeat of the General Strike in 1926. But so too did propaganda depicting the unemployed as helpless and incompetent authors of their own misfortune who burdened the public with their discontents and incapacities (1990c: 288–90).

Classes and Cultures (1998)

In *Classes and Cultures* McKibbin further develops some of these arguments while exploring many aspects of class culture in immense detail. The Labour Party, as I said at the outset, drops largely out of view and there is much in the book that can be ignored here. For my purposes it is relevant that McKibbin now recognises that 'the First World War seriously disturbed the pattern of English class relations' (1998: 528). The war is the origin of middle-class discontent. By 1918 the middle class (just 13–15 per cent of the population) was defined by, more than anything else, its 'anti-working class' outlook (1998: 50). The war and its immediate after-math eroded its money and property by inflation and taxation. At the same time powerful and growing trade unions had emerged. The Lloyd George coalition further inflamed middle-class hatred. It was perceived as a 'rapacious and extravagant plutocracy' that was nevertheless always ready to placate the unions. The Tories turned this situation to their advantage by giving priority to the defence of the middle class – portrayed as the defence of the public and the constitution. The propertied regrouped and a broad 'anti-socialist' coalition was created which survived into the 1930s. From as early as 1920 the balance of class power, disturbed by the war, was 'normalised' by deflation and rising unemployment. But middle-class perceptions scarcely altered in response to their improving relative position. Embittered class relations remained a factor throughout the decade as middle-class priorities dominated government policy. The intense fear of loss of social esteem and relative status simply persisted as a factor in middle-class attitudes well after the wartime conditions which first gave them substance had disappeared (1998: 104–5). The success of Warwick Deeping's *Sorrell and Son* (1925) – which McKibbin discusses as an example of a 'literature of conflict', a genre popular with the middle class in which class conflict was a central theme – is indicative of this fear and loathing. The book went through forty-one editions and innumerable impressions, and 'was read and re-read long out of its time' (1998: 481). It was distinguished by 'its unvarnished hostility to the working class'. By the 1930s the mood has changed, according to McKibbin; the more self-confident middle-class tone of A. J. Cronin's 1937 novel *The Citadel* is taken as indicative of the trend.

But what of the working class, constituting 78–72 per cent of the population in the years up to 1951? For those in work living standards rose in the inter-war years, as prices fell after 1920. But nearly all working-class men and women experienced some period of unemployment (1998: 151). Unemployment was heavily concentrated by industry and region, of course, but long-term unemployment was largely a 1930s' phenomenon. Those affected were impoverished, marginalised and humiliated by the experience. The trade unions at best organised only 55 per cent of working men, 45 per cent of the workforce. Only one-quarter of eligible women joined a union. In no year did the number of days lost through strikes even exceed days lost by one public holiday (1998: 144). Union members complained that their leaders were not radical enough, and McKibbin admits that they did indeed seek to avoid strikes. Yet their public image was one of strike proneness. The working class was in reality divided. Its experience varied by region, occupation and gender. McKibbin depicts a working-class family that was often politically fractured. The female proportion of the workforce was stable at around 30 per cent, but the proportion who worked on a more or less equal basis with men declined and the great majority of working women were single rather than married. Role segregation was thus entrenched in the family and promoted different views of the world. The greater propensity of women to vote Conservative may have something to do with this (1998: 518). Unfortunately, McKibbin says nothing about Labour's success in recruiting women – they made up 40 per cent of its individual membership by 1930 – and their role in the evolution of its social and welfare policies is unexamined.

Let us not forget, however, that the bigger issue is why the British working class gave the Conservatives more support than Centre-Right parties elsewhere in Europe normally received from blue-collar workers. I will not repeat the arguments already employed on this issue. Suffice to say that McKibbin portrays a defensive, introverted working class and a defeatist and fatalistic working-class culture. The workers demanded only to be left alone (1998:161). Men may have occupied a public world centred on work, but collective opinion prohibited any enthusiasm for work that may have separated the individual from the norms of the larger group. A churlish 'folk-Marxism', independent of actual party-political allegiances, was not uncommon. Manual labour was the source of all value, in this view, though not white-collar clerical labour or that of officialdom – both of which, according to popular prejudice, contributed 'nothing' to wealth production. Pilfering was 'intrinsic to factory culture' and seen as legitimate. Long memories of real or imagined grievances hung over 'many industries'.

Though a sense of historical grievance underpinned the Labour Party itself, grievances did not always translate into a political affirmation of working-class interests. The working class was accustomed to being talked down to. Though sports' mad, it allowed almost all sporting bodies to be run by a self-selecting, all-male, upper and upper-middle-class clique (cricket, racing, rugby union, tennis, athletics, golf, boxing), when they were not run by local brewers, butchers and bakers (football). McKibbin discusses some of the ways in which the authorities sought to reinforce working-class deference. The Reithian BBC excluded the working class and treated it with a snobbish paternalism. Censorship was used against 'anything which undermined respect for authority' (1998: 424). Lord Tyrell, president of the British Board of Film Censors, quoted in illustration of this point, said in 1937: 'we may take pride in observing that there is not a single film showing in London today which deals with any of the burning issues of the day' (1998: 425). But it is fair to say that conscious manipulation of this sort – though we have already encountered it in the 'politically necessary stereotypes' – occupies a minor place in McKibbin's argument; the structural barriers to a combative, pro-Labour class consciousness seem far more potent in producing the Tory hegemony than did mere propaganda, even when it had institutional reinforcement.

The only threat to the huge coalition of popular support for Conservatism which loomed on the horizon in the 1930s was external, according to McKibbin. It was the Second World War that 'threw British history and, even more, English history off course' (1998: 531). The war eroded deference and renewed the traditional working class by restoring the old staple industries on which it depended. Full employment was the context for trade union growth, and the growth of the north and its political culture, at the expense of the south and its political culture. The war universalised working-class political culture and allowed Labour to recruit men and women who had stood outside that culture in the 1930s, as in Birmingham. An unprecedented politicisation took place and a social democratic definition of *democracy* came to prevail over the middle-class individualism that had ruled in the 1930s. The Labour Government of 1945 failed to exploit this situation to the full, according to McKibbin, by remaining outside the sphere of civil society and leaving most of its conservative bastions untouched. The old social oligarchies in sport and education survived unscathed, as did the institutions of the State, including its 'ideological apparatus'. 'Outside the realm of social services or nationalized industries the visitor would not have observed a social democracy', with the result that the political settlement of 1945 depended on the physical survival of the industrial working class, rather than the diffusion within civil society of social democracy as an ideology (1998: 535–6).

Concluding remarks

If our understanding of a party cannot fail to depend on our understanding of the social classes which form its main constituency, Labour history must be rooted in working-class history. Conservatism and liberalism necessarily loom larger in the analysis once we examine twentieth-century working-class politics. McKibbin's argument sees this and realises that it involves class relationships and class cultures. The prolonged exclusion of Labour from government also invites us to examine the role of the State in managing class conflicts and class cultures to the party's disadvantage. But it is clear that this approach assumes that it is the underlying historical situation of the working class, its relationship to society and its consciousness that matter. McKibbin, in this mode, is arguing that the social is determinant, while politics and ideology are merely reflective. The new-born Labour Party was thus the product of the temper and situation of the working class and the intellectuals associated with it as these had evolved during the second half of the nineteenth century. The working class had been remade in these decades and a distinctively new pattern of working-class culture had come into existence, characterised by an introverted and defensive conservatism. The subaltern class was conscious of itself as different and separate. This sectional or corporate self-consciousness enabled it to create organisations confirming its social apartheid. Such organisations could be aggressive in their defence of 'the workers', but they accepted the conservative hierarchy of British society. There was no radical, alienated intelligentsia in Britain and the working class had no use for one.

These arguments have been fashioned over the years by historians such as Anderson (1964), Nairn (1964) and Stedman Jones (1974 and 1983), as well as by McKibbin. Missing from them all is the sort of comparative analysis which would seem to be essential if a case for British exceptionalism is to be sustained. Did 'other countries' have stronger trades union movements, industrial establishments that were typically bigger, workforces that were more homogenous and more engaged in politics than the British? Was British collectivism really weaker than it was in the relatively backward rural societies of Europe – many of which, nonetheless, had Marxist parties? Many items in McKibbin's list are unconvincing as ingredients of a British exceptionalism. The 'other countries' which this implicit comparison rests upon really boils down to just one – Wilhemine Germany. But close analysis of Germany before 1914 demonstrates that the differences were not as great as is often supposed. Large sections of the party were never much influenced by Marxism; the growing power of the trade unions within the SPD was pragmatic and reformist in impetus; and many millions of workers lay beyond the party's orbit (Berger 1994; Berger and Boughton 1995). As in Britain, a deep loyalty to the State was evident in Germany (Van der Linden 1998: 286), and it is not clear that the associational life of the German working class was more conducive to political class consciousness than it was in Britain. Even 'the distinction which is commonly made between a British party which was merely an electoral machine and a German community-oriented party proves on inspection to have little basis in fact', according to one thorough analysis of the subject (Berger 1994: 142). The gap between working-class life and the culture of the labour movement, which McKibbin makes so much of for Britain, was on this reading common to both countries.

The relatively open, rule-based, political system may be a stronger contender for 'special' status, but this too can be over-drawn. Here McKibbin also concurs with earlier analyses, such as that by Nairn (1970: 14–20), in seeing the British constitution as the main institutional mechanism of conservative rule. The Conservative hegemony was based on a paternalist authority, in this view, rather than on a coercive power. It drew upon traditions and customs of deference but made significant concessions, too, such as in tolerating free collective bargaining. The German State and employers were undoubtedly more repressive than their British counterparts where organised labour and the socialists were concerned in the period 1880–1914. There is a good case for believing that this was related to the fact that Germany was experiencing the immense social stresses engendered by industrial capitalism which Britain had already passed through in the first half of the nineteenth century. In that earlier period the British State had been just as repressive as the German State was after 1870. Nevertheless, the Labour Party and the Social Democratic Party grew up in different worlds in this respect, and it is arguable that the more liberal State and the more conciliatory employers played a significant role in integrating and moderating the Labour movement in Britain (Geary 1989: 3–4).

The Labour Party was born after the craft unions had already established a *modus vivendi* with the British State and the employers. Labour was marked from the outset by the outlook associated with these organisations of the working-class elite. Both accepted the existing institutional order as the inevitable political framework of action, and action was accordingly conservative and economistic. Labour was joined to the unions at birth, and for McKibbin the party could not avoid a corresponding class identity, despite the national pretensions of some of its leaders. But in this view politics was always, in any case, marginal in most working-class lives. Outside its narrow reaches, in the private realm, a multitude of pastimes and hobbies, clubs and societies flourished in the working-class towns. These provided a relatively rich associational and recreational culture to which individual historians have attached differing meanings. Thus these activities variously entertained and compensated the working class, perhaps diverting and distracting it from politics (as Stedman Jones suggests of the music hall) or (in McKibbin's emphasis) creatively engaged the lower orders in civil society and gave them an identification with it.

McKibbin's work closely engages with this culture but supplies no compelling reasons to refute the old argument that a relatively rich associational culture broadly encourages political participation. *Classes and Cultures* supplies a mass of interesting detail but much of it is largely divorced from the political generalisations that appear in the book's Preface and Conclusion. The social and cultural history of a class or classes are complex matters. What counts in our attempt to investigate class politics? Though McKibbin writes entertainingly about working-class gambling, for example, his discussion adds nothing to the declared central purpose of his study, which is to disclose the importance of culture in shaping working-class political behaviour and explain why those who had authority in 1918 still possessed it in 1951. A bigger and related cultural problem is left ambivalently unresolved – namely the relation of working-class culture to ruling-class culture. We are told that 'England had no common culture, rather a set of overlapping cultures' (1998: 527). It took the Second World War, on this account, to assimilate the working class into the ruling 'moral consensus' (1998: 535–6).

These contentions are consistent with the portrait of the working class as set apart, little affected by official culture, introverted, defeatist and fatalistic. But what was the inter-war 'public', which I discussed earlier, if it did not contain much, if not most, of the working class? Surely this suggests common values and beliefs uniting millions of working-class men and women with the classes above them in the social hierarchy? McKibbin supplies plenty of evidence of the hegemony of the dominant culture, as I have shown. Members of the upper class are said to have had ideological authority; the monarchy is depicted as culturally central to British life; patriotic etiquette is widely and spontaneously observed. He also argues that the State played a significant role in shaping the 'ideologically necessary stereotypes' of the unemployed. The working class does not seem so insulated in the light of these considerations. Indeed, it is arguable that all sorts of middle-class values permeated the working class through church and chapel, work (particularly domestic service and small-scale establishments) and leisure. The massive working-class Tory vote is clearly related to all of this, though it is not clear whether McKibbin sees Conservative electoral dominance as the effect or the cause of what he calls 'the structural and ideological bases of the pre-war system' (1990c: 290).

The realm of politics and public discourse is an unexplored continent in McKibbin's work on class cultures. Governments, parties, pressure groups, newspapers, local government, the education and the intellectual formation of the working class are conspicuously absent from the analysis. In *The Intellectual Life of the British Working Classes* (2001), Rose makes use of numerous unpublished working-class sources, as well as published memoirs, autobiographies, diaries and surveys. McKibbin's 'eye-witness' sources in *Classes and Cultures* are by comparison relatively narrow and predictable, and are faithfully adhered to rather than critically engaged with. This problem is not confined to *Classes and Cultures*. The State is only ever the focus of McKibbins's analysis in relation to one issue – the management of unemployment. On that subject, McKibbin concedes to the State a role which is absent from the social determinism informing most of his writings. Yet the period 1880–1950 was one of unprecedented tumult in political affairs, both foreign and domestic. It must be considered a major flaw in McKibbin's account of the formation and evolution of the Labour Party that imperialism and foreign relations, the impact of the wars and many significant domestic conflicts are absent from the analysis. Why should active politics be confined to explaining attitudes to the unemployed?

The role of the State and the political parties has a bearing on many of the issues raised by McKibbin's work. The three periods of Labour governance up to 1950, for example, clearly bear on the question of Labour's identity as a sectional or (if only in aspiration) a national force, but they are never considered at any length. The exception is the essay 'The economic policy of the second Labour Government' in *The Ideologies of Class* (1990), but this is concerned with the specific issue of whether the Government could have reflated the economy in the circumstances of 1929–31. There can be no doubt that Labour sought to govern in 'the national interest', and it is counter-intuitive to suppose that those spells in office made no impression on 'the public'. Even if we root the Labour Party in the social history of the working class we still have to ask what the party did to shape the politics of its natural constituency?

The same question can be asked of the affiliated trade unions and the socialists. This side of the equation receives scant attention in McKibbin's work. For one so interested in culture the neglect of the Labour movement's own political discourse is a major lacuna. For Labour – trade unionist or socialist – was in competition with some of the dominant values discussed above. It is not at all clear that the 'intense class consciousness' which McKibbin refers to was purely defensive. This is to underestimate the extent to which even the mundane but central slogan of labourism – 'a fair day's work for a fair day's pay' – implied a critique of the existing order. Socialist values could be made to connect to widely held views about the injustices of work and pay, and even the middle class was not immune to the critique of *laissez-faire* capitalism which existed in British politics throughout McKibbin's period – as the history of the relation of the middle-class to the welfare state shows. McKibbin sees that the economic and social experiences of the inter-war years may have unsettled the ruling orthodoxies, but he does not pursue this insight.

The discontinuities which I referred to at the beginning of this chapter deprive McKibbin's work of a possible historical dynamic. So do the silences. The two world wars supply material for assertions rather than for sustained analysis. The industrial unrest of 1910–20 is mentioned only in passing, as is the conflict in industry during the embittered 1920s. Class conflict is an acknowledged factor in McKibbin's argument but is never examined as an element in industrial conflict and in many of the disciplinary economic and social policies exercised by both the State and the employers. The consciousness of the working class appears largely unaffected by such class conflict as McKibbin does discuss, if only because he does not address the question of how the major political experiences of Britain since 1914 have made and remade working-class beliefs and values. The emergence of socialism in relation to the formation of working-class consciousness is neglected perhaps because of this lacuna. *Socialism*, indeed, is a word that McKibbin rarely has any use for, and it is difficult to find any basis for its emergence as the dominant discourse of the Labour Party after 1931 in anything that he finds important in the previous thirty years.

The working-class institutions which McKibbin tracks up to 1951 actually peaked after his period closes and important features of working-class culture survived for another twenty years alongside the discourse of socialism, the party's dominant doctrine. If the working class was remade in the last quarter of the nineteenth century, it seems plausible to assume that its characteristic way of life took some time to become embedded and generalised. Though the working class has never been a single homogenous entity, the images associated with it in the period 1870–1950 – the urban terraced houses, the mass employees of heavy industry, the crowds of flat-capped men at football matches – are images which reveal a nationalisation–standardisation of culture that was real enough. It is a pity that the sorts of questions which McKibbin asks about the Edwardian working class are not pursued in his later work. Surely we would find that at least some of the aspects of its fractured character prior to 1914 were subjected to processes of convergence and homogeneity? The widespread experience of unemployment, economic and other forms of insecurity, employment in similar types of manual work, common experiences of urban life, the rise of Labour in local government – surely there are nationalising trends here to counter the localising influences which McKibbin dwells on pre-1914?

It remains true, in the face of these trends, that Labour never managed more than 37 per cent of the total vote prior to 1945 and that the Conservative Party enjoyed greater working-class support. McKibbin's work has forced us to acknowledge and seek to explain these facts, and his discussion of class relations, the State's management of unemployment and the Conservative defence of the 'public' has provided signposts for others to follow in search of answers.

References

Unless indicated, the place of publication is London.

Anderson, P. (1964) 'Origins of the present crisis', *New Left Review*, 23.

Berger, S. (1994) *The British Labour Party and the German Social Democrats*, Oxford

Berger, S. and Boughton, D. (eds) (1995) *The Force of Labour: The Western European Labour Movement and the Working Class in the Twentieth Century*, Oxford

Geary, D. (ed.) (1989) *Labour and Socialist Movements in Europe Before 1914*, Oxford

McKibbin, R. (1974) *The Evolution of the Labour Party*, Oxford

McKibbin, R. (1990) *The Ideologies of Class: Social Relations in Britain 1880–1950*, Oxford

McKibbin, R.(1990a [1984]) 'Why was there no Marxism in Britain?' Reprinted in McKibbin, R., *The Ideologies of Class: Social Relations in Britain 1880–1950*, Oxford

McKibbin, R. (1990b [1978]) 'Arthur Henderson as Labour leader', reprinted in McKibbin, R., *The Ideologies of Class: Social Relations in Britain 1880–1950*, Oxford

McKibbin, R. (1990c [1988]) 'Class and conventional wisdom: the Conservative Party and the "public" in inter-war Britain', reprinted in McKibbin, R., *The Ideologies of Class: Social Relations in Britain 1880–1950*, Oxford

McKibbin, R. (1990d [1987]) 'The "social psychology" of unemployment in inter-war Britain', reprinted in McKibbin, R., *The Ideologies of Class: Social Relations in Britain 1880–1950*, Oxford

McKibbin, R. (1998) *Classes and Cultures: England 1918–1951*, Oxford

McKibbin, R., Matthew, C. and Kay, J. (1990 [1976]) 'The franchise factor in the rise of the Labour Party', reprinted in McKibbin, R., *The Ideologies of Class: Social Relations in Britain 1880–1950*, Oxford

Nairn, T. (1964) 'The English working class', *New Left Review*, 24.

Nairn, T. (1970) 'The fateful meridian', *New Left Review*, 60.

Rose, J. (2001) *The Intellectual Life of the British Working Classes*

Stedman Jones, G. (1974) 'Working class culture and working class politics in London, 1870–1900', *Journal of Social History*, 7:4

Stedman Jones, G. (1983) *Languages of Class: Studies in English Working Class History*, Cambridge

Tanner, D. (1990) *Political Change and the Labour Party, 1900–1918*, Cambridge

Van der Linden, M. (1998) 'The national integration of European working classes, 1871–1914', *International Review of Social History*, 33

9

The Progressive Dilemma and the social democratic perspective

Steven Fielding and Declan McHugh

The object of this chapter is to consider the notion of the 'progressive dilemma' as outlined by David Marquand in his collection of essays of the same name (Marquand 1999). Marquand sought to explain Labour's historically poor electoral performance by focusing on the party's inability to unite a sufficient number of working-class and middle-class voters in a sustained anti-Conservative coalition. As will be explained in more detail later, he believed Labour's attachment to the trade unions was too close and prevented the party making a strong appeal to those outside the labour movement.

Marquand was by no means the first academic to alight on this as possible cause of Labour's disappointing electoral performance (for example, see Stedman Jones 1983). However, the particular means by which he explained Labour's failure enjoyed a unique purchase among students of the Party, as well as those most responsible for the creation of 'New' Labour. Many of Tony Blair's early speeches delivered as leader owed more than a little to Marquand's perspective. One of the 'New' Labour leader's closest advisers, Phillip Gould, even used it to justify the policy and organisational changes fostered by Neil Kinnock and Blair since 1983 (Gould 1998: 1–17). Despite Marquand's own reservations about 'New' Labour, the perspective outlined in *The Progressive Dilemma* obviously resonated with those pursuing what Blair described during the 2001 election campaign as a 'radical, modern, social democratic' agenda. Indeed, as Marquand (1997: 78–9) conceded after Labour's 1997 landslide victory, 'modernisers' like Blair had gone some way to resolving his 'dilemma'.

The Progressive Dilemma is here taken as the exemplar of a wider 'social democratic' interpretation of the Labour Party. There are, in truth, few historical accounts that explicitly employ this form of analysis – but only because it is such an insidious a part of many leading authorities' 'common-sense' view of the party (see in particular, Crewe and King 1995: 3–26 and Williams 1979). Marquand's work is worthy of close attention, not the least because he is rare in foregrounding many of that tradition's most significant assumptions and he employs them in a particularly lucid manner.

It should nonetheless be borne in mind that the social democratic view of the party, like all others, has not stood still. Thus, *The Progressive Dilemma* was the product of a particular moment – after the collapse of the Social Democratic Party (SDP) in the late 1980s but before Blair assumed the Labour leadership in 1994 – in the history of British social democracy. Therefore, while Marquand aspired to present an interpretation of general historical relevance, it is a product of its time. Consequently, the chapter first historicises *The Progressive Dilemma* before scrutinising it as a piece of political analysis.

Social democrats and Labour

Before outlining the social democratic perspective, it is necessary to characterise the outlook of those described as social democrats; in accomplishing this task the work of Peter Clarke (1983) is particularly useful. Clarke was interested in those intellectuals-cum-politicians who wished to gain control of the State through democratic means so as to create a more equal society. This could be achieved, they believed, within a reformed capitalism, one in which most of the damaging consequences of a wholly free market had been curtailed by government action. While the chapter is also concerned with those who took a leading role in formulating this social democratic outlook, not all of its adherents, it should be stressed, were Oxbridge-educated, academically inclined, aspiring cabinet ministers. For, while Labour activists are regarded as drawn predominantly to radical socialism, a substantial minority taken from solidly proletarian backgrounds looked favourably on social democracy. Thus, in the early 1960s' fight against the Left's attempt to win Labour over to unilateral nuclear disarmament, the parliamentary leadership won the support of over half of conference delegates (Hindell and Williams 1962). During this period, social democrats attempted to give a lead to supporters in the country by creating the Campaign for Democratic Socialism (CDS). Despite some early success, however, they let the CDS fall into abeyance and thereby allowed the Labour Left freedom to extend its influence within constituency parties (Brivati 1996: 359–64, 380–403).

According to Clarke, social democratic intellectuals were committed to an ultimately untenable position. They saw the promotion of class conflict as an undesirable, indeed unnecessary, means of achieving their ends: as the future Labour Cabinet Minister Anthony Crosland stated in the 1950s, there was no 'irreconcilable conflict' between the classes. Social democrats looked on co-operation as the best, if not the only, way of advancing their cause. Instead of promoting the interests of a particular social group, they wished to mobilise a communal interest that transcended class. Despite this, for much of the twentieth century the majority of social democrats found themselves identifying with, belonging to and sometimes leading a Labour Party seen by many of its supporters in the trade unions as a 'class' party. Moreover, many such trade unionists expected it to advance their particular interests – at the expense of others', if necessary.

Even so, not all social democrats worked within Labour's ranks. In particular when the New Liberals – Edwardian Liberal intellectuals who approved a significant degree of state intervention to promote a more equal society – considered leaving their disintegrating party and joining Labour after 1918, they had to ask themselves a difficult question. Could they accept the union influence within the party? Some answered this question in the negative: the economist John Maynard Keynes was one of those who remained in the Liberal Party (Desai 1994: 50–2). Indeed, whether such 'progressive' thinkers should join with Labour, for all its apparent shortcomings, or stand aloof and passively contribute to the continued success of the Conservatives, lies at the heart of Marquand's dilemma. Clarke claims that those social democrats working within the party resolved the contradiction between some of the implications of their outlook and Labour's apparent character by accepting the self-interested nature of the labour movement. Ingenuously, however, they persuaded themselves that the unions' claims for redress were consistent with their own aim of social justice. On the way to a more equal society, the demands of the unions would of necessity have to be met; as Clarke (1983: 15–16) puts it, the unions' self-interest was conceptualised as 'incipient altruism'.

Living with the unions

While Labour's 1918 constitution was not considered ideal, given the extent of the influence which it granted the unions, it still had its advantages. Writing in the early 1950s, the leading social democratic intellectual R. H. Tawney (1966: 177) believed the unions provided the party with 'broad popular foundations' that prevented Labour becoming dogmatic – unlike other continental left-wing parties which did not enjoy such close links with their indigenous labour movements. Moreover, the constitution enabled social democrats to lead the unions in directions they might not otherwise have taken. In 1955 Bill Rodgers, who would later help found the SDP, conceded that union dominance of the Labour Party Conference was sometimes 'undesirable'. 'The important thing', however, was 'to keep the trade unions in politics and on the side of Labour . . . [Trade union leaders] want to be liked: they even want to be guided' (Fielding 1997: 45–6). If this appeared arrogant, Rodgers's comments echoed those of Graham Wallas, made earlier in the century, that intellectuals like himself were charged with the 'duty of thinking on behalf of the working class' (quoted in Clarke 1978: 139). This sounded more like the assumption of an onerous responsibility and formed the basis for Hugh Gaitskell's opinion, that fellow-middle-class Labour MPs should observe a 'profound humility' towards the party's working-class supporters, as 'we've got to lead them because they can't do it without us, without our abilities' (quoted in Morgan 1981: 769–70). Marquand also bluntly suggested, though in more acrimonious times, that without social democratic intellectuals, Labour would have been 'all brawn and no brain': had the party achieved power without their guidance, 'it would not have had the remotest idea what to do with it' (1979: 9).

As Labour's social democrats are agreed to have attained their greatest influence within the party at mid-century, it is especially instructive to analyse what they thought of their political home at this point. Their outlook is best encapsulated in the 1960 CDS manifesto, which stated that social democrats viewed the party's 'central tradition' as 'a non-doctrinal, practical, humanitarian socialism – a creed of conscience and reform rather than of class hatred'. The labour movement, it went on, owed 'its inspiration to British radicals, trade unionists, co-operators, nonconformists and christian socialists, not to Marx or Lenin'. Moreover, the manifesto asserted, Labour 'should be a broadly-based national party of all the people . . . A democratic socialist party must be based predominantly on working people. But a purely sectional, one-class party would . . . be a betrayal of the ideal of a classless society'. Thus, the 'socialism' to which social democrats adhered was not 'an arid economic dogma' but one of 'freedom, equality, social justice and world co-operation' based on 'an idealistic appeal to remedy real evils by practical and radical reform' (quoted in Fielding 1997: 61–2).

Labour never fully adhered to the CDS vision, and as the 1960s gave way to the 1970s the party seemed to move ever-further away from its ideal. Under Gaitskell's leadership, social democrats had relied on the brute force of the union block vote to achieve their ends, viewing it as the lesser of two evils. Such a reliance on union power, however, brought fewer returns after 1966. Moreover, the identification of the unions as comprising a materially deprived working class became questionable: many trade unionists were by any measure fairly well off. By the late 1960s, a few social democrats came to view the unions as less like the universal-interest-in-waiting and more as a selfish, vested interest, just like any other. This minority began to consider that Labour's connection with the unions – indeed, with the working class as a whole – prevented the party achieving a socialism 'based on co-operation, neighbourliness and readiness to help other people'. To such eyes, Labour's over-reliance on working-class voters also endangered social reform, as many workers virulently opposed black immigration, homosexuality, abortion, divorce and the abolition of capital punishment (Mayhew 1969: 94–5).

By the late 1970s, Rodgers's earlier confidence in the effect of his 'guidance' on the unions had disappeared. Writing of those years, he criticised Labour politicians for 'defer[ring] uncritically' to union demands; the unions, he stated, were locked into a time-warp, 'fighting a by now irrelevant "them" and "us" battle', despite the fact that social and economic change made class hostility irrelevant. Their influence, he asserted, undermined Labour's ability to 'have a mind' – presumably a social democratic mind – 'of its own' (Rodgers 1982: 167–70). By the start of the 1980s, a Labour Party that apparently allowed the unions such dominance appeared to some as an impediment to social democracy. The unions were certainly neither help nor hindrance in stopping the party's move leftwards. They were also at best uninterested in issues of importance to social democrats, such as individual freedom; opposed reforms thought necessary to revitalise the economy; were apparently unpopular with the electorate; and, finally, believed to not even represent their own members' views (Jenkins, Aaronovitch and Hall 1982: 16; Minkin 1991: 208–21). Even MPs who, like Denis Healey, were strongly influenced by revisionism but stayed within the Labour Party broadly agreed with much of this analysis (Healey 1990: 467–8).

David Marquand

By the time David Marquand was helping to found the SDP he had been active in Labour politics for about 25 years. He entered the Commons in 1966 after a short career as a journalist. One of the second wave of Labour's post-war revisionists that included David Owen and Roy Hattersley, Marquand like them became part of Roy Jenkins's entourage. When Jenkins left the Cabinet in 1976 to become president of the European Economic Community, Marquand resigned as an MP and followed him to Brussels; when Jenkins returned to establish the SDP, Marquand assisted in the enterprise. Indeed, in 1979 he wrote – after voting Liberal in the general election of that year – what has been described as the SDP's 'founding text' in outlining why it had become impossible for those like him to remain loyal to Labour (Desai 1994: 178). In his essay 'Inquest on a movement: Labour's defeat and its consequences' (1979), Marquand argued that Labour had failed to develop into the organisation desired by social democrats. Instead, during the 1970s it had assumed the mien of an aggressive 'proletarianism'. This asserted that Labour should be 'not merely a predominantly but an exclusively working-class party; that the working class can be properly represented only by people of working-class origin who alone understand its aspirations and have its interest at heart'. The 'elaborate intellectual constructs' of middle-class progressives were consequently viewed as at best unnecessary, as 'the party can be guided much more satisfactorily by the gut reactions of its working-class members, and at worst positively dangerous, since they may lead the party away from its working-class roots'. The lesson drawn by the party from the industrial discontent of the 1970s was, Marquand believed, that people like him were now surplus to requirements (Marquand 1979: 14, 16).

Following more of an academic than a political career subsequently, Marquand became a Liberal Democrat when the SDP split between the Liberal-inclined Jenkinsites and the go-it-alone Owenites. Like a number of other social democratic *émigrés* he rejoined Labour after Blair became leader; in doing so, he announced that 'New' Labour was now an 'unequivocally social-democratic party' located in the 'mainstream of North European social democracy' (Marquand 1995: 18–19). In contrast to certain other ex-Labour MPs who joined the SDP, Marquand continued to advocate many of the policies associated with post-war Keynesian social democracy. It was not so much Labour's social democratic policies which had been at fault, he suggested: instead, the triumph of Thatcherism had derived more from the flawed political practices employed by successive Labour Governments to enact them. Like many of those who left Labour, Marquand became increasingly preoccupied with the forms in which politics was articulated. If he did not question the basic intellectual foundations of much of post-1945 social democracy, Marquand (1988) explored different constitutional means of ensuring its successful implantation in British society. Thus, on the basis of his desire for constitutional change but continued faith in some of the assumptions underlying Croslandite social democracy, Marquand became a keen critic of 'New' Labour.

The Progressive Dilemma

Publication of *The Progressive Dilemma* occurred at a particularly pregnant moment in British political history. As Marquand characterises the period, the neo-liberalism of the 1980s was on the wane, Margaret Thatcher having been displaced as prime minister after the poll tax revolts. There was a 'new mood' stressing the drawbacks of the form of capitalism engendered by the Thatcher Governments' neo-liberal reforms. To address these problems, a 'new intellectual and political paradigm' had emerged which combined insights from 'traditional social liberalism' and 'traditional social democracy' (Marquand 1991: 227–30). At the same time, Kinnock's 'modernisation' of Labour's formal attitude to key areas of policy made some observers believe that he was moving the party from 'its distinctively British, labourist roots' and transforming it into a 'social-democratic party on the European model' (Mulgan 1989: 28–9). Such a body should have been the ideal agency for putting the *rapprochement* between liberalism and socialism into practice. Indeed, given the slump in the fortunes of the centre parties since the SDP–Liberal merger, Labour appeared to be the only practicable means of advance. Marquand, however, looked on that prospect with a sceptical eye. If yet hopeful that the divided anti-Conservative majority would unite, he believed Kinnock's Labour was still too much in awe of the unions to allow it to assume command (Marquand 1989: 375–8). *The Progressive Dilemma* was Marquand's attempt to think these matters through.

The ostensible focus of Marquand's celebrated essay was Labour's inability to hold national office for much longer than a single term. The party, at the time Marquand wrote, had only twice won a working Commons' majority, but neither the 1945 nor the 1966 victory led to a sustained period in power. Marquand considered Labour's inability to make a strong appeal to those beyond the manual working class as the key reason for this failure. The party, he argued, was tied too closely to that group, to the industrial trade unions, in particular, to construct a long-term socially diverse anti-Conservative coalition. The basic reasons for Labour's poor record were its 'structure and beliefs', its very nature – at least as codified in the 1918 constitution. Had Labour's character been different – had the party assumed the one outlined by Marquand – its electoral record would have been more respectable.

According to Marquand, Labour should have emulated the model established by the Liberal-led Edwardian 'progressive alliance'. Indeed, he effectively argued that it would have been better all round had Labour not sought independence but remained within a coalition 'reconstituted' to take better account of the unions' interests (Marquand 1991: 18–20). He appeared to believe that, had it not been for the First World War, and had Labour been sufficiently patient, the Liberals would have accommodated the working class on more favourable terms than those on offer prior to 1914. Even so, the Liberals between 1906 and 1914 had tried to establish a 'middle way' between *laissez-faire* capitalism and the collectivist State. The New Liberals, most notably, hoped to chart a course between capital and labour with the aim of incorporating the labour movement within a suitably reformed capitalism. Marquand was not slow to suggest that such a programme anticipated those embraced by post-war European social democrats in general and Labour figures such as Gaitskell in particular.

The appropriate political context for the enactment of these policies was, he suggested, one where the unions formed part of a 'broad-based, cross-class coalition', and within which they could enjoy a 'crucial, but not dominating, part'. Marquand suggested that this arrangement – similar to the vision of the CDS – was more than feasible by pointing out that it had been achieved elsewhere. The Democrats in the USA and most other European social democratic parties had built similar multi-class coalitions. Britain was the exception, for here the labour interest dominated, and was indeed embodied in, the Labour Party. As he asserted, Labour 'deliberately' – and, on the basis of his analysis, perversely – chose to 'identify itself as the instrument of the labour interest rather than as the vehicle for any ideology'. Thus,

> in a sense not true of its social democratic counterparts on the mainland of Europe, it has been a trade union party, created, financed and, in the last analysis, controlled by a highly decentralised trade union movement, which was already in existence before it came into being. Above all, its ethos – the symbols, rituals, shared memories and unwritten understandings, which have shaped the life of the party and given it its unmistakable identity – had been saturated with the ethos of trade unionism. (1991: 17)

As Labour was so tied to the unions, reflecting their defensive 'us-and-them' *labourist* outlook to the exclusion of all others, the party enjoyed solid support in its proletarian fortresses but could evoke little enthusiasm beyond them. Agreeing that parties enjoy the ability to 'shape' voters' attitudes and transform their appreciation of their own interests, Marquand stressed how Labour's internal character prevented it from addressing those outside its union-dominated redoubts in language that may have evoked a more positive response. The party's essential reliance on a 'class' appeal meant that it was incapable of making the intellectual leap necessary to draw in those for whom class meant little – or something different from what it meant to those in the heartlands. The confining 'structure and mentality' of the unions meant, therefore, that Labour lacked the necessary political imagination to sustain itself in office. Here the progressive alliance's very heterogeneity was seen as giving it a further advantage over its 'labourist' successor. As Marquand wrote elsewhere, for much of the post-war period, Labour had sought to use the State merely to protect workers in declining industries against the consequences of economic change. As Labour had based its electoral appeal on its ability to provide material improvement, it possessed no moral language that might have appealed to those less dependent on that kind of protection (Marquand 1988: 19–20, 141–3, and 1989: 375–8). It would have been so much better had Labour approached the electorate in a different manner: it did not – could not – do so because of the kind of organisation it was.

Marquand's essay contains many subtle points that do not bear compression, yet it proceeds, in effect, from the following five assumptions.

- The Liberals were not a spent force and could have fully integrated the labour interest within a progressive alliance had it not been for the First World War.

- Labour's own nature, confirmed in the 1918 constitution, prevented it from 'shaping' non-working-class voters' preferences.
- Had Labour assumed a different character – akin to the New Liberals' – it would have enjoyed a happier electoral history.
- Within continental social democracy, Labour was the exception rather than the rule: the experience of other countries confirmed the feasibility of Marquand's model.
- Social democracy's failure was due less to programmatic weakness and more to the flawed means by which it was articulated.

Marquand's view of Labour was influenced by considerations which feature in accounts that could in no way be described as social democratic: hence the belief in British exceptionalism in general and of Labour in particular, and the related assumption that it embodied a 'labourism' directly traceable to the outlook of manual trade unions. If Marquand and other social democrats saw this 'labourism' as blocking the development of social democracy, then socialists such as Ralph Miliband and John Saville saw it in similar terms with regard to their own political ambitions (Fielding 2000). Closer to home, the account was influenced also by a keenly contested historiographical debate about the electoral viability of the Liberals after 1914. In particular, Marquand was impressed by Clarke's optimistic account of Edwardian Liberalism's engagement with class politics. Indeed, belief in the viability of the Liberal Party is probably one of the two hallmarks of many late twentieth-century social democrats. The other is that Labour was too closely tied to the trade unions to have been a successful vehicle for social democracy. It is now time to scrutinise those two assumptions in the light of some of the available historical evidence.

The progressive alliance

To test Marquand's key historical suppositions, it is useful to concentrate on the first quarter of the twentieth century and make particular reference to the situation in Manchester. Historians generally regard Manchester as one of the most clear-cut examples of harmonious Liberal–Labour relations prior to 1914 and in that partnership the Liberals are thought to have held the whip hand (Clarke 1971; Tanner 1990: 157). It might be thought that if the progressive alliance was on the verge of collapse in Edwardian Manchester then important questions should be asked of its future in less favoured locations across the country.

In his study of politics in industrial Lancashire, the product of a PhD supervised by Henry Pelling, Clarke claimed that although social class was an increasingly important factor in determining political affiliations prior to 1914, it did not guarantee Labour's rise. Rather, he argued that the Liberal Party, by adopting policies such as old-age pensions and national insurance, and by virtue of its electoral pact with Labour, was set for a bright future as the senior partner in a progressive alliance. As evidence of the successful operation of this coalition, he referred to the situation in Manchester, where Lib–Lab cooperation had transformed a Tory citadel into a progressive heartland. Ostensibly, the Lib–Lab understanding offered considerable advantages to both sides, and, according to Clarke and others, was growing stronger on the eve of 1914 (Adams 2000: 29; Tanner 1990:157). Closer inspection suggests this to be a rather sanguine view. By looking at relations between the parties more closely, it is clear that even in Manchester tensions were becoming unmanageable and were boiling over well before the outbreak of the First World War (McHugh 2002).

As early as 1907, municipal elections had become the occasion for Liberal–Labour conflict in Manchester. While most local Liberal Associations fought shy of standing against Labour candidates, some supported Conservatives in the hope of defeating their putative partner. In 1908 Liberals and Conservatives went so far as to run joint-Independent candidates in two Labour wards (*Manchester Guardian*, 3 November 1908; see Nuttall 1908). The Liberal Party was, then, not exactly united in its adherence to progressivism: a significant number of its members were very close to the Conservatives. Indeed, in the years immediately after 1918, when their organisation had fallen into disarray, a substantial minority of Liberal councillors sat on the Conservative benches in Manchester's municipal chamber (*Manchester Guardian*, 5 and 12 October 1920).

Many Labour activists were also unhappy about cooperating with the Liberals. Prior to the 1910 municipal elections those wishing to make the break to independence formed a Socialist Representation Committee (SRC) in the city. The SRC aimed to 'promote Socialist Representation on public bodies, and to form a National Socialist Party, uniting all militant socialists' (*Clarion*, 21 July 1911). Within a year, the Manchester SRC had joined with others to form the British Socialist Party (BSP), which held its foundation conference in neighbouring Salford, attracting numerous ex-Labour supporters into its ranks. It was to halt the flow of defections to this new body that the Manchester and Salford Labour Representation Committee (MSLRC) took steps to emphasise its autonomy by aiming to contest Liberal seats in what would have been the 1915 general election (MSLRC 1912). This belligerence provoked a greater determination on the part of certain Liberals to call for an end to their party's alliance with Labour (Hertz 1912: 93; Manchester Liberal Federation 1913).

Most Liberals hoped to avoid conflict by supporting electoral reform, principally some type of proportional system. This would allow both parties, advocates believed, to compete in the same seats without splitting the anti-Conservative vote. This suggests that specific ideological inconsistencies were not the main bone of contention for most Liberals. Rather, the unwillingness of many members to concede their own position to Labour owed much to the socially constructed 'tribalism' that underpinned organised politics. More than differences in political outlook, however, the division between Liberals and Labour rested on the contrasting class composition of the two parties. It had, after all, been the refusal of the Manchester Liberal Union (MLU) to run working men candidates before 1900 that had given impetus to the creation of the MSLRC in the first place. Dominated by a wealthy elite, the MLU was happy to represent workers, even tailoring some of the party's policies to suit their needs, but members did not want to be represented by proletarians. As a result, the Independent Labour Party converted the Manchester and Salford Trades Council, which acted for skilled trade unionists historically close to the Liberals, to independent labour representation. Subsequently, the Trades Council played a key role in the formation of the MSLRC, a development that effectively ended the possibility of organised labour ever being subsumed within local Liberalism (Hill 1981: 192–7).

Thus, social differences, as much as political disagreements imperilled the long-term survival of the 'progressive alliance' in Manchester. Indeed, it is arguable that it would have survived the General Election due to be held in 1915. Despite good intentions at the national level, differences among local activists were profound and set to end the possibility of cooperation. In this process, Manchester was typical of other towns and cities across Britain where the progressive alliance showed signs of weakness even before 1914 and afterwards quickly unravelled (Belchem 1996; Berger 1993).

The 1918 constitution

If the continuation of the Lib–Lab coalition was in doubt even prior to the intervention of the First World War, the repercussions of the European conflict made its demise certain. The split in the Liberals and the proposal to extend the franchise to all men and most women presented Labour with a chance to become the main anti-Conservative alternative. Recognising this opening, the party's leadership devised a plan for Labour's reorganisation, which they hoped would transform it from a trade-union pressure group into a national independent body capable of winning majority support. Thus, Labour's membership had to be broadened, its machinery made sound and the party equipped with a comprehensive programme serving an ultimate aim (*Fabian News*, 29 (1918): 6; Henderson 1918).

According to Marquand, the choices made at this juncture would prove fatal. Instead of creating a pluralistic party and furnishing Labour with a programme that meshed 'labourism' with Liberalism, the leadership re-established Labour, as Gould put it, as 'a socialist party immutably linked to trade unionism'. Clause 4, in particular, committed Labour to pursuing public ownership as its ultimate goal, while concessions to the unions confirmed their dominance over the annual conference and the National Executive Committee. As a result, 'discipline was gained, but flexibility and the influence of ordinary members was weakened'. The capacity to 'modernise and adapt was to be the ultimate casualty', while other 'possible options, which were still open at the start of the century, were closed down' (Gould 1998: 26–7).

There is some truth in this argument. Powers granted to the unions proved crucial in shaping Labour's future path. At critical moments in the party's history – notably Gaitskell's thwarted attempt to revise Clause 4 and Harold Wilson's efforts to reform industrial relations in 1969 – the unions vetoed moves that would have significantly altered the course of both party and national history. Moreover, the unions' influence could be felt throughout the organisation: because they offered Labour unrivalled access to money, personnel and facilities the unions often dominated branches in industrial areas.

It is doubtful that there could have been any other outcome in 1918. Those most responsible for change nonetheless strove to transform Labour from a union pressure group to a party open to all classes. As Arthur Henderson, then party chair, explained (1918: 124), the new constitution sought to make Labour 'the party of the producers – of the workers, in the widest sense of that noble word: of all the people, without distinction of class or sex, who labour to enrich the community'. The adoption of Clause 4, with its references to 'workers by hand or brain', was meant to further that process and was not designed to cast Labour in a class-conscious socialist mould. Indeed, the ideological aspect of the constitution was largely ignored at the time – although it came to attract substantially greater interest in later years.

Far more important to contemporaries were the structural changes instituted by the new constitution, and here the unions largely enjoyed their own way, if only on a *quid pro quo* basis. Nevertheless, the agreement to construct a national network of local parties, populated for the first time by individual members, was a significant step. Indeed, some hoped that these new branches would drain power away from the unions. Herbert Drinkwater, one of Labour's senior organisers, claimed (1923: 15) that 'individual membership had in it the genesis of a revolutionary transference of weight and power within the party'. For him, 1918 was 'nowhere a final and last word regarding [Labour's] structure . . . it will adapt itself to circumstances as it grows' (Drinkwater 1921: 7).

If the unions remained the formally dominant force in Labour's organisation, this was not necessarily meant to be a permanent state of affairs. Eventually, it was hoped, power would be devolved to the members, a development seen to be crucial if Labour was to become a truly national body. For, according to Sidney Webb (1917: 152), it was through the provision of individual membership that 'those younger men who have enjoyed the advantages of a wider education than the workman can secure, and of a training other than that of life at the forge, [will] come into the Labour Party'. Many of these, it was anticipated, would be former Liberals who were thought to be 'looking longingly' at Labour from their slowly sinking ship (Wilson Harris 1917).

In essence, Labour's leadership strove to achieve precisely the results that Marquand has accused them of neglecting. Indeed, in some respects, the changes implemented in 1918 represent the original 'New' Labour project – an attempt to broaden Labour's political and electoral scope by loosening the grip of the unions. While not exactly a great success, these reforms were by no means a complete failure. After all, several commentators – in particular Lewis Minkin – believe that the powers enjoyed in theory by the unions often amounted in practice to less. This was, they consider, largely due to the fact that most unions did not want to dictate to the party leadership, fearing the wider electoral consequences should they do so. The formula defining how relations between MPs and the unions-dominated conference was in fact agreed as early at 1907. This stipulated that parliamentarians enjoyed the final power to determine the 'time and method of giving effect' to conference decisions – a discretion they went on to exploit with some gusto (Minkin 1978: 5–6 and 1990).

Even in the immediate wake of 1918, Ramsay MacDonald showed little concern for union sensitivities, and during the 1920s he represented his party as a body that sought to transcend notions of class through a commitment to create 'community'. In 1929 Labour achieved a level of electoral strength that suggested it was developing support both within and without its working-class bastions. Had the second Labour Government of 1929–31 operated in more benign economic circumstances, MacDonald may have eventually resolved Marquand's 'dilemma'. The onset of a world depression and the difficult choices that followed drew the curtain down on that possibility. It also shifted power back to the unions – but only because the PLP had been smashed at the 1931 general election and was bereft of effective leadership after MacDonald defected to form a National Government (Riddell 1999).

For much of the post-war period, Labour leaders enjoyed a near-autonomous position within the party, one deriving from the largely unconditional support of the largest unions. This gave Hugh Gaistkell and Harold Wilson, in particular, the freedom to pursue electoral strategies designed to appeal to moderate 'floating' voters outside of the labour movement. When this autonomy came to an end, in the 1970s and 1980s, it was due largely to the demands of the party's radicalised active members, rather than the unions. Ironically, given Marquand's complaints about the party's 'proletarianism' at that time, Labour's activists were increasingly middle-class in origin. Moreover, those working to end their leaders' freedom of action and supporting policies meant to serve working-class interests over all others were led by the former hereditary peer Tony Benn (Whiteley 1983: 53–80).

No alternative?

On the whole, the 1918 constitution failed to create a greater distance between Labour and the unions and thus, it could be argued, handicapped the party's development. Against that view, some final comments should be made.

First, if the 1918 constitution did not develop in the ways intended, that was not necessarily due to the actions of Labour's leadership. At least in part, the failing was down to 'the people', who simply could not be induced to join and become active in the party. Although it might be argued that it was because they were alienated by the image and operation of the party machine that people did not commit to Labour, the reasons for popular political inactivity were more deep-rooted (McHugh 2001: 147–74).

Second, even accepting that the changes instituted in 1918 were defective, it is doubtful that another, more attractive, course was open. While some may lament Labour's trade union origins, those origins remain a fact, and one that restricted the leadership's room for manoeuvre. Indeed, before he temporarily gave up on Labour as a vehicle for progressive change, even Marquand accepted this. In his biography of MacDonald (1977: 229), he conceded that 'in the circumstances of 1918, Henderson's constitution was probably the best obtainable'. The unions were being asked to pay higher affiliation fees – essential if Labour was to compete in an enlarged electorate – and 'they were hardly likely to do so without a *quid pro quo*'.

Consequently, in the context of the time, the party that emerged, although by no means an ideal body for the promotion of social democracy, was the best on offer. As Henderson asked Labour's 1918 Conference delegates, while they considered his proposed new constitution:

> Should they have no longer a Federation and begin to build up from a new foundation a political organisation depending only upon individual membership? Speaking as an old electioneer he did not mind saying that if he had to begin afresh that would be the goal at which he would aim . . . But apart from the nearness of a general election it would be practically impossible to attempt such a course. Imagine the Executive saying to the Trade Unions upon whom the party had depended that they had no formal use for them. He thought the Conference would give short shrift to such a proposition. (Labour Party 1918: 99)

It is this point that is often lost on some, at least, of Labour's social democratic critics. Eager to argue that things should have been much different, they can go too far in asserting that things *could* have been much different. At least one reading of Labour's history, however, suggests that party leaders in 1918 had few options open to them. The party had been established with the crucial help of the unions and without their continued support its future was uncertain: the alternative of a truly membership-based party appeared too much of a risk. With the unions Labour may have been a flawed vehicle for progressive politics; but without them, as Robert Taylor (2000: 43) has firmly put it, it would have been 'nothing'. The history of the SDP indicates the wisdom of the 1918 settlement. Unlike Marquand and colleagues in the 1980s, Henderson and Webb appreciated the electoral, financial and organisational strengths offered by the unions, and realised that at least for the time being it was impossible to proceed without them.

The progressive dilemma resolved?

By now it should be clear that the social democratic interpretation of the Labour Party, as exemplified by *The Progressive Dilemma*, should be viewed with some caution. Its central proposition, regarding the role of the unions, was the product of a particular political tradition with its own peculiar trajectory. In this generic sense, the social democratic perspective is just like any other: self-interested, partial and subject to variation over time. It should not be assumed, however, that by criticising the social democrats in such terms, we adhere to some alternative analytical 'golden mean', for none presently exists. It might, indeed, be ventured that if the social democratic interpretation was flawed, it possessed fewer faults than those propounded by Labour's many socialist critics.

To question the social democratic perspective, two of Marquand's central contentions have been scrutinised in the light of the evidence that presently exists. That exercise has revealed the extent to which this viewpoint was informed as much by hopeful speculation about how the past *should* have been as it was by sober analysis of real historical possibilities. Again, it would be wrong to condemn

social democrats as uniquely unsound in this respect: many historians travel back-
wards determined to discover what they have already decided to find.

In conclusion, there is a final thought that further undermines the utility of the
social democratic approach. One of Marquand's key propositions was that, had
Labour been able to alter its character in such a way as to make a sustained appeal
to those beyond the 'traditional' working class, it would have enjoyed a rosier electoral history. This presumed that Labour's gains within the middle class would not
have been offset by losses in the working class, a view sharply contradicted by
Adam Przeworski's analysis of the electoral history of European Social Democracy.
For he discerned that as soon as Centre-Left parties reduced the salience of class in
their electoral strategies, so as to appeal to middle-class voters, they found it all the
harder to mobilise workers' support (see Przeworski and Sprague 1986: 57–79).

Table 9.1 The Labour vote, 1964–70

	1964	1966	1970	Difference 1964–70
Higher service	18	19	22	+4
Lower service	20	29	32	+12
Routine non-manual	26	41	40	+14
Petty bourgeoisie	15	20	20	+5
Foremen/technicians	48	61	56	+8
Skilled working class	70	73	63	−7
Unskilled working class	66	70	61	−5

Source: Evans, Heath and Payne (1999: 90).

British election survey data generated during the 1960s endorses Przeworski's
pessimism over Marquand's optimism. In the general election of 1966 Wilson
increased his party's appeal to voters in all social classes compared to 1964 (see
Table 9.1). The result was a Labour majority in the Commons of some ninety-
seven seats, which included the newly elected MP David Marquand. In office,
Wilson's ministers believed they would best maintain that majority by continuing
to do what they had done for some years: pitch their policies most directly at fickle
suburban voters with no attachment to the labour movement. They imagined that
the manual working class would remain that which they had always been: loyal
Labour voters (Fielding 2004: chapter 2). The result of the 1970 general election
showed the disadvantages of this eminently social democratic strategy: while
Labour held on to or even increased non-manual support won during the 1964–66
period it lost support in the working class and found itself once more in opposition (Butler and Pinto-Duschinsky 1971).

As 'New' Labour approached re-election in 2001, many feared the party would
suffer a similar fate. They believed Blair's focus on the concerns of 'middle England', which had helped him capture power in 1997, had to a dangerous degree
alienated the party's working-class supporters (Fielding 2003: 85–115). In the end,
the party held on to most, not all, of its non-manual voters but lost support within

its working-class heartlands, although perhaps not to the extent that some Jeremiahs had forecast (Denver 2002). Unlike in 1970, however, Labour retained its majority. Given the expansion of non-manual and lightly unionised occupations, and given also the decline of the 'traditional' working class since the 1950s, this trade-off in votes was evidently acceptable to certain party strategists at the start of the new millennium. Time will tell how far this is a wise course to follow for the rest of the twenty-first century. It is, however, unlikely – despite Marquand's valiant attempt to convince us otherwise – that it would have been the electoral basis for a 'progressive' twentieth century.

References

Unless indicated, the place of publication is London.

Adams, T. (2000) 'Labour vanguard, Tory bastion or the triumph of New Liberalism? Manchester politics 1900 to 1914 in comparative perspective', *Manchester Region History Review*, 14

Belchem, J. (1996) *Popular Radicalism in Nineteenth Century Britain*

Berger, S. (1993) 'The decline of Liberalism and the rise of Labour – the regional approach', *Parliamentary History*, 22:1

Brivati, B. (1996) *Hugh Gaitskell*

Butler, D. and Pinto-Duschinsky, M. (1971) *The British General Election of 1970*

Clarke, P. (1971) *Lancashire and the New Liberalism*, Cambridge

Clarke, P. (1978) *Liberals and Social Democrats*, Cambridge

Clarke, P. (1983) 'The social democratic theory of the class struggle', in Winter, J. (ed.) *The Working Class in Modern British History*, Cambridge

Crewe, I. and King, A. (1995) *SDP. The Birth, Life and Death of the Social Democratic Party*, Oxford

Denver. D. (2002) 'The results: how Britain voted (or didn't)', in Geddes, A. and Tonge, J. (eds) *Labour's Second Landslide*, Manchester

Desai, R. (1994) *Intellectuals and Socialism*

Drinkwater, H. (1921) 'The constitution of the Labour Party', *Labour Organiser*, 6

Drinkwater, H. (1923) 'The outlook: from an organiser's standpoint', *Labour Organiser*, 35

Evans, G., Heath, A. and Payne, C. (1999) 'Class: Labour as a catch-all party?', in Evans, G. and Norris, P. (eds) *Critical Elections*

Fielding, S. (1997) *The Labour Party. 'Socialism' and Society Since 1951*, Manchester

Fielding, S. (2000) '"Labourism" and the British Labour Party', in the Collection de l'ecole francaise de rome – 267, *Les Familles politiques en europe occidentale au XXe siécle*, Rome

Fielding, S. (2003) *The Labour Party. Continuity and Change in the Making of 'New' Labour*

Fielding, S. (2004) *The Labour Governments, 1964–70, vol. 1: Labour and Cultural Change*, Manchester

Gould, P. (1998) *The Unfinished Revolution*

Healey, D. (1990) *Time of My Life*, Harmondsworth

Henderson, A. (1918) 'The outlook for Labour', *Contemporary Review*, 113

Hertz, G. B. (1912) *The Manchester Politician, 1750–1912*

Hill, J. (1981) 'Manchester and Salford politics and the early development of the Independent Labour Party', *International Review of Social History*, 26

Hindell, K. and Williams, P. (1962) 'Scarborough and Blackpool: an analysis of some votes at the Labour Party Conferences of 1960 and 1961', *Political Quarterly*, 3:3

Jenkins, P., Aaronovitch, S. and Hall, S. (1982) 'Redrawing the political map', *Marxism Today*, December

Labour Party (1918) *Labour Party Annual Conference Report*

McHugh, D. (2001) 'A mass party frustrated? The development of the Labour Party in Manchester, 1918–31', unpublished PhD thesis, University of Salford

McHugh, D. (2002) 'Labour, the Liberals and the progressive alliance in Manchester, 1900–14', *Northern History*, 39:1

Manchester Liberal Federation (1912) Executive Committee Minutes, 6 and 22 June, Manchester Reference Library Archive

Manchester Liberal Federation (1913) Executive Committee Minutes, 9 July, Manchester Reference Library Archive

Manchester and Salford Labour Representation Committee (1912) Letter to the National Executive Committee Elections Sub-Committee, NEC Minutes, 10 October, National Museum of Labour History.

Marquand, D. (1977) *Ramsay MacDonald*

Marquand, D. (1979) 'Inquest on a movement: Labour's defeat and its consequences', *Encounter*, July

Marquand, D. (1988) *The Unprincipled Society*

Marquand, D. (1989) 'Beyond Left and Right: the need for a new politics', in Hall, S. and Jacques, M. (eds) *New Times*

Marquand, D. (1995) 'Joining the "new" ship', *New Statesman and Society*, 6 October

Marquand, D. (1997) *The New Reckoning*, Cambridge

Marquand, D. (1999 [1991]) *The Progressive Dilemma*, 2nd edition

Mayhew, D. (1969) *Party Games*

Minkin, L. (1978) *The Labour Party Conference*

Minkin, L. (1991) *The Contentious Alliance*, Edinburgh

Morgan, J. (ed) (1981) *The Backbench Diaries of R. H. S. Crossman*

Mulgan, G. (1989) 'The vision thing', *Marxism Today*, August

Nuttall, J. (1908) Letter to Labour's national organiser, 5 November, LP/EP/08/1/113, National Museum of Labour History

Przeworski, A. and Sprague, J. (1986) *Paper Stones. A History of Electoral Socialism*, Chicago, IL

Riddell, N. (1999) *Labour in Crisis. The Second Labour Government, 1929–31*, Manchester

Rodgers, W. (1982) *The Politics of Change*

Stedman Jones, G. (1983) 'Why is the Labour Party in a mess?', in Stedman Jones, G., *Languages of Class*, Cambridge

Tanner, D. (1990) *Political Change and the Labour Party, 1900–18*, Cambridge

Taylor, R. (2000) 'Out of the bowels of the movement: the trade unions and the origins of the Labour Party, 1900–1918', in Brivati, B. and Heffernan, R. (eds) *The Labour Party. A Centenary History*

Tawney, R. H. (1966) 'British socialism today', in Tawney, R. H., *The Radical Tradition*, Harmondsworth

Webb, S. (1917) 'The reorganisation of the British Labor Party', *New Republic*, 8 December

Whiteley, P. (1983) *The Labour Party in Crisis*

Williams, P. M. (1979) *Hugh Gaitskell*

Wilson Harris, H. (1917) 'British Labor in the ascendant', *New Republic*, 1 December

10

Too much pluralism, not enough socialism: interpreting the unions–party link

Steve Ludlam

A central object of Labour's re-branding as 'New Labour' was to distance it from its trade union affiliates (Gould 1998: 257–8). The relationship was tense before and after the 1997 election, when Blair reduced the unions' formal power in the party, and restricted employment policy initiatives largely to his predecessors' promises (Ludlam 2001). But discontent was limited by real union gains, and tension eased markedly between Labour's mid-term election losses in 1999 and the 2001 election campaign, in which the unions played a crucial role. After the 2001 campaign, though, bitter conflict erupted over the Government's drive to place more public services under private sector management, and discontent over New Labour's stance on EU labour market policy became more intense. To younger students of British politics, this public conflict may have appeared novel. Since the mid-1980s most unions had supported Labour's organisational and policy modernisation under Neil Kinnock and John Smith. Only the occasional public reference to the allegedly 'bad old days' of the 1970s acted as a reminder of earlier conflicts.

Yet in the first post-war study of the labour alliance – the unions–Labour Party link – Martin Harrison (1960: 12) had dubbed it 'the most controversial relationship in British politics'. And thirty years later Lewis Minkin (1992: 646) echoed Harrison, describing 'a disputatious and controversial relationship – the most contentious in British political life'. Nevertheless, the relationship has attracted little specialist scholarship.

Between Harrison's and Minkin's seminal studies, just seven other monographs appeared: Irving Richter's studies of the politics of three affiliated unions (1973); Leo Panitch's study of incomes policy (1976); William Muller's study of union-sponsored MPs (1977); Lewis Minkin's study of the Labour Party Conference (1978); Derek Fatchett's study of the first struggle over political fund ballots (1987); Andrew Taylor's analysis of the link during the Social Contract era and its aftermath (1987); and Paul Webb's study of the link's institutional forms and of union members' electoral behaviour (1992).

These monographs have not generated a sustained academic dialogue about the linkage, although Minkin's *Contentious Alliance* was the result of an extended engagement with the 'new and dominant myth', from the 1960s, that it was the unions 'which, by finance and votes, controlled the Labour Party' (1997: 78ff.), a 'myth' equally dismissed by Harrison in his earlier study (1960: 336ff.; see also chapter 11 of the present volume, by Eric Shaw).

Of course, many shorter studies of the linkage have appeared as chapters in more general works on trade unionism, economic policy and the Labour Party, and in biographical studies and memoirs, and it is probably from these scattered sources that students have mostly learned about the contentious alliance. This wider literature does, though, contain the perspectives of two distinct schools of thought: the liberal–social democratic pluralist perspective; and the perspective of socialist and Marxist writers. This chapter seeks to outline key features of the two perspectives and indicates some limitations to which they are subject. It illustrates these limitations by discussing neglected aspects of the crucial period that falls, roughly, between 1974 and 1983, years that cover both the collapse of the Social Contract and the labour alliance's subsequent civil war.

Too much pluralism . . .

Pluralism, as political theory, celebrated the liberal democratic political system and portrayed it as driven by the free competition of parties and interest groups, from which preferences emerged that parliamentarians and a neutral state machine implemented. A good starting point for understanding the post-war perspective on the unions–party link of liberal and social democratic pluralists is the concept of 'pluralistic stagnation', applied to British politics by Samuel Beer (1965 and 1982), and in a series of studies of British unions by Gerald Dorfman (1974, 1979 and 1983) and Robert Taylor (1980, 1993 and 2000). The concept of 'pluralistic stagnation' depicted post-war Britain as characterised by a new producer-group politics, in which capital, labour and the State bargained collectively on a range of public policy issues. This pluralistic governance emerged from the war economy, and had underpinned the post-war settlement, above all the prioritisation of full employment. The latter implied restraint in wage bargaining. When, during the war, William Beveridge sought reassurance over this implication, the TUC insisted that the employment objective would have to be modified if it implied 'methods incompatible with the rights of workpeople and the objects of Trade Unionism'; but it conceded that free collective bargaining might be restrained given a context of socially progressive economic intervention (TUC 1944: 419–20; and see Taylor 1993: 20ff.). Wage restraint thus became, in Allan Flanders's words, 'the greatest unresolved problem in existing relations between the trade unions and the state' (1957: 159).

After Sterling had become fully convertible in 1958, so that governments could no longer restrict its sale, its vulnerability, and the perception of relative decline, pushed governments towards indicative planning and wage controls. Here the 'stagnation' component of 'pluralistic stagnation' emerged, as the TUC proved, on this view, to have insufficient authority to police wage behaviour among its affiliates and permit stable economic growth. Unions appeared unable to control shop stewards and members in their multi-union, leap-frogging, wage drifting, work-places. Here was *far too much pluralism*, and the 'union problem' became a central focus of political and academic debate. Dorfman (1983: 131) summarised it thus:

> Collectivist politics thus failed to work in relation to the speed at which government took control of the economy and made consequent demands for union participation in bargaining and implementing economic and industrial policies. By the late sixties, the gap between government 'demand' and TUC 'delivery' had widened to a politically unacceptable degree.

When the (eminently pluralist) recommendations of the Donovan Commission (HMSO 1968) proved politically inadequate, Labour attempted to legislate against unofficial strikes, but failed to overcome opposition in the TUC, the Government and the party. Another pluralist writer echoed Flanders, commenting on this outcome of Labour's *In Place of Strife* proposals: 'The Social Democratic dilemma – how to contain the interests of organised labour within a broadly-based political party, and how to combine free trade unionism with the efficient management of the economy – remained unsolved' (Jenkins 1970: 166).

This background gives the pluralist literature its overwhelming focus: unions–government relations. This focus produced, in the 1970s, a burgeoning neo-pluralist literature on 'corporatism', a growth industry largely shut down, like so many others, by Margaret Thatcher. The link between affiliated unions and the party was thus viewed very largely, and narrowly, as an aspect of the conflict over wages and industrial relations. This perspective produces a number of problems.

In the first place, there is a tendency to *conflate* the appearance of union power in the institutions of tripartism with union power in the Labour Party. With so much constitutional weight in the party, union affiliates were portrayed as dominating party policy and management. As noted above, both Harrison and Minkin have comprehensively dismissed this portrayal on the basis of detailed analysis of the internal unions–party linkage (see chapter 11).

A second tendency, a kind of *monolithism*, treats unions as a single political entity. Students of politics, as a rule, do not make statements of the kind: 'In 1956, the political parties decided to invade the Suez Canal Zone', or, for that matter 'In the 1980s, the political parties decided to destroy the National Union of Mineworkers'. Yet the literature is replete with indiscriminate references to the actions of 'the unions', although even in the era when the unions' 'praetorian guard' fixed party conferences, several large unions routinely defied the party leadership, one reason why 'the stereotyped image of the unions as a sort of orthodox lump of suet pudding clogging the Party's progress is a potentially disastrous over-simplification' (Harrison 1960: 238). And, indeed, scholars in this school have conducted important disaggregated studies of individual unions (Richter 1973; Taylor 1980). Nevertheless, writing on the unions' role in Labour's civil war after 1979, Ben Pimlott identified 'a union decision to move into Labour Party politics more decisively than ever before, and to throw their weight heavily against the parliamentary leadership' (1991: 217). This particular belief is demolished by Minkin (1992: 194–5), who shows that union votes were evenly balanced on key issues.

Needless to say, these two assessments have deeply contrasting consequences for understanding the recent history of the unions–party link.

A third tendency is to explain the unions–party relationship in terms of a *bipolar* conflict between union leaders and union members, again emphasising the formers' inadequate authority. In his analysis of the 'progressive dilemma' – how to reconcile Labour's working class origins with its electoral need to appeal to other classes – David Marquand discusses the collapse of the Social Contract. Portraying Labour ministers as slow to control wages, he asserts (1992: 196) that 'in spite of their assiduous servility to the union leaders, opposition from the rank and file of the trade unions eventually made their policies inoperative too' (see also chapter 9, by Steven Fielding and Declan McHugh). An undifferentiated union leadership was apparently confronted by a force from below. Yet by 1978 union leaders themselves were hopelessly divided over the Social Contract. In November 1978, the TUC Economic Committee's recommendation to re-open wage talks was dramatically abandoned, with the General Council split 14 votes to 14. By then, as I will suggest, the unions had been badly divided for some time.

A fourth tendency is to treat union leaders as mere *cyphers*, reactively defending industrial voluntarism. Where they used their clout in the party, they did so defensively, directing it industrially, Irving Richter (1973: 218) insisted, at 'simply the achievement, maintenance or restoration of "free collective bargaining", or, within the party, as Robert Taylor notes (1980: 100), at providing 'the only real counterweight to combat the negative extremism of the constituency rank and file'. Yet union leaders have frequently participated as activists in Labour politics, often ignoring their unions' policies in the process. Biographical accounts often reveal political activists trying to drive Labour policy well beyond industrial relations' concerns: Frank Chapple (1984) on foreign policy; Frank Cousins on nuclear arms (see Goodman 1979); and Jack Jones (1986) on pensions.

The argument here, then, is that the pluralist focus on unions as unreliable partners in economic management, usually reflecting a normative commitment to Keynesian political economy, often neglects the full complexities of the unions–party relationship, and of union–union relationships, and thus inhibits full understanding of the labour alliance.

. . . not enough socialism

The other principal academic perspective on the post-war labour alliance is that of socialist and Marxist writers, who rejected the pluralist claim that the State was politically neutral, portraying it as overwhelmingly on the side of capital in its class struggle against labour. Much of this perspective was inspired by Ralph Miliband's *Parliamentary Socialism* (1961; see chapter 5 of this volume, by David Coates and Leo Panitch). This school explicitly aims to help identify viable socialist political strategies. The starting point is Miliband's analysis of Labour as an overwhelmingly parliamentarist party, whose political function was to integrate organised workers into parliamentary modes of action. Applied to the party–unions link, Leo Panitch elaborated:

The function of the Labour Party in the British political system consists not only of representing working class interests, but of acting as one of the chief mechanisms for inculcating the organised working class with national values and symbols and of restraining and reinterpreting working class demands in this light.

In particular, he argued, when Labour mobilised support for the (liberal capitalist) 'national interest' against union 'sectional' behaviour, it acted 'as a highly effective agency of social control against the objective expression of working class dissent' (Panitch 1976: 235–6).

Panitch's 1976 study focused on incomes policy and hence mainly on the party–government link. It portrayed a political economy context mirroring that of the pluralists: an emphasis on the relative weakness of British capital, its exposed currency, inadequate productivity and investment, and wage militancy. In this problematical world, Labour played an 'enhanced integrative role', promoting indicative planning and incomes policy. Labour's success, and part of its electoral appeal, 'depended primarily on its structural ties with the trade unions' (Panitch 1976: 240). In the clash between class and national interests, however, the unions–party link also acted as 'a structural constraint upon the ability of the Labour Party to act out its integrative role', not least when 'the basic dilemma of corporatism – coercion in the name of harmony – comes to rear its ugly head' (Panitch 1976: 247; 1986: 69, 73). Nevertheless, as David Coates (1980: 215) put it, the loyalty of key union leaders helped sustain Labour Governments when such dilemmas 'generated tension among the rank and file of the trade union movement which, had the Government been Conservative, the trade union leadership would have articulated more fully'.

Much of the emphasis in socialist work is thus on exposing the consequences for the labour movement of 'enhanced' incorporation of unions within the institutions and strategies of tripartite economic management. Socialist writers have insisted that while unions place their key social power over wage bargaining on the corporatist table, business keeps to itself its key power over investment. Hence where pluralist *bipolarism* saw union leaders immobilised by mass militancy, socialists saw militancy pacified by union leaders, and in some Marxist accounts this pacifying role is portrayed as far more significant than Left-Right factionalism inside unions (Cliff and Gluckstein 1988).

The socialist school sometimes shares the pluralist tendency to *monolithism*. Not that the role of factionalism – generalised internal political struggle – in the labour alliance is ignored: the school's founding purpose was to engage with such factionalism, and recent work is in this vein (Panitch and Leys 1997). Abstract opposition of Labour to 'the unions' is nevertheless sometimes characteristic. In an early essay Panitch (1986: 74) wrote: 'The result [of the party's integrationist ideology] is conflict between the unions and Labour Party over the very integrative character of the party and over party policy towards the economy and industrial relations'. Coates commented (1989: 96):

Between 1974 and 1979 the historic connections binding Labour politicians and union officialdom, the positive commitments of union leaders to the Labour Party, and the close links that they enjoyed with Labour politicians, all left union leaders particularly prone to subordinate trade union demands to the general drift of government policy.

Such shorthand may be unavoidable – certainly Coates himself has warned that it is 'always a mistake to treat the national trade unions as a homogeneous and undifferentiated bloc' (1980: 212) – but it should be treated with caution by students of labour, and it may divert attention from insights that a disaggregated approach can produce, as I suggest below.

A second tendency of the socialist school is its emphasis on national *industrial* policy, a focus linked to identifying underinvestment in British industry as a principal explanation for relative economic decline, an alternative to the pluralist focus on labour militancy. This can divert attention from other policy conflicts. In his discussion of the political power of trade unionism in 1974–79, Coates concludes (1980: 226) that unions and the Labour Government were not ideologically divided over economic policy: 'On the contrary, with the exception of left-wing pre-occupation with free collective bargaining, both groups operated within roughly similar definitions of the causes and consequences, the necessities and policy options that the crisis generated.' It is suggested below that a disaggregated approach to the economic policy conflicts in the period reveals serious union division along another crucial dimension of the ideologically integrative role of Labour, namely the promotion of a *residualist* or *productivist* ideology in respect of public, and sometimes private, service sector work at a time of the neo-liberal assault on the welfare state. 'Productivist' here means the designation of some forms of work as economically productive, and others as unproductive; 'residualist' means the perception of public service spending as being limited to the resources left over after the needs of productive economic activities have been met.

The suggestion here then, is that accounts from the socialist perspective, for all the scholarship and passion it brings to the understanding of the labour alliance, can share with the pluralists some tendencies to what are here being termed monolithism and bipolarism, and a focus on industrial policy that underestimates the significance of sectoral divisions over fiscal policy within the alliance for both unions–government and unions–party relations.

The last but one Labour Government

To put into historical context the criticisms made above, the focus of this chapter is the decade after 1974, not because the criticisms are applicable only to this period, but because this was when the corporatist dilemmas identified by both schools as straining the labour alliance were most intense. This was a period, historically, of the closest integration of the alliance in the programme and institutions of the Social Contract, notably the new TUC–Labour Party Liaison Committee, in which the TUC, the party's National Executive Committee (NEC) and the parliamentary leadership/Government were equally represented. It was a period of accelerating international inflation and currency instability, massive deflation in the industrial states whose wealth was being redistributed to oil-producers and the return of mass unemployment. The period also witnessed the rise in ideological influence of neo-liberal political economy, incorporating a new assault on state spending for, allegedly, 'crowding out' the 'wealth-creating' sectors. A Marxist political economy of this 'fiscal crisis' (Gough 1979; O'Connor 1973) suggested new fractures within labour movements (Offe 1984), but was little pursued at the time in relation to the British movement (exceptions were McDonnell 1978; Fryer 1979). Fractions of capital proved much more interesting to Marxist academics than did fractions of labour. Responding to these economic and political crises, the Labour Government introduced 'the largest cuts in real public expenditure that have occurred in the last fifty years' (Jackson 1991: 73). These cuts, it should be emphasised, largely pre-dated the over-mythologised International Monetary Fund (IMF) deal of 1976 when, in a highly public manner, the Government was forced to announce more public spending cuts in return for loans to stabilise the Sterling exchange rate (Ludlam 1992). The social and industrial policy trade-offs in the Social Contract, supposed to reward wage restraint, were hit hard in the process, as, consequently, was the unions–party link.

A final justification for the emphasis on this period is its relative absence from the monographs. Even in Minkin's monumental studies the late 1970s receive less attention than, arguably, they deserve. They feature in the epilogue to the second edition of *The Labour Party Conference*, and more extensively in *The Contentious Alliance*, where divisions over fiscal policy are noted, but are treated only to a few suggestive paragraphs. Andrew Taylor's study (1987) contained the first detailed examination of TUC–government relations over fiscal policy in the 1970s, but did not directly address the sectoral division that, I argue, emerged at the time.

Three arguments are presented here about the unions–party link in this period, addressing the limitations of monolithism, of a bipolar counterposing of union leaders to members, and of overemphasis on industrial policy. Firstly, it is suggested that the period witnessed an under-analysed union division along public–private sectoral lines which revealed the presence within labourist ideology of a profoundly capitalist commitment to the primacy of 'productive' labour – the productivism or residualism referred to above. Secondly, this division is presented as central in understanding the collapse of the Social Contract. And, thirdly, it is argued that the hostilities thus generated help explain factional realignments within the unions–party link between 1979 and 1983.

Deserving versus undeserving workers: productivism and residualism

Over half the TUC's membership worked in the public sector by 1974. But public sector unions were grossly under-represented on senior TUC economic committees. The National and Local Government Officers' Association (NALGO) and the National Union of Public Employees (NUPE), the fourth and fifth largest unions, were excluded until 1977–78. This mattered because the TUC generally endorsed fiscal policy in 1975–76, as the biggest spending cuts and the non-inflation-proofed 'cash limits' on spending were introduced.

Anti-cuts motions were routinely adopted at TUC Conferences, but frustration at the TUC General Council's reluctance to act on them led NUPE and NALGO to picket the 1976 TUC and Labour Conferences, lead a huge national demonstration against cuts in November 1976 and then launch the National Steering Committee Against the Cuts (NSCAC). This unprecedented sectoral union pressure group was 'the official body established by eleven public sector trade unions and associations to combat the cuts in public expenditure' (NSCAC 1977: i). Like the TUC General Council, the giant general unions – the Transport and General Workers' Union (TGWU) and the General and Municipal Workers' Union (GMWU) – declined to support the pickets or the mass demonstration. A public service union's research officer wrote: 'The issue of cuts brought about a major split within the trade union movement in the mid-1970s . . . cuts were the primary union issue from 1975 to 1977' (Hall 1983: 10–11). The new sectoral cleavage may have been cross-cut by older factional loyalties, but its emergence is beyond dispute.

A major factor producing the public sector alliance was the need to confront the alarming new ideological discourse, the neo-liberal assault on public spending, that echoed older discourses on the 'unproductive labour' question (see Boss 1990). Contemporary socialist analysis of the 'fiscal crisis of the state', a 'good riddance' version of the neo-liberal analysis, offered anti-cuts unions little ammunition (Gough 1979; O'Connor 1973). The Left's AES did not break cleanly from liberal political economy on this point. As one union research officer put it: 'The way the AES treats public services is heartbreaking. They remain a problem of financing, a residual in the arithmetic of capitalism' (Hall 1983: 96). And the new Cambridge group of Keynesians, whose analysis of import controls appealed to the unions' Left, prescribed even deeper cuts than the Treasury (Crosland 1982: 342).

The labour movement echoed to the sound of residualist arguments, most dramatically from Hugh Scanlon at the TUC's 1976 Special Congress on economic policy. The Amalgamated Union of Engineering Workers' (AUEW) leader backed spending cuts because, 'if Britain is to get out of her undoubted economic difficulties, she can only do it on the basis of a viable, efficient manufacturing industry with emphasis on those who make and sell and, if necessary, somewhat less emphasis on those who serve' (TUC 1976a: 28). Of the 'crowding out' line (that a bloated public sector was asphyxiating free enterprise), NSCAC noted: 'This argument has been used by the Government to divide the trade union Movement. Cut back on the public sector, argues the Chancellor, and there will be more investment and therefore more jobs for trade unionists and the unemployed in the private manufacturing sector' (1977: 18). The records of unions in different economic sectors amply confirm this perception, though more often in the relative privacy of their journals and conferences (Ludlam 1991, 1995). The position in the giant general unions was more complex. Both had significant memberships in the public sector. In the TGWU the authority and political loyalty of Jack Jones moderated open protest, but public sector anger surfaced in the union's newspaper as soon as Jones was succeeded by Moss Evans. The GMWU's traditional loyalty to Labour leaders similarly constrained official expressions of anger until its leader, David Basnett, became alarmed at the mass employment that followed fiscal deflation. At its conference in 1976, the GMWU's public services officer succinctly addressed the sectoral division and the resulting political dilemma for general unions:

> The policy is intended to channel resources away from consumption and into pro-ductive investment. So those unions whose membership lies wholly in industry find no conflict whatsoever here between the public interest and their private interest. On the other hand those unions whose membership lies wholly in the public sector have an obvious interest in opposing the cuts . . . the real dilemma is forced on unions like our own who have a membership interested in both camps and which can either lose or gain. (GMWU 1976: 522)

A disaggregated approach to the unions–party link in this period, then, reveals the limitation of monolithism, and a dimension of Labour's 'integrative ideology' lying beyond corporatist industrial policy. This dimension reflects a fundamental tenet of capitalist ideology: the absolute primacy of traded commodity produc-tion, and an associated prejudice against the burden of 'unproductive' labour. The following sections consider the effects of this sectoral cleavage on union–govern-ment relations and on power relations within the party.

Sectoral division and the fate of the unions–party-in-government link

The Social Contract's disintegration in the 'winter of discontent' is blamed, con-ventionally, on the wage policy that inflicted the most serious real wage cuts in living memory and squeezed skilled workers' differentials (Ludlam 1999). This explanation neglects the impact of fiscal policy on union tolerance of wage restraint, and the related impact of the TUC's loss of cohesion as a bargaining part-ner, arising from the sectoral division noted above.

Wage restraint had been sold as part of a 'wider Social Contract' that included industrial relations' reform, industrial intervention and democracy, and, above all, social policy commitments – the 'social wage'. Demanding wage restraint at the 1974 TUC Conference, future Prime Minister James Callaghan insisted: 'The Social Contract was devised as a whole, and it will stand or fall as a whole. No one . . . is entitled to say that he accepts the part that pleases him but rejects the rest' (TUC 1974: 396). The Government's inability to maintain its end of this package deal progressively undermined the Social Contract wage deal.

Following early education cuts, the TUC's General Council threatened that 'restoration of the cuts must be regarded as part of the Social Contract' (TUC 1975: 167). The unexpected introduction of new cash limits on public spending almost reversed the TGWU Conference's approval of the 1975 incomes policy (Jones 1986: 297), and the 1975 TUC Conference passed an anti-cuts motion declaring that, 'further cuts in public expenditure . . . will be regarded as . . . a fun-damental breach of the social contract' (TUC 1975: 483, 462). The TUC statement *The Social Contract 1976–77* subsequently accepted cuts already announced, but insisted that avoiding further cuts was central to the contract's progress (TUC 1976a: 40). In the wake of the IMF crisis, the TUC's 1977 *Economic Review* (1977a: 10) warned that unions could not oversee further wage restraint until the fiscal policy issue was settled. When Callaghan, as prime minister, appealed to the 1977

TUC Conference to maintain wage controls, the miners' spokesperson retorted: 'We have a mass of cuts in the social services that we were told would not take place if we accepted the Social Contract. I believe that this is the biggest con trick that has ever been pulled' (TUC 1977b: 459–60).

Larry Whitty recalled how opinion shifted in the conferences of the ultra-loyal GMWU:

> By [19]77 from being pretty docile, they suddenly turned into quite substantial attacks on the union, attacks on the party and so on . . . you couldn't actually see the social policy being delivered. We know aspects of it were being delivered, but also publicly, and to a large extent in real terms, the Government's direction was to cut public expenditure covering those aspects of the social wage. (Interview)

Jones' successor as TGWU leader, Moss Evans, held a similar view:

> The principle cause of undermining any sort of hope in a Social Contract with the government or any sense of understanding were the terms agreed by Denis Healey with the IMF . . . in layman's terms it would appear that the quid pro quos for the Social Contract could not be met by the Government because of the terms of the IMF loan . . . This disillusioned lots of people. (Interview)

NUPE's 1977 economic review *Fight Back!*, the most savage official union attack on the Social Contract, concluded:

> Because the Government has failed to meet the expectations it raised among workers when it entered into the bargain, the Social Contract has been transformed, in the eyes of trade unionists, from an agreement about economic and social priorities into a vehicle for implementing a policy of wage restraint – and nothing more. (NUPE 1977: 9)

TUC General Secretary Lionel Murray recalled (in interview): 'In the end, it was the decision to batten down the hatches in the public sector that led to the uprising, to the so-called winter of discontent. That was the strongest thing.' Crucially, the frustration of public service unions at the TUC leadership's initial acceptance of Labour's fiscal policy, manifested in the formation of the sectoral NSCAC and its mass demonstrations described above, had, by 1978, undermined the cohesion of the TUC as a peak organisation. By the time the Social Contract collapsed, in 1978, distrust among unions over the top-table bargaining with Labour had made the TUC's core negotiating machinery unworkable. Moss Evans (in interview) recalled: '[T]here was so much suspicion that the whole of the General Council would have to turn up to meet the prime minister and the chancellor of the exchequer and the secretary of state for employment. The suspicion that had emerged had to be seen to be believed.'

If monolithism is abandoned, then, there is overwhelming evidence that sectoral division produced a catastrophic loss of cohesion within the TUC, rendering it impossible for the Social Contract negotiations to continue past 1977–78. So, did this less well-known dimension of labour movement politics produce new factional alignments that contradict the tendency, noted above, to treat union leaders as mere cyphers? Did it have implications for the cohesion of the party itself?

Realignment in Labour's civil war: the unions–party-in-opposition link

This section addresses two main questions. Was there a Hard Left–Soft Left division in the unions in the mid-1970s, related to sectoral divisions, that in any way prefigured the realignment in the party associated with the 1980s? And, if so, what impact did it have on the trajectory of the Labour Left in the late 1970s and early 1980s?

By the Soft Left–Hard Left split is meant the division that is conventionally dated from 1981 when Neil Kinnock led a group of Left – *Tribune* Group – MPs in opposition to Tony Benn's challenge for the party's deputy leadership. This realignment was crucial to Kinnock's construction of the Centre-Left block that gave him a clear run at the policy and party reforms that built the foundations for New Labour (Kinnock 1994). This conventional periodisation needs modification, irrespective of whether it was prefigured among the unions. We know that Michael Foot and Tony Benn had split over the party's 1973 public ownership programme, that Foot did not mobilise against Benn's sacking as industry secretary in 1975, and about Foot's estrangement from the *Tribune* Group in the mid-1970s (Castle 1980: 469; Hatfield 1978: 211; Jones, M. 1994: 358). Is there evidence of a similar Hard Left–Soft Left union split in the mid-1970s?

Firstly, the realignment of Jones and Scanlon is noted by academics, by cabinet diarists and by both men themselves (Benn 1989: 46, 61, 166; Castle 1980: 469–71, 679; Jones 1986: 304, 325; Minkin 1992: 163–182; Wickham-Jones 1996: 150 *et passim*; Scanlon 1979: 394; Scanlon interview). The reasons were straightforward: fear of hyperinflation; and a determination to keep Labour in office and Thatcher out. The divergence was occasionally very public, as when Jones attacked veteran Left MP Ian Mikardo at the 1975 annual *Tribune* rally, for suggesting that the unions were failing to protect workers. For Benn, this episode 'ended the pretence of a Left fighting a Right'. As Larry Whitty put it (in interview): 'Jack and Hughie, by that time, 1975–76, from being on the Left of the general council, had become the anti-public sector element.' Jones, Scanlon and GMWU leader David Basnett blocked calls for a TUC Special Congress on rising unemployment in January 1976, and lambasted *Tribune* Group MPs who voted against the March 1976 public expenditure White Paper – the most deflationary of the whole government (*Tribune* 19 March 1976).

The three leaders also called for a TUC–Labour Party Liaison Committee statement to override existing TUC and party policies, producing more factional tensions. In the early 1970s, the balance of political forces in the Liaison Committee had favoured NEC and trade union members of the Tribunite Left. By 1976, with Jones and Scanlon defending wage controls and public spending cuts, NEC Tribunites were outgunned by an alliance of TUC and government representatives (Minkin 1978: 480; Taylor 1987: 71–2). Liaison Committee minutes in 1976 reveal a bitter struggle, lasting several months, over the wording of Treasury drafts on public spending for the key Social Contract statement *The Next Three Years and the Question of Priorities* (TUC 1976b: 416–24; see Liaison Committee Minutes of 26 April, 24 May, 21 June and 26 July 1976). Left-wing NEC members then published a report comparing this statement with Labour and TUC Conference policies, demonstrating how far the Liaison Committee was abandoning the latter. Such disputes highlight a struggle by the NEC-based Labour Left against a Soft Left alliance of Foot with Jones and Scanlon.

So where, if anywhere, is a realigned union Hard Left emerging? The argument here is that two wings of the union left resisted the Liaison Committee line. Communist Party-influenced unions, and allied unions in the contemporary Broad Left, promoted a hard-line version of the 'Alternative Economic Strategy' (AES). After 1974, these unions systematically attacked the Social Contract and pushed the AES. What was new from 1975 was the Broad Left's alliance with newly-radicalised public service unions, behind resolution-mongering against the cuts and deflation, and for Hard Left versions of the AES. Murray's view (in interview), some years later, was that these two groupings 'did coalesce for the purposes of the campaign – very often for very different reasons. And I don't think there was a clear ideology underlying the joint action.' Murray had warned the Government of this alliance, fearing it might carry an anti-Social Contract motion at the 1975 TUC, if more cuts were announced.

However, although this Hard Left realignment was real, it was not easily sustained. From 1976 onwards softer versions of the AES were passed at the TUC, and to some of the anti-cuts' unions the argument seemed to have been won. Previously excluded unions were gradually admitted to the TUC's top committees, and the benefits were outweighing the costs of continued factionalism (NSCAC was wound up by 1981). And although 1976–78 saw the worst impact of pre-IMF deal cuts and 'cash limits', budgets after the IMF deal were all reflationary (if more by tax cuts than by restoration of spending cuts). Furthermore, the AES did not provide a very firm platform. Union versions of the AES differed widely in scope and radicalism (Sharples 1981). The Treasury worked hard to convince union leaders that retaliation against AES protectionism would be devastating. And the Social Contract years took a toll: the more service cuts and closures went through without successful resistance, the harder it became to mobilise (Neale 1983).

If the realignment of the union Left was relatively limited within the TUC, though, did it carry into the Labour Party? Apart from its NSCAC work, NUPE greatly intensified work inside the party. It increased its national affiliation to the party, and thus its conference vote, from 150,000 to 600,000 between 1974 and 1980. This has even led some, ignoring other unions' changed affiliations, to argue that NUPE's increased vote led to the party leadership's defeats over constitutional reforms (Healey 1989: 470; Minkin 1992: 199). NUPE, TGWU and the Association of Scientific, Technical and Managerial Staffs (ASTMS) routinely supported all three of the constitutional reformers' key demands: automatic reselection of MPs; widening the leadership election franchise; and giving the NEC the final word over election manifestos. The first two were adopted. The unions *en bloc* did not, as noted above, force reforms through after 1979, but, as Minkin (1992: 194–5) makes clear, enough did to get two of the demands through. But NUPE went further, becoming an early affiliate, along with other unions in the new leftist alliance, of the CLPD. Between 1975 and 1979, unions grew from 6 per cent to 49 per cent of CLPD affiliates. NUPE's Research Director Bernard Dix became CLPD vice-president, and permitted his staff to devote union resources to the cause (Dix in interview). Dix and other NUPE officers became important union contacts in the proto-Bennite movement of the last years of the Labour Government (Benn 1989: 258; Kogan and Kogan 1982: 108).

The threat of Thatcherism was, however, acute by 1981, when Benn's deputy-leadership challenge against Denis Healey split the parliamentary Tribunites, causing consternation on the union Left. Bill Keys, a pivotal union left-winger on the party NEC, the TGWU's Evans and ASTMS' Clive Jenkins all opposed Benn's candidacy. NUPE held a branch ballot, which Healey won. The TGWU first backed Soft Left 'spoiler' John Silkin, then voted for Benn in the second round. In the first round Benn took 36.5 per cent of the union vote to Healey's 61.2 per cent. At the same conference, NEC election results revealed that a revived union Right had removed five left-wingers, which, combined with the Soft Left shift of some MPs, gave Foot an anti-Bennite NEC majority for the first time. Key unions now imposed a truce inside the party, in the so-called 'Peace of Bishop's Stortford' brokered at the ASTMS training college.

So there was realignment on the union Left in the 1970s, and it was the newly radicalised public service unions, seeking allies as sectoral division in the TUC left them vulnerable to Labour's fiscal deflation, that gave it a reach beyond the traditional Broad Left. And it did prefigure the Hard Left–Soft Left division of the 1980s. It was not a coherent force within the TUC for long, more a tactical alliance. There was intensive activity in 1975 and 1976, but much less thereafter, as the TUC as a whole became more critical of economic policy, and the outsider public service unions were permitted to come inside. The realignment did help to precipitate party divisions, by promoting the CLPD and providing enough block votes to give the reformers their victories. But, facing electoral disaster and anti-union legislation, key unions called it a day as far as generalised factionalism was concerned.

Conclusions

This chapter has suggested some limitations of the two main interpretative schools, and has demonstrated historically that important dimensions of the unions–party link need additional perspectives and more disaggregated methods of study if we are to deepen our understanding. It suggests, above all, that analysis should avoid both monolithism, treating the unions as Harrison's 'orthodox lump of suet pudding', and bipolarism, treating the labour alliance as a simple combination of 'the unions' with 'the party'. The existence of virtually permanent cross-cutting factionalism, in which individual unions take up opposing positions alongside distinct groups of party members and leaders, must be recognised. It is certainly difficult otherwise to make sense of the link in the New Labour era – for example, in relation to key issues on which unions are divided, such as the Private Finance Initiative (PFI) for the private financing and management of public services, employment law reform and European monetary union. The fact that the cross-cutting organised Labour Left of old has been less in evidence in the New Labour era does not mean that there are no alliances on key issues between different unions and distinct groupings of party activists and leaders.

This chapter also suggests that analysis of the dynamics of the role of the unions in the labour alliance should also include a disaggregated perspective that pays attention to sectoral factors. Certainly union divisions in the face of New Labour's reform of the funding and management of public services has once again revealed, among Britain's merged super-unions, the contours of the sectoral divisions that were so significant in the 1970s. A most striking example was the support of the manufacturing union AMICUS–AEEU for PFI, a policy despised by public service unions. And, in that same area of dispute under New Labour we can see compelling evidence of the need to study union leaders as independent political actors, in particular as political agents within the party, rather than simply as political cyphers, or as subordinate bureaucrats, in the behaviour of the leadership of the General, Municipal and Boilermakers' union (GMB). In 2001, the GMB withdrew £2m of funding from Labour and launched an advertising campaign bitterly critical of PFI.

All interpretative approaches can benefit from a large dose of the sort of contemporary historiographical methods that Minkin's work exemplifies, combining documentary and interview-based materials with the study of values and ideas among union leaders and activists and the study of party constitutional and policy issues. In this last respect, what is suggested is specifically the extension of the 'integrationist' argument – on the ideological subordination of the labour movement to national capitalist economic policy strategies – to a discussion of subordination to more fundamental and abstract assumptions of liberal political economy, notably about the centrality to prosperity of the production of traded commodities as opposed to the provision of human services.

Analysing the unions–party link is not easy. Important aspects are hidden from scholarly view unless, like Minkin, the scholar is a lifelong participant observer. The political complexities of the important unions are subject to a variety of influences, both personal and constitutional, and above all to the unpredictable impact of economic change. In one decade, one of the most powerful and political of Labour's affiliated unions, the NUM, all but disappeared. But without attempting an understanding of Britain's unique and complex labour alliance, a complete understanding of Labour in Britain is not possible.

References

Unless indicated, the place of publication is London.

Beer, S. (1965) *Modern British Politics*

Beer, S. (1982) *Britain Against Itself: The Political Consequences of Collectivism*

Benn, T. (1989) *Against the Tide: Diaries 1973–76*

Boss, H. (1990) *Theories of Surplus and Transfer: Parasites and Producers in Economic Thought*

Castle, B. (1980) *The Castle Diaries 1974–76*

Chapple, F. (1984) *Sparks Fly!*

Cliff, T. and Gluckstein, D. (1988) *The Labour Party: A Marxist History*

Coates, D. (1980) *Labour in Power? A Study of the Labour Government 1974–1979*

Coates, D. (1989) *The Crisis of Labour: Industrial Relations and the State in Contemporary Britain*, Oxford

Crosland, S. (1982) *Tony Crosland*

Dorfman, G. (1974) *Wage Politics in Britain 1945–67*, Ames, IA

Dorfman, G. (1979) *Government versus Trade Unionism in British Politics Since 1968*

Dorfman, G. (1983) *British Trade Unionism Against the Trades Union Congress*

Fatchett, D. (1987) *Trade Unions and Politics in the 1980s*

Flanders, A. (1957) *Trade Unions*, Tillicoultry

Fryer, R. (1979) 'British trade unionism and the cuts', *Capital and Class*, 8

GMWU (1976) *GMWU Congress Report*

Goodman, G. (1979) *The Awkward Warrior. Frank Cousins: His Life and Times*

Gough, I. (1979) *The Political Economy of the Welfare State*

Gould, P. (1998) *The Unfinished Revolution: How the Modernisers Saved the Labour Party*

Hall, D. (1983) *The Cuts Machine: The Politics of Public Expenditure*

Harrison, M. (1960) *Trade Unions and the Labour Party*

Hatfield, M. (1978) *The House the Left Built: Inside Labour Policy-Making 1970–1975*

Healey, D. (1989) *The Time of My Life*, Harmondsworth

HMSO (1968) *Report of the Royal Commission on Trades Unions and Employers Associations 1965–1968*

Jackson, P.M. (1991) 'Public expenditure', in Artis, M. and Cobham, D. (eds) *Labour's Economic Policies 1974–79*, Manchester

Jenkins, P. (1970) *The Battle of Downing Street*

Jones, J. (1986) *Union Man: An Autobiography*

Kinnock, N. (1994) 'Reforming the Labour Party', *Contemporary Record*, 8:3

Kogan, D. and Kogan, M. (1982) *The Battle for the Labour Party*

Labour Party (1974–79) *Reports of the Annual Conference of the Labour Party*

Liaison Committee (1976) Minutes of the Trades Union Congress – Labour Party Liaison Committee

Ludlam, S. (1991) 'Labourism and the disintegration of the postwar consensus: disunited trade union economic policy responses to public expenditure cuts, 1974–79', unpublished PhD thesis, University of Sheffield

Ludlam, S. (1992) 'The gnomes of Washington: four myths of the 1976 IMF crisis', *Political Studies*, 40:4

Ludlam, S. (1995) 'The impact of sectoral cleavage and spending cuts on Labour Party/trade union relations: the Social Contract experience', in Broughton, D., Farrell, D., Denver, D. and Rallings, C. (eds) *British Elections and Parties Yearbook 1994*

Ludlam, S. (1999) 'Myths of the winter of discontent', *Politics Review*, 9:2

Ludlam, S. (2001) 'New Labour and the unions: the end of the contentious alliance?' In Ludlam, S. and Smith, M. J. (2001) *New Labour in Government*

Marquand, D. (1992) *The Progressive Dilemma: From Lloyd George to Kinnock*

McDonnell, K. (1978) 'Ideology, crisis and the cuts', *Capital and Class*, 4

Milliband, R. (1961) *Parliamentary Socialism: A Study in the Politics of Labour*

Minkin, L. (1978) *The Labour Party Conference*

Minkin, L. (1992) *The Contentious Alliance: Trade Unions and the Labour Party*, Edinburgh

Minkin, L. (1997) *Exits and Entrances: Political Research as a Creative Art*, Sheffield

Muller, W. D. (1977) *The Kept Men? The First Century of Trade Unoin Representation in the British House of Commons 1874–1975*, Hassocks

Neale, J. (1983) *Memoirs of a Callous Picket*

NSCAC (1977) *Breakdown: The Crisis in Your Public Services*

NUPE (1977) *Fight Back!*

O'Connor, J. (1973) *The Fiscal Crisis of the State*, New York

Offe, C. (1984) *Contradictions of the Welfare State*

Panitch, L. (1976) *Social Democracy and Industrial Militancy: The Labour Party, Trade Unions and Incomes Policy, 1945–74*, Cambridge

Panitch, L. (1986) 'Ideology and integration: the case of the British Labour Party', in Panitch, L., *Working Class Politics in Crisis: Essays on Labour and the State*

Panitch, L. and Leys, C. (1997) *The End of Parliamentary Socialism: From New Left to New Labour*

Pimlott, B. (1991) 'Trade unions and the second coming of CND', in Pimlott, B. and Cook, C., *Trade Unions in British Politics: The First 250 Years*

Richter, I. (1973) *Political Purpose in Trade Unions*

Scanlon, H. (1979) 'Why the Social Contract failed' (text of televised debate), *The Listener*, 27 September

Sharples, A. (1981) 'Alternative economic strategies – Labour movement responses to the crisis', *Socialist Economic Review 1981*

Taylor, A. J. (1987) *The Trade Unions and the Labour Party*

Taylor, R. (1980) *The Fifth Estate: Britain's Unions in the Modern World*

Taylor, R. (1993) *The Trade Union Question in British Politics: Government and Unions Since 1945*, Oxford

Taylor, R. (2000) *The TUC: From the General Strike to New Unionism*

TUC (1944) *Report of the Annual Trades Union Congress*

TUC (1974) *Report of the Annual Trades Union Congress*

TUC (1975) *Report of the Annual Trades Union Congress*

TUC (1976a) *Report of the Special Trades Union Congress on the Social Contract 1976–77*

TUC (1976b) *Report of the Annual Trades Union Congress*

TUC (1977a) *Trades Union Congress Economic Review*

TUC (1977b) *Report of the Annual Trades Union Congress*

Webb, P. (1992) *Trade Unions and the British Electorate*, Aldershot

Wickham-Jones, M. (1996) *Economic Strategy and the Labour Party: Politics and Policy-Making, 1970–83*

Interviews cited

Bernard Dix, former assistant general secretary, NUPE. Mynnyd Cerrig, 23 January 1992

Moss Evans, former general secretary, TGWU. Heacham, 14 July 1992

Lionel Murray, former general secretary, TUC. London, 29 January 1992

Hugh Scanlon, former president, AUEW. Broadstairs, 28 May 1992

Larry Whitty, former national research officer, GMWU. London, 2 June 1992

11

Lewis Minkin and the party–unions link

Eric Shaw

'For over 80 years', Minkin declares in his magisterial survey *The Contentious Alliance* (1991: xii), the Labour Party–trade unions link 'has shaped the structure and, in various ways, the character of the British Left'. His core proposition can be encapsulated simply: trade union 'restraint has been the central characteristic' of the link (1991: 26). This constitutes a frontal challenge to received wisdom – endlessly repeated, recycled and amplified by Britain's media – that, until the 'modernisation' of the party, initiated by Neil Kinnock and accelerated by Tony Blair, the unions ran the party. So ingrained is this wisdom in British political culture that no discussion of party–unions relations in the media can endure for long without some reference to the days when 'the union barons controlled the party'. This view, Minkin holds, is a gross over-simplification and, to a degree, downright misleading. The relationship is infinitely more subtle and complex, and far more balanced than the conventional view allows. The task Minkin sets himself in *The Contentious Alliance* is twofold: on the one hand to explain why and how he reached that conclusion; and, on the other – the core of the book – to lay bare the inner dynamics of the party–unions connection.

What is most distinctive and enduring about Minkin's work? In what ways has it most contributed to our understanding of the labour movement? Does it still offer insights for scholars of Labour politics? In the first section of this paper, I examine how Minkin contests the premises underpinning the orthodox thesis of trade union 'baronial power'; in the second, I analyse the 'sociological' frame of reference he devised as an analytical tool to uncover the roots and essential properties of the party–unions connection; in the third section, I address the question of the relevance of Minkin today.

The 'baronial power' thesis

I call the received wisdom about party–unions relationship the thesis of 'baronial power'. It can be stated simply. 'In a sense not true of its social democratic counterparts on the mainland of Europe', Marquand (1991: 25) contends, Labour, 'has been a trade union party, created, financed and, in the last analysis, controlled by a highly decentralised trade union movement'. The link has been widely held responsible for Labour's post-1979 long sojourn in the wilderness, because the concessions needed to rally the union leaders behind the parliamentary leadership in the 1970s were 'so substantial . . . that they helped to undermine the leader's stature and the Party's credibility' (Harrison 1996: 199). Kitschelt, in a much-cited work (1994), concludes that the Labour Party affords the closest approximation to what he calls the unions-control model. In a neat distillation of the conventional wisdom he writes that not only are they 'the major party financiers, but [they] control the Conference Arrangement Committee, which sets the agenda at national party conferences, and the bulk of the conference votes, which are cast in blocks by the leaders of individual unions'. Moreover, the unions elected a majority of the party's National Executive Committee, enjoyed a powerful role in the selection of parliamentary candidates, and sponsored a large number of MPs (1994: 251; see also Barnes and Reid 1980: 222). These organisational characteristics can surely admit to no other conclusion than that the unions will naturally 'dominate the party elite by controlling key appointments and placing their own leadership in important executive and legislative party offices' (Kitschelt 1994: 225). Yet this conclusion Minkin shows, in the most heavily researched and meticulous survey of the party–unions connection yet published, to be wrong on all counts.

The Contentious Alliance – building in a number of respects on Minkin's path-finding first study *The Labour Party Conference* – provides chapter and verse in explaining why it is wrong. At one level it is, like its predecessor, an indispensable source book on Labour, chronicling the history of the relationship between (what were once called) the two wings of the movement. But its purpose is much more ambitious, for it seeks to understand why established orthodoxy is wrong. This greatly extends and deepens its intellectual horizon, for Minkin is, in effect, asking a most challenging question: why do political actors – and especially those who wield power – behave as they do?

Minkin began systematically exploring the nature of the party–unions relationship in the period of the 1974–79 Labour Government (Minkin 1978a). In these years the baronial power thesis was taken for granted. Few queried the judgement that Jack Jones, head of the largest union, the TGWU, had become 'arguably the most powerful politician within the Labour Party' (Barnes and Reid 1980: 191–2), and it was generally accepted that Labour ministers exhibited a 'pervasive deference to the trade union movement' (Artis and Cobham 1991: 276).

Minkin was one of the few who dissented. In 1978 his definitive study *The Labour Party Conference* was published. Given the massive role the unions played in the party's policy machinery it was inevitable that the nature of the party–unions relationship would be one of its major concerns. Having conducted extremely detailed and exhaustive empirical research – a hallmark of the Minkin style – what struck him was the complexity and dialectical quality of that relationship. On the one hand, anticipation of the reaction of the major unions, on issues that impinged directly on their own functions, was an integral feature of the policy process. Thus, with employment and industrial relations' matters, the unions expected, indeed insisted, that policy-making should be a joint party–unions exercise and reacted with hostility and deep resentment in the period of the 1964–70 Labour Government, when major initiatives were taken unilaterally over incomes policy and trade union legislation (in the famous White Paper *In Place of Strife*). On the other hand, the unions were prepared in all other policy sectors to give the parliamentary leadership very substantial latitude: indeed they believed that it *should* have overall primacy (Minkin 1978b: 317).

A more methodical investigation of the nature and roots of the party–unions connection was the natural next step after the *Labour Party Conference*. 'I write', Minkin noted, 'with glacier-like speed; architect, bricklayer and painter' (Minkin 1991: xi). In fact, the dozen years he spend compiling the work involved undertaking a considerable research programme, conducting a large number of interviews, inspecting a mound of documentary material, and interweaving and fusing the empirical, the analytical and the explanatory. He has elucidated how he set about the task:

> Primarily, I aim to construct a coherent and adequate conceptual framework grounded in the repeated occurrences found in my empirical investigations. This framework is always analytical in the attempt to establish a pattern which makes sense in describing and categorising relationships and developments across time, but it also aspires to be explanatory, organising the material in such a way as to indicate solutions to the core problem (or problems) and related questions under investigation, seeking to account for all cases within a particular historical and cultural setting. (Minkin 1997: 173)

The ambition – to produce a definitive work – was realised. This made his conclusion – a direct challenge to 'baronial power' thesis – all the more compelling. Whatever the formal organisational structure of the party would seem to suggest, he stated emphatically, it was 'virtually always misleading to say that the unions "run the Labour Party"' (Minkin 1991: 629). Minkin's concern is not simply to demonstrate, through methodical empirical analysis, that the 'union control' model is wrong, but to explain *why* it is wrong. The book accomplishes two major goals. Firstly, it exposes to the most rigorous and exacting scrutiny the features of the party–unions link, chronicling its evolution since the party's founding in 1900. Secondly, it offers an explanation of the forces governing 'the contentious alliance'. What this chapter seeks to do is to lay bare the nature of his conceptual framework, his analytical categories and his explanatory mode. But to do this adequately I need to place Minkin's interpretation in a broader intellectual context.

Minkin's sociological frame

Homo economicus

Elster (1989: 99) has written that

> one of the most persistent cleavages in the social sciences is the opposition between two lines of thought conveniently associated with Adam Smith and Emile Durkheim, between *homo economicus* and *homo sociologicus*. Of these, the former is supposed to be guided by instrumental rationality, while the behaviour of the latter is dictated by social norms.

The popularity curve of the former in the study of political organisations has for a number of years been steadily rising with the increasing use of 'rational choice' models. 'Rational choice theories', the noted scholar Aaron Wildavsky commented (1994: 132), 'have been among the most successful in the social sciences.' *Homo sociologicus*, in contrast, though at present languishing in political science as a whole, lies at the centre of Minkin's explanatory universe. In considering the value of Minkin's approach we are also, implicitly, making judgements of the relative heuristic merits of economic and sociological perspectives on human behaviour. I would go further: Minkin's work, most notably *The Contentious Alliance*, is perhaps the best example (in terms of its thoroughness, depth of thought and analytical sophistication) of the value of *homo sociologicus* to the study of political parties.

Rational choice theory, in essence, involves the application of neo-classical economic models to the study of political phenomena (its proponents claim that is provides the rigour so often lacking in the academic study of politics). As one scholar has recently observed, 'in contemporary social science, rational-choice theory is perhaps the most coherent and best known approach based on principles of methodological individualism' (Sil 2000: 362). The kernel of this methodology is the belief that 'the elementary unit of social life is individual human action. To explain social institutions and social change is to show how they arise as the result of the action and interaction of individuals' (Elster 1989: 13).

More specifically, it makes two claims. All social action is reducible to individual action. There are, of course, other major forces, public and private institutions, voluntary associations, and so forth, but, in the last resort, they aggregate the behaviour of individuals. It follows that 'all general propositions about the interactions or relations among individuals can be reduced without loss of meaning to the qualities, dispositions and actions of individuals themselves' (Sil 2000: 361).

Acting rationally entails selecting the most economical means to achieve given ends. The theory of instrumental rationality stipulates that social actors are utility maximisers, motivated by a desire to promote their own interests. They are goal-directed, in that they consistently follow courses of action that will afford them greater personal satisfaction. Applied specifically to political parties, this means that political influentials will 'act solely in order to attain income, prestige and power which comes from being in power'. They will seek power either for the pleasure it affords (in terms of personal self-esteem or gratification) or as the means to procure valued goods, such as office, status or material benefits. Hence securing power is, for the rational actor, the overriding objective (Downs 1957: 27–8).

Rational choice institutionalism, which has applied the theory to the study of political organisations, accepts that actors operate within frameworks of rules and arrangements. But their role is limited to providing the stage – the parts, scripts, props and so forth – on which individual actors strive for personal advancement. Institutions provide the strategic context in which optimising behaviour takes place by determining the identity of the key players, the power resources available to them, the rules to which they must adhere and the type of strategic calculations they make (Shepsle 1989: 135).

So the key rational choice postulates (for our purposes) are as follows:

- decision-making is ultimately reducible to conscious, deliberate individual action;
- behaviour is driven by desire to maximise personal or institutional advantage;
- preferences are fixed and consistent, and derive from an accurate awareness of interests; and
- political action is strategic: that is, it involves utilising all available power resources, within set institutional contexts to achieve given goals.

If we apply this approach to the unions–party relationship, the following propositions will naturally emerge (here, for purposes of exposition, I concentrate on the unions):

- Action will be primarily motivated by the aims, interests and calculations of individual union leaders.
- They will be self-interested, that is they will seek to maximise their own interests, those of their organisations and (to the extent that it benefits them) those of the people they represent.
- An identifiable and consistent pattern of preferences – reflecting an informed understanding of where their interests lie – will underpin their choices.
- They will behave strategically by utilising all available resources taking account of costs and benefits of the various options open to them within given institutional settings.

In operational terms, it follows that union leaders would routinely use their entrenched position within the party structure to determine its policy. Two propositions are relevant. Firstly, the party was heavily reliant on union funding, constantly circulating the begging bowl, and this gave unions a lever to influence policy decisions. Secondly, the unions directly elect the trade union section of the NEC (historically over 55 per cent of the total), and would act to push union interests. Minkin subjects both these propositions to detailed scrutiny.

Controlling the purse strings

Drawing on a most impressive body of research, Minkin shows that unions' money was not used as leverage to procure favourable policy outcomes. Indeed, any attempt to do so was regarded as improper: 'there were and remain unwritten prohibitions against open threats of financial sanctions, and there were and are inhibitions and constraints which limit the implementation of such sanctions' (Minkin 1991: 626). As Ben Pimlott expressed it: 'He who paid the piper merely played the tuba and the big bass drum' (quoted in Minkin 1991: 626).

Controlling the votes

With a battery of examples, Minkin demonstrates that, far from operating as a trade union bridgehead, the NEC's trade union section (with only minor and temporary exceptions) afforded successive Labour leaders a solid block of loyalists. Throughout most of Labour's history (and it remains largely true to this day) 'the historic role the Trade Union Section of the NEC has been to act as a loyal base responding to the initiatives of the "politicians", particularly the Parliamentary leadership' (Minkin 1991: 626).

Let's explore another rational choice postulate: that trade union leaders will have a 1set and stable pattern of preferences derived from their union interests. If we apply it the 1974–79 Labour Government, when the unions' power reached its peak, we do indeed find that they used their weight to secure the repeal of the Conservatives' Industrial Relations Act and the enactment of series of measures designed to augment the individual and collective rights of labour (e.g. the Trade Union and Labour Relations Act, the Equal Pay Act). In the early years of the Government many of the pledges hammered out in negotiations between the parliamentary and TUC leadership prior to the 1974 election were fully implemented – often in the teeth of opposition from business and elements within the civil service.

But this is only part of the story. In his searching analysis of 'left-wing unionism', which rehearses the role of Jack Jones and Hugh Scanlon of the AUEW – the left-wing 'terrible twins' – Minkin uncovers portraits of Scanlon and Jones that diverge quite radically from the figure of the 'instrumentally rational' power-maximising 'baron'. In some areas (as noted) they had a clear set of preferences that they consistently pursued. But elsewhere their stance was characterised by uncertainty, flux, lack of confidence and a general willingness to accommodate to the Government. Indeed 'Jones and Scanlon had no particularly distinctive economic position' (Minkin 1991: 169). Trade union officials were frequently to be seen stalking (sometimes to the dismay of the denizens) the corridors of power, but the outcome was less straightforward than is usually supposed. While ministers displayed an unprecedented degree of sensitivity to union preferences those preferences were, in turn, altered, sometimes markedly, in response to the new reference groups and pressures to which their holders were exposed. Both Scanlon and Jones were increasingly persuaded of the validity of the Treasury's definition of the UK's economic policies (though not always of their prescriptions) producing a growing gap between the TUC policies to which the two leaders were officially committed and their real views. More generally, while Minkin agrees that union access to and influence over legislation was indeed greater during the 1974–79 Labour Government than in any other peacetime administration, he holds that the orthodox view has exaggerated its scale, ignores its variability and understates its limits (Minkin 1991: 176). Thus the unions played a very prominent role in the shaping of industrial relations and employment legislation, though their influence in other policy sectors was much more modest and, in a number of areas (such as defence policy), negligible.

But the political trajectory pursued by the two by no means ran in parallel. The one-time Marxist Scanlon moved significantly to the Right as he came to accept the so-called Bacon–Eltis thesis, 'heavily pushed by economic journalists and by the Treasury at this time . . . high levels of public expenditure were starving the market sector of resources, causing deindustrialisation and weakening the economy', and, for that reason, largely acquiesced in the Government's shift to a more monetarist orientation in economic policy (Minkin 1991: 170). Jack Jones, in contrast, remained a (cautious) proponent of higher public spending. How can we account for this?

Rational choice could provide part of the explanation. The AUEW's membership base was in private manufacturing industry, and, therefore, could be seen as a potential beneficiary of cutbacks in public spending (though only on the much-contested assumption that the Bacon–Eltis thesis was correct). The TGWU membership, in contrast, straddled both public and private sectors, manufacturing and services (see Steve Ludlam's discussion in chapter 10). But, equally important – as Minkin stresses – were the two men's differing views on politics and on their respective industrial roles. Scanlon always strictly compartmentalised 'the industrial and the political' and moved increasingly to the Right (he was eventually to be ennobled). Jones's trade unionism, in contrast, was much more infused 'with ideological values of democratic and economic egalitarianism' – a difference reflected in the quite disparate views of the two men on the issue of industrial democracy – and was a relentless campaigner against poverty, especially that of the elderly (Minkin 1991: 165). He was to spend two decades after his retirement as a tireless crusader for higher pensions.

More fundamentally, Minkin challenges the notion that the key motive-force of union leaders, in their relationship with the Labour Party and government, is primarily defined by their desire to maximise their personal and institutional interest. This implies that the unions and the Labour Party constitute two quite separate units. In reality, Minkin shows, union leaders regarded themselves not as outsiders but as insiders, members of the party *they* helped to found: they were as much part of the party as MPs or constituency organisations. Although the issue of the degree of power the unions possessed – as manifested, for instance, in the size of the unions' vote at the Labour Party Conference – was, as they came to acknowledge, a legitimate ground for concern, they insisted that they had as much *right* as any other unit within 'the labour movement' to participate in the party's affairs. This party–unions alliance was, in part, instrumental, a matter of interest and power; it was, however, no less ideological (a shared inventory of values and goals), and expressive and solidaristic (common origins, history and experiences). But this brings us out of the territory of *homo economicus* into that of *homo sociologicus.*

Homo sociologicus

Homo sociologicus is grounded in a notion of 'social action' which differs markedly from that of *homo economicus*, both conceptually and methodologically. It repudiates the notion that all social interaction is explicable in terms of individually driven behaviour, insisting instead on the irreducibility of specifically *social* facts: phenomena that exist outside the minds of individuals – though which are internalised by them (Durkheim 1982). This key methodological premiss derives from Durkheim's understanding of society as 'not a mere sum of individuals; rather the system formed by their association represents a specific reality which has its own characteristic' (quoted in Lukes 1973: 19). *Only* individuals can act, but *how and why* they act as they do is explicable only in terms of the social milieu they inhabit, their upbringing and their social experiences and relationships. What some have called 'methodological collectivism' (or 'holism') contends that collectivities of one sort or another (including society itself) have their own properties, their own regularised patterns which imprint themselves on individuals and shape the way in which they act. Social action is not simply a function of calculated self-interest – since selves themselves are social constructs; and notions of self-interest are therefore contingent upon how the self is constructed (Wildavsky 1994: 140).

Minkin draws heavily from this tradition in developing his three central concepts: 'rules', roles and relations. In a core proposition Minkin contends (1991: 27) that 'it is impossible to understand the trade union–Labour Party relationship (and much else about the Labour Movement) without understanding the powerful and long-lasting restraints produced by adherence to [the] "rules"'. Minkin's concept is put within inverted commas to distinguish it from formal rules, for they are unwritten codes and are only rarely given constitutional status: in effect, they constitute norms and conventions. Norms can be defined as precepts stipulating socially prescribed and acceptable behaviour, 'ideas about how classes or categories ought to behave in specified situations' (Haas and Drabek 1973: 110–11). Here we have a clear contrast between *homo economicus* and *homo sociologicus*. March and Olsen (1984: 741) illustrate the point in comparing the 'choice metaphor' and the 'duty metaphor':

> In a choice metaphor, we assume that political actors consult personal preferences and subjective expectations, then select actions that are as consistent as possible with those preferences and expectations. In a duty metaphor, we assume that political actors associate certain actions with certain situations by rules of appropriateness. What is appropriate for a particular person in a particular situation is defined by the political and social system and transmitted through socialisation.

Minkin follows the 'duty metaphor'.

We must be cautious about over-dichotomous thinking here. *Homo sociologicus* does not (or should not) discount the role of self-interest and ambition – of vanity, status-seeking, greed, even – whose part in the politics of labour receives, from Minkin, its due attention. The point is that such action is 'embedded in an institutional structure of rules, norms, expectations, and traditions that severely limited the free play of individual will and calculation' (March and Olsen 1984: 736).

For Minkin, the key to understanding why the trade unions have not dominated the Labour Party lies in the 'playing of different roles' in a system of functional differentiation (Minkin 1991: 26). Along with the 'rules', *role* is a central organising concept in Minkin's work. A role comprises 'a cluster of norms that applies to any single unit of social interaction' (see Haas and Drabek 1973: 110–1). In other words, the role of, say, a trade union member of the NEC comprises the various norms and conventions attached to it. Role theory posits that role-holders will behave in accordance with role requirements – as formally laid down, as conceived by themselves and as expected by others in the organisation. Thus Minkin contends (1991: 396) that the fundamental flaw of conventional wisdom, with its image of the 'union baron', is that it takes no account of 'the crucial inhibitions involved in trade union role-playing and their obedience to "rules" of the relationship'.

Roles, in turn, mould relationships by shaping the way in which members interact, laying down sets of mutual expectations and anticipations. Established relations between political and trade union role-holders comprised the superstructure of understanding that knits the party together. Conversely, the belief that roles were being transgressed could rupture relations and cause acute internal dissension. Those who refused to enact their roles in the appropriate manner – Arthur Scargill of the National Union of Miners being a classic example – would always be outriders. Understanding purposive conduct within an organisation, then, is not simply a matter of analysing how power-and interest-maximising individuals navigate institutional rules, constraints and opportunities the better to satisfy their goals, for those very goals, and the choice of means to realise them, are shaped by the ethos of the organisation.

Roles and 'rules'

Minkin applies these analytical categories by considering the roles that trade union and party leaders play: 'How and when did it happen that union leaders adopted particular rules? What agency or processes continued to socialise new union leaders into the codes of conduct?' (Minkin 1997: 283). The main organising motif in the conceptual structure of *The Contentious Alliance* is his painstaking elaboration of the 'rules'. These 'rules' are akin to Durkheim's *conscience collective*: 'the beliefs, tendencies and practices of the group taken collectively' and, by virtue of their collective provenance, 'invested with a special authority' (Durkheim 1982: 55). Minkin's central proposition (1991: xiv) is that power relations between the unions and the party 'cannot be fully understood without appreciating the inhibitions, restrictions and constraints that the "rules" produced'. These rules 'acted as boundaries producing inhibitions which prevented the absolute supremacy of leadership groups in either wing of the relationship'.

What are these 'rules'? Minkin enumerates the following: freedom, democracy, unity and solidarity, to which is coupled, slightly awkwardly, priority – 'the operative principle of trade unionism'.

- *Freedom* is defined in terms of autonomy: 'the collective capacity to promote the industrial freedom of workers and the right to realise this with minimum interference from political bodies'. By extension this came to encompass mutual respect for the independence and institutional integrity of the labour movement's industrial and political wings, a respect which, in turn, was interpreted to bar the application by trade unionists of party sanctions to bring party policy into line with that of the TUC – 'a conscious self-restraint in the use of potential levers of power' (Minkin 1991: 28, 30). Irrespective of the precise wording of the formal rules, neither political nor industrial leaders were expected to encroach upon the territory of the other, defined by its functional responsibilities.

- By *democracy* was meant a commitment to collective majoritarian decision-making – though firmly qualified by respect for the autonomy of the PLP and the frontbench over the prioritising and method of implementing Labour Party Conference decisions.
- *Unity* referred to the striving after maximum consensus and the containing of disagreements, and was associated also with an ingrained belief that parliamentary leadership should be pre-eminent on the NEC.
- *Solidarity* was an application of the 'fundamental ethics of trade unionism', which prescribed 'loyalty to the collective community [and] the sacrifice, if necessary, of immediate sectional interest'. In the context of party–unions relations it took the form of trade union leaders assuming a 'parental obligation to the Party to play a stabilising role' (Minkin 1991: 37–8). These emotional and moral compulsions of solidarity with party and (when in office) Government could ' be so great times to produce a denial of immediate interest' (1991: 178). An interesting example of this was the position – or, rather, the reluctance to take a position – of trade union leaderswhen the Labour Cabinet engaged in its prolonged struggle over whether to accept the harsh conditions of the IMF loan in 1976. Tony Crosland proved a formidable and lucid critic of the severe cutbacks in public spending – which were to lead an actual *fall* in health spending – demanded by the IMF (and its controllers in Washington), but trade union leaders like Scanlon and Jones, historically and formally still well to Crosland's Left, kept quiet. The survival of the Labour Government, they believed, was at stake and it was *not* the role of union leaders in such circumstances to rock the boat.
- These values are supplemented by the principle of *priority* (Minkin 1991: 40–2). While the unions had policies on a very wide range of issues, not all are actively promoted. Lifetime immersion in collective bargaining encouraged 'a pragmatic approach to problem-solving, a reliance on experience as a guide to appropriate response and a stress on the best available outcome'. Conceptions of realism and practical politics fused with a focus on those matters which impinged most forcefully on the institutional needs of unions, and which were uppermost in the minds of their members to determine those goals and policies that were accorded priority. Thus in practice the willingness of union leaders to assert their power was shaped and constrained by a range of factors: the relevance of particular issues to their unions; the extent to which they were bound by unequivocal union mandates; the preferences of the parliamentary leadership; and the need to sustain the unity and the electoral appeal of the party.

How did the 'rules' and the performance of the roles they engendered operate to form regular and discernible patterns of behaviour? Let us return to the comparison between *homo economicus* and *homo sociologicus*. For the former the relationship between subject and object, between actor and the external environment, is relatively unproblematical. If actors are 'rational' – that is, if understanding is informed and open-minded, interests clearly and precisely identified, and 'realities' dispassionately appraised – a cool assessment can be made as to how their ends can be most efficiently achieved. As events are observed, feedback allows experience to guide judgement and amend behaviour accordingly (March and Olsen 1988: 343). The analyst, accordingly, can (in a way broadly comparable to that of the natural scientist) observe, classify, explain and perhaps even predict patterned behaviour. *Homo sociologicus*, however, construes the relationship between actor and setting quite differently. Social and natural phenomena differ fundamentally because in the former conscious actors invest with meaning the events they experience. Accordingly, since 'the distinctive trait of human behaviour is . . . that there are connections and rules that can be interpretively understood', the task of the social scientist is decipher them – to explore how people make sense of the situations they encounter (Weber quoted in Eckstein 1996: 483). This is the task Minkin sets for himself.

His first step is to determine the process by which the 'rules' emerged. It is characteristic of Minkin's method (first elaborated in *The Labour Party Conference*) to explain institutions by tracing their development historically. The evolution of the 'rules' he sees as 'in the main, an organic process', the products of the 'fundamental values of trade unionism', derived ultimately from the encounter between institutional needs and industrial experience. In a way typical of the institutions of labour in Britain, it took the form of 'unwritten understandings and a strong sense of the protocol of rule-governed behaviour' (Minkin 1991: 27). The content of the 'rules' stemmed from functional differentiation, the growing division of responsibilities between what came to be labelled the industrial and political wings of 'the movement': each had its own needs, tasks and interests, with the relationship regulated by common norms. Each new generation was inducted into the culture by organisational socialisation, that process by which 'the beliefs, norms and perspectives of participants are brought into line with those of the organisation' (Etzioni 1965: 246). Minkin (1991: 46) writes:

> Trade union leaders were socialised into understanding role responsibilities and constraints. General Council definitions of 'appropriate behaviour' became a measure of what was perceived as 'political maturity'. This socialisation process was enforced primarily by normative pressures, by 'embarrassment, guilt and group hostility' rather than by sanctions though these . . . were available.

He charts how new left-wing members of the NEC's trade union section were encouraged to 'integrate within "the union group" and play the loyal game as it had been played in the past' (1991: 404–5). Tom Sawyer, who rose to prominence as a senior official of NUPE (the National Union of Public Employees) in the late 1970s, and joined the NEC as a keen 'Bennite', gradually evolved into a stalwart of the trade union section (and, indeed, eventually became general secretary of the party) as he increasingly conformed to expectations as to how the role of a trade union NEC member should be properly discharged. More generally, Minkin uncovers the process by which left-wing leaders – notably Jack Jones and Hugh Scanlon – who initially queried some of the 'rules', increasingly came to subscribe to them. They became more loath to challenge the policy-making prerogative of the parliamentary leadership (outside of those areas designated as appropriate objectives for joint party–unions determination) and increasingly adopted a 'protective' role.

All this explains persistence – recurrent and stable patterns in party–union relations: the 'rules' were 'essentially rules of anchorage', locating 'a base and moorings from which it was dangerous to move too far' (Minkin 1991: 42). But how do we then account for conflict and change? Minkin's purpose is not only to characterise the parameters which were shaped by the party–unions connection but to identify the forces that allowed it to develop; equally, not only to explain what held it together but what pulled it apart. What, above all, imparted the dynamic to the alliance was that it was, Minkin stresses throughout, always a *contentious* one defined not only by normatively regulated co-operation but by clashes of interest, priorities and aspirations. 'To understand fully the relationship between trade unions and the Labour Party', he observes (1991: 628), 'we have to appreciate both its consistencies and its variabilities.' His perspective can best be defined as 'interactionist', one that envisages norms, roles and relationships coming into conflict and being perpetually revised as circumstances, pressures, political alignments all mutate. From this perspective, organisations can be conceived as arenas characterised by the on-going processes of negotiation and bargaining, where 'rules', roles and relationships constantly evolve in response to shifts in the balance of power, in the pattern of political alignments, and in the face of conflicting interests and priorities and environmental shocks. Thus there is always a disparity between, on the one hand, role *prescriptions* and expectations (not least from the rank and file) and, on the other, leaders' role *performances*, with the latter influenced by multiple forces ranging from role demands, personal role definitions (and idiosyncrasies) and the sheer pressure of events and conflicting demands. This disparity often surfaced in accusations (with varying degrees of credibility) by disillusioned rank-and-filers that a union leader had 'sold-out' and had been 'bought'

Minkin also notes that the 'rules' were not immutable. They were always 'clearer in what they excluded than what they prescribed', supplying abundant room for interpretation and reworking. There was sufficient plasticity to allow for trade union diversity, the shifting balance of Left and Right political traditions, and different views as to how role responsibilities could best be discharged (Minkin 1991: 43). One instance of this plasticity was 'multiple-role playing'. As already noted the relations of Jones and Scanlon with former allies on the party's Left deteriorated after 1974 and, at times, became quite strained. Notwithstanding, when casting union votes, at the Labour Party Conference or for the women's section of the NEC, they continued to back left-wing candidates. What was appropriate conduct in one forum was not necessarily appropriate in another.

The continued relevance of Minkin

The aforementioned account allows for and helps to explain incremental change in the relationship – but what if the change was qualitative? The 'rules' – the whole labourist culture – have since the election of Tony Blair to Labour's leadership been under sustained assault. Blair, it has been noted, has 'no sympathy, enthusiasm or concern for the collective values of trade unionism such as solidarity and feels no need to identify himself with them' (Taylor 2000). The fact that the party–unions relationship 'had changed in quite fundamental ways' (Howell 2000: 34) is a judgement from which few would dissent. The party–unions connection acquired many of its defining properties, it has been seen in this chapter, from a process of functional differentiation. But this notion implies the existence of a common organism, a system each of whose inter-related parts had a distinct function to discharge but which operated for the survival and advancement of the whole. But is this any long true – has functional specialisation and differentiation metamorphosed into separation?

Minkin identifies four variables determining the extent to which harmony characterised the relationship:

- *ideology* registers the degree to which there was 'general ideological agreement on aims and values';
- *interest* registers the degree of correspondence between unions' definitions of the interests of the workforce and the party leadership's notion of the national interest;
- *social affinity* registers the degree of social affinity between the leaderships of the two wings; and
- *strategic convergence* registers the degree of strategic compatibility between the party and the unions.

To the extent that there was sufficient overlap in these four areas, unity of purpose could be sustained. There was enough commonality to sustain the alliance, though 'there was also enough divergence to engender permanent tensions' (Minkin 1991: 9).

As a preliminary to exploring the argument further I want to point to what seems to me to be a weakness in Minkin's account. He suggests that the 'rules', and the role responsibilities they engendered, related to *political* as much as *industrial* leaders of the movement. Though there were 'some important variations in definition and emphasis', he held that the 'rules' enmeshed both parliamentary and trade union leadership in 'mutual expectations and obligations' (1991: 286–7, 47). But is this claim really substantiated? He himself acknowledges (1991: 45) that the '"rules" laid down a network of obligations, mutual in form but most restrictive in effect, upon the potentially omnipotent trade unions and their senior leaders'. I think we need to take this further. There was always much greater variation in the degree to which the outlook of political leaders was permeated by the 'rules'. This has been taken much further with the emergence of 'New Labour', which is characterised as a whole (there are individual differences) by a wariness towards anything that smacks too much of (what the 'New' chooses to label) 'Old Labour'. For some, indeed, proximity to the unions seems to cause profound discomfort. Invocation of 'This Great Movement of Ours' (TIGMOO) was a staple of the Conference's rhetoric, but for many reflected a real sense of common traditions, loyalties and symbols. For many within New Labour circles, TIGMOO belongs to the dark days, an old skin now cast off. It may well be that one of the most profound changes signalled by New Labour is the rapid dwindling among the parliamentary leadership of any real feeling of involvement in a shared movement.

Weakening if not terminating the alliance, Chris Howell argues, is 'the defining core of the [Blairite] modernisation project'. He adduces as evidence the following points: that both in setting the new minimum wage and in reshaping industrial relations legislation closer attention was paid to the concerns of business than to those of the unions. The overwhelming bulk of Conservative industrial relations legislation remains in force, and has been endorsed by New Labour, including strict regulation of, and limits upon, industrial action and the survival of a highly flexible labour market. Procedurally, business is far better represented in the numerous government task forces than by the unions, while union influence is heavily reliant on informal and personal contacts (Howell 2000: 33).

Nevertheless, as Ludlam (2001) has pointed out, the alliance has displayed unexpected resilience. Though there is no doubt that the influence and access the unions possess now is much less than under any previous majority Labour Government, they are still appreciably greater than under the Tories – and that is unlikely to change. In some major areas of policy – notably the growing private sector involvement in the delivery of public services and the enthusiasm for 'labour market flexibility' – the gap between the Government and the unions is now alarmingly wide, though in other areas the balance sheet for the unions is much more positive. North-European-style corporatism will not be introduced, one can confidently predict, under New Labour, but at least the unions are once more 'insiders'. Conversely, though the party is much less reliant on trade union money than in the past, it is still heavily dependent for the effective conduct of election campaigns on the unions' resources – manpower, office space and equipment. Indeed, as evidence mounts that the number and commitment of constituency activists is rapidly shrinking – the grass is coming away at the roots – that dependence will almost certainly intensify. Equally, trade union organisations and networks have proved invaluable allies for New Labourites (Blairites and Brownites) – whether in terms of promoting leaders (there have been setbacks here!), securing parliamentary nominations, or competing for places in party organs such as the NEC, the Policy Forum and the Scottish, Welsh and London Executives (Shaw 2001). And 'parental obligation to the Party to play a stabilising role' continues to manifest itself mainly in protective loyalty to a Labour Government in the face of left-wing criticism – as demonstrated by the behaviour of the trade union section of the NEC (Davies 2001). It is noticeable that calls from New Labour circles for a loosening of the connection are now more muted.

There are, however, warning signs. For the first time, union funding is being used as an instrument of pressure, though largely due to demands from an increasingly disenchanted rank and file within the public sector unions. In July 2001 the GMBU (General Workers' and Boilermakers' Union) – an organisation which has never been associated with the Left – decided to cut £1 million over four years from its funding of the party. In the public service union UNISON, rank and file pressure forced the passage of a motion calling for a review of the party–unions link

(*Guardian*, 18 July 2001) Indeed, some commentators have suggested that the unions should consider giving priority to representing their members' interests 'rather than being expected to dance to the tune of a piper they pay' (Kevin Maguire in *Guardian*, 26 June 2001). The party–unions connection is entering upon its most turbulent phase yet.

Conclusion

Minkin has demolished the image of the 'bullies with the block vote', of 'union barons' lording it over the party. By a relentless accumulation of detail he punctures one myth after another. But he goes well beyond correcting the historical record: he explains why the baronial power thesis is wrong. In so doing, he uncovers the limits of rational-choice-style theories of political behaviour. Political actors are role-players and their roles combine into complexes and are enshrined in organisational forms. Roles comprise norms and conventions, or the 'rules', and these, he convincingly establishes, have profoundly affected power- and policy-making within the party. Above all, they have structured the party–unions connection. Minkin argues (1991: 27):

> The role playing, the 'rules' and the protocol which went with them produced a syndrome of inhibition and self-control which was the most remarkable feature of a relationship in which all the potential levers of power appeared to lie in the hands of the unions. But they also provided a network of *mutual* restraint specifying obligations which were a duty on both sides of the relationship.

And role-playing, we see, was a matter of constant renegotiation and mutual adjustment – a creative exercise, and a source of change and of conflict as well as of persistence. Parties, he shows, are social as well as political systems, intricate fabrics of positions, roles, rules and relationships, as well as a forum for competing ideas and interests.

But is Minkin the historian of a movement that is reaching the end of its natural life? The degree of general ideological agreement on aims and values between 'New' Labour and the bulk of the affiliated unions has substantially diminished. Equally significant is the fraying of the functional and solidaristic bases of cohesion: the old 'ties of sentiment and loyalty and agreed ideological commitment', as Robert Taylor (2000) has put it, are now fading away. The Labour Party, certainly, is undergoing a process of transformation. Is the link (as a growing number within the unions are beginning to argue) now a handicap for the unions and their members? Has the party's metamorphosis into 'New' Labour fundamentally altered the rules and norms governing the relationship? We do not know the answers. But only by studying the changing norms, conventions, role conceptions and aspirations – the cultural fabric of organisational life – can we commence the search for answers. In short, *homo sociologicus*, as *The Contentious Alliance* demonstrates so well, still has much more to offer than does *homo economicus*.

References

Unless indicated, the place of publication is London.

Artis, M. and Cobham, D. (1991) *Labour's Economic Policies 1974–79*, Manchester

Barnes, D. and Reid, E. (1980) *Governments and Trade Unions: The British Experience, 1964–79*

Davies, L. (2001) *Through the Looking Glass*

Downs, A. (1957) *An Economic Theory of Democracy*

Durkheim, E. (1982) *The Rules of the Sociological Method*, 8th edition, New York

Eckstein, H. (1996) 'Culture as a foundation concept for the social sciences', *Journal of Theoretical Politics*, 8:4

Elster, J. (1989) 'Social norms and economic theory', *Journal of Economic Perspectives*, 3:4

Etzioni, A. (1965) *The Comparative Analysis of Complex Organisations*

Haas, J. E. and Drabek, T. E. (1973) *Complex Organisations: A Sociological Perspective*

Harrison, B. (1996) *The Transformation of British Politics 1860–1995*, Oxford

Howell, C. (2000) 'Is there a Third Way for the party–union relationship? The industrial relations project of New Labour', paper presented at the Political Studies Association Annual Conference

Kitschelt, H. (1994) *The Transformation of European Social Democracy*, Cambridge

Ludlam, S. (2001) 'New Labour and the unions: the end of the contentious alliance?', in Ludlam, S. and Smith, M. J. (eds) *New Labour in Government*

Lukes, S. (1973) *Emile Durkheim: His Life and Works*, Harmondsworth

March, J. G. and Olsen, J. P. (1975) 'The uncertainty of the past: organizational learning under ambiguity', *European Journal of Political Research*, 3

March, J. G. and Olsen, J. P. (1984) 'The new institutionalism: organisational factors in political life', *American Political Science Review*, 78:3

Marquand, D. (1991) *The Progressive Dilemma*

Minkin, L. (1978a) 'The party connection: divergence and convergence in the British labour movement', *Government and Opposition*, 13:4

Minkin, L. (1978b) *The Labour Party Conference: A Study in the Politics of Intra-Party Democracy*, Manchester

Minkin, L. (1991) *The Contentious Alliance: Trade Unions and the Labour Party*, Edinburgh

Minkin, L. (1997) *Exits and Entrances: Political Research as a Creative Art*, Sheffield

Shaw, E. (2001) 'New Labour: new pathways to Parliament', *Parliamentary Affairs*, 54:1

Shepsle, K. (1989) 'Studying institutions: some lessons from the rational choice approach', *Journal of Theoretical Politics*, 1

Sil, R. (2000) 'The foundations of eclecticism', *Journal of Theoretical Politics*, 12:3

Taylor, R. (2000) 'Economic reform and new industrial relations', available online: www.europaprogrammet.no/sider/4_publikasjoner/4_bokerhefter/hefter/98_5/taylor.html

Wildavsky, A. (1994) 'Self-interest and rational choice', *Journal of Theoretical Politics*, 6:2

12

How to study the Labour Party: contextual, analytical and theoretical issues

Colin Hay

The political analysis and the political economy of the British Labour Party have tended to concern themselves principally with the concrete and the substantive. This is both unremarkable and entirely legitimate. Yet something is potentially lost. For while an aim of the present collection is to discuss the principal positions of some of the leading exponents in this literature, it cannot be doubted that the literature rests largely on rarely acknowledged and generally unstated assumptions about basic analytical questions. If we are to encourage dialogue between competing interpretations of Labour, we might benefit from rendering such assumptions explicit. Moreover, the present is a particularly opportune time for such reflections, as contemporary political analysis is perhaps more conscious than it has ever been of its most fundamental analytical assumptions (see Hay 2002a).

In what follows four core themes are identified, each of which can be associated with what might tentatively be termed the 'new political science of British politics'. Each serves to highlight a distinctive aspect of the issue of causality; and each has a special relevance to labour studies in general and to the political science and the political economy of Labour in particular. They are:

- the relationship between structure and agency, context and conduct;
- the relationship between the discursive and the material, between the ideas held about the world and that world itself;
- the relative significance of political, economic and cultural factors; and
- the relative significance of domestic, international and transnational factors.

Before considering each of these themes in more detail, it is important to enter a few cautionary remarks. Arguments such as that presented here are unavoidably controversial and they need to be handled with care: after all, political scientists are, by convention, wary of analytical prescription. It is important, then, at the outset that to clarify the aims and intentions of what follows, while cautioning against certain potential misinterpretations.

First, although the argument presented here has important implications for the conduct of labour studies more generally, and although the chapter does make the general case for reinserting labour within the analysis of the Labour Party, the substantive contribution of this chapter is more limited. Given constraints of space I confine my observations to writings on the political science and the political economy of the British Labour Party published since the 1980s. Second, and crucially, while the argument will not be entirely neutral in respect of interpretations of Labour, I do not aim to champion a particular interpretation (for that, see Coates and Hay 2001; Hay 1999). This chapter is not so much concerned with the substantive detail of particular accounts of recent Labour history as it is with the compatibility of specific interpretations with the theoretical assumptions which ostensibly inform them. Consequently, what follows is consistent with a range of diverse descriptive accounts, substantive interpretations and theoretical positions – positions the author does not necessarily share. The chapter is a call for greater theoretical reflexivity, clarity and internal consistency rather than a more partisan appeal for a particular approach.

My aim is, in essence, two-fold. First I highlight a series of key analytical issues. These divide the protagonists in what at first appear to be substantive disputes that might be adjudicated empirically (such as the roles of political volition and economic imperatives in the trajectory of Labour's economic policy since the mid-1980s). Frequently, in such controversies, it is not so much the empirical evidence as the selection of what counts as evidence in the first place and the interpretation placed on it that divides analysts. Here the trading of empirical claim and counter-claim may serve only to institutionalise a dialogue of the deaf. The result is that underlying disagreements in fundamental theoretical or analytical assumptions remain unacknowledged and unexamined. Drawing attention to the implicit and often intuitive assumptions on which such contemporary disputes so frequently hinge, may serve to, first, promote greater analytical clarity; second, facilitate theoretical dialogue and reflexivity; and, finally, encourage analysts to render explicit the core analytical assumptions on which their work is premised and of which one might legitimately expect a degree of internal consistency.

This is part and parcel of an approach to the conduct of theoretical and empirical debate which judges accounts by the standards they themselves propose rather than those foisted upon them externally. It places a premium on theoretical consistency, but is largely neutral with regard to the substantive content of accounts consistent with a given set of (acknowledged) analytical assumptions. Of course, this is not to suggest that in evaluating contending accounts we should restrict ourselves to judgements based purely on criteria of theoretical consistency. Work that draws freely on implicit but nonetheless incommensurate analytical assumptions should be exposed as doing so. This, however, is much easier if we can make such issues as explicit as possible in the first place.

The second objective is perhaps rather more prescriptive. I seek to highlight a range of issues which, though perhaps characteristic of a 'new political science of British politics', have arguably tended to be overlooked or, at least, are insufficiently developed in the political analysis and the political economy of Labour. Three issues in particular might here be noted as structuring much of the discussion in the sections that follow. They relate to the needs to:

- contextualise contemporary political dynamics economically and contemporary economic dynamics politically;
- transcend the artificial distinction between domestic, comparative and international or transnational analysis and develop further the capacity to relate political and economic dynamics at a variety of spatial scales; and
- exercise greater sensitivity to the role of ideas as causal variables in the analysis and interpretation of political and economic processes.

As may already be clear, the agenda of this chapter is informed by a growing sense of the emergence of a more reflexive, more modest and more consciously theory-informed political analysis. It is with this 'new political science of British politics' that I should perhaps begin.

A new political science of British politics?

Some might think it premature to suggest there is now a 'new political science of British politics' – and the label is undoubtedly one that few would volunteer as a badge of self-identification. Moreover, the political science of British politics has always been characterised by diversity and intellectual pluralism. Nonetheless, a series of common and consistent themes has emerged in recent work that reflects a new sprit of analytical reflexivity among more theory-inclined analysts. While such themes are by no means confined to studies of British politics, their effects are now filtering into more substantive analyses, including contemporary work on the political development of Britain (see, for instance, Bevir and Rhodes 1998, 1999; English and Kenny 1999; Kerr 2001; Marsh, Buller, Hay, Johnston, Kerr, McAnulla and Watson 1999; Smith 1999). What is perhaps most interesting about this emergent political science is the extent to which its distinctive analytical concerns are shared by an unlikely assortment of authors defending a variety of otherwise antagonistic theoretical approaches. Though divided by the absence of a common theoretical perspective, self-styled behaviouralists, philosophical realists, neo-institutionalists, constructivists and interpretetivists increasingly appeal to a common set of core analytical concerns.

In summarising these concerns (Hay 2002b: 11), it can be said that there is

- a tendency to place contemporary dynamics in their historical (that is temporal) and national (or spatial) context;
- a desire to emphasise how institutions and ideas mediate the political process, along with a related concern to track change from inputs (intentions and context) to outcomes (whether intended or unintended);
- a greater willingness to recognise the uncertainty of outcomes and hence to acknowledge the significance of unintended consequences;
- the more open acknowledgement of the need to locate events in Britain in relation to those in comparable countries;
- a recognition of the blurring of a once rigid demarcation between domestic and international politics and a growing recognition of the significance of

institutional forces, such as the European Union, that operate above the lone nation state;
- a broadening of what might legitimately be studied by political analysts. This is reflected in a greater recognition, say, of the role of cultural or economic factors in determining what might appear to be purely political developments; and
- a greater appreciation of the contribution to political outcomes of ideational variables (such as values, paradigms, ideology and rhetoric).

Taken together these closely related concerns constitute, just as they also reflect, a challenge to the modes of analysis that have hitherto dominated the political science and political economy of post-war British politics. They have implications for the analysis of the Labour Party and for labour studies more generally. It is to these that I now turn, beginning with factors specific to the political analysis of Labour, before turning to those that might be thought to apply more generally to contemporary political analysis.

Revisiting the political analysis of labour/Labour

It is tempting to suggest that while the new political science of British politics, tentatively outlined above, has important implications for political analysis in general it has no specific implications for the political analysis of Labour. For the analysis of Labour is, in the end, an exercise in analysis like any other. In so far as the new political science poses challenges, it does so largely independently of the specific object of their analytical attentions.

This is undoubtedly the case. However, there is perhaps one exception that follows directly from the above. It can be stated simply: labour studies should not be regarded, as sometimes it is, as a separate or independent sphere of analysis. This is, in fact, a specific implication of a more general point. The new political science identified above is distinctly post-disciplinary in its outlook. It is deeply suspicious of arbitrarily imposed boundaries and the associated apportioning of primary variables (party variables to political science, macro-economic variables to economics, interactive variables to sociology, and so forth). It has, if anything, even less sympathy with sub-disciplinary sectarianism. While labour studies can, then, be seen as a sub-field of political economy, political science or political history, it can also be more progressively presented as a post-disciplinary arena in which the tools appropriate to the analysis and interpretation of labour – whatever their origins – can be brought together. In so far as this describes the practice of contemporary labour studies, it might be seen to herald the emergence of the new political science of British politics; in so far as it does not, it can only benefit from such a development.

If there are few, if any, specific implications of the new political science for the political analysis of Labour, then there are nonetheless a series of points which, though potentially generalisable, might be regarded as having particular purchase for a post-disciplinary labour studies. The first of these is, again, stated simply, though its implications are more involved. It concerns the place of labour within labour–Labour studies: labour, in terms of the organised or disorganised working class, needs to be reinserted into the analysis of Labour the political organisation. It might seem strange to associate such a claim with contemporary currents in British political science. It would be perverse indeed to suggest that there is anything terribly original or innovative about putting the 'L' back into labour studies. Yet, though not, perhaps, immediately obvious, there are clear links between the latter's more reflexive and integrated approach to political analysis and the return to labour in labour studies.

At this point it is important to note that there are plenty of analysts of both Labour (Party) and labour (movement) who need no reminder of labour studies' erstwhile object of analysis. The point, however, is that here new political science and traditional labour studies might speak with one voice. For, in their attempts to scrutinise and interrogate its previously unacknowledged and intuitive assumptions, exponents of the new political science have tended to broaden their concept of 'the political' and to reject the pervasive and corrosive legacy of pluralist assumptions (Marsh 2002). The result has been:

- a rejection of input-loaded models of political processes (such as pluralism and elitism);
- an associated reconnection of political inputs and outcomes;
- a far greater emphasis upon the uneven distribution of strategic resources; and,
- a related concern with a range of distributional asymmetries (such as class, gender and ethnicity).

Each serves to reposition the analysis of labour at the heart of labour studies – where it rightly belongs.

A second observation also chimes with traditional labour studies. We should be careful to interrogate assumptions we may be tempted to internalise relating to Labour's highly mythologised past (see also Fielding 2000a, 2000b). With a Labour prime minister currently resident in Downing Street, a fact attributed by many to the party's ability to distance itself in opposition from a particular construction of a previous incarnation ('Old Labour'), it is more important than ever that we scrutinise such constructions. It is perhaps equally imperative that we acknowledge the significance of such popular fictions as potential causal factors in their own right (a point to which we return). Thus, the appeal of such constructions should itself be of interest. The point is, however, that there is world of difference between internalising such convenient fictions as baseline assumptions that might inform analysis of the present and examining their conditions of emergence, diffusion and persuasion. Collectively, students of Labour need to engage in rather more of the latter and rather less of the former. The pressures on political analysts of all persuasions to incorporate an ever-greater range of variables in a (supposedly) ever-more complex and interdependent world are considerable and growing. Arguably, they make analysis of the present increasingly difficult. Yet in such a context, it is, if anything, more important that we refuse to trade in our historical sense for the mistaken promise of achieving a greater purchase on the present by concentrating on more obviously immediate factors (for useful attempts to locate recent developments in a historical context, see Brivati and Bale 1997; Brivati and Heffernan 2000; Tanner, Thane and Tiratsoo 2000).

Third, it is important (as arguably it always was) to examine and re-examine Labour's complex associations with the highly distinctive European tradition of social democracy, a distinctiveness we overlook at our peril. The term *social democracy* has become increasingly slippery as it has become ever-more-loosely invoked and ever-more-intimately connected to discussions of the future of Centre-Left political parties across Europe. What this suggests is the value of comparative labour studies. Important points follow from an attempt to locate contemporary British political dynamics comparatively. In particular, Labour's connection to European social democracy was always somewhat tenuous and indirect (see, for instance, Clift 2001; Drucker 1979; George and Haythorne 1996; Minkin 1991). It is surely telling, for instance, that Jose Harris's exhaustive survey (2000) of Labour's social and political thought for the centenary history of the party makes no reference, explicit or implicit, to the European tradition of social democracy. The influence of continental social democracy on Labour's thinking has been modest indeed.

Additionally, by any institutional definition of social democracy which looks at outcomes rather than merely at articulated aspirations, Labour's much-vaunted post-war social democratic past looks rather different. Such a definition of social democracy (as a regime-type as distinct from a political ideology or ethos) is conventional in comparative political economy, though rare in British labour studies. For the authors who deploy such a conception (for instance, Berman 1998; Garrett 1998; Pontusson 1992), Britain is – and throughout the post-war period always has been – the European archetype of market liberalism, not of social democracy.

Moreover, as Mark Wickham-Jones (2000) has persuasively argued, Labour's early 'modernisation' process under Kinnock and Smith – a process more conventionally seen as a slow march from social democracy – was in fact animated, perhaps for the first time in the party's history, by a genuine attempt to embrace the European social democratic tradition (see also Clift 2001; George and Haythorne 1996; Sassoon 1998; and, for evidence of this kind of thinking among Kinnock's closest advisors, Eatwell 1992). Of course, this abortive strategy was never more than aspirational – and, as aspirations go, a rather optimistic one at that. Certainly the completion of the modernisation process under Blair represented a systematic repudiation of such a vision and an attempt, instead, to project a 'Third Way', 'renewed' or 'post'-social democratic alternative. Ironically, in recent years, this has increasingly come to be re-packaged for export as a modernised 'European social model', appropriate, where the European tradition of social democracy was not, to the new competitive environment summoned by an era of globalisation.

As this perhaps suggests, whether Labour is seen as a party with a social democratic past, a party with a social democratic present but not past, or a party that has never been nor is ever likely to become social democratic depends on one's definition of social democracy. Yet if it is accepted that Labour's origins do not reside in the continental European social democratic tradition, but in a rather more Anglophone 'labourism' (as, for instance, in Drucker 1979; Minkin 1991), then whether New Labour represents a reclaiming, disavowal or betrayal of that tradition is not especially significant. For what it is worth, my own opinion is that it is wrong to see Labour as part of the European social democratic tradition; and at a time when the current Government claims to offer a 'renewed' social democratic model for European export, it may well be appropriate to say so.

A final consideration may serve as an important point of departure for the concluding section of this chapter. It is stated simply, though its implications, if taken seriously, are considerable. As political analysts and, perhaps especially, as political economists of Labour, we should be extremely careful not to confine ourselves only to holding opinions on matters in which we might present the Labour Party or movement as an obvious or significant agent. There is, understandably, a certain tendency in labour studies to restrict the analytical enterprise to the description of processes and the elucidation of causal mechanisms in which Labour and labour feature as prominent agents. The result may be a certain tendency to silence on the key question of the exogenous constraints invariably held to circumscribe the realm of feasible political agency for such actors. In an era of putative globalisation, in which the logic of non-negotiable external economic constraint is frequently invoked, self-declared political economists of Labour–labour cannot but afford to have an opinion on the empirical content of such claims. If that entails a temporary suspension of their analyses of Labour, until such time as they are better informed as to the nature of Britain's external economic exposure, then so be it.

Towards a post–disciplinary political analysis of Labour

The preceding section identified some of the principal substantive issues that any balanced assessment and evaluation of Labour's recent history must surely consider. The rest of the chapter moves from factors specific to the political analysis and political economy of Labour to those that are more general. To reiterate, the argument here echoes that of an earlier collaborative study of the post-war period, *Postwar British Politics in Perspective* (Marsh *et al.* 1999), and it is that the principal positions in debates which characterise labour studies today, like those on the periodisation of political development in post-war Britain, rest on generally unstated assumptions about a core set of basic analytical questions. Rendering these explicit should clarify the nature of the debate and the precise character of the specific positions adopted by the principal protagonists, thereby contributing to what otherwise threatens to become a dialogue of the deaf.

In making this argument, we should return to the four central issues introduced at the opening of the chapter, each of which serves to highlight a distinct aspect of the question of causality. Before considering each in turn, however, it is perhaps important to emphasise that what unites these issues in the new political science of British politics is a common emphasis on interconnectedness and what is sometimes termed 'complex interdependence'. Thus, the remainder of the chapter aims to trace the implications of such a condition of interdependence for the practice of political analysis – and of labour studies as an exercise in political analysis.

Interconnectedness and interdependence

It is tempting to argue, as many have, that the world we inhabit is more complex, interdependent and interconnected than ever before. Yet for present purposes what matters is not whether contemporary levels of interdependence are unprecedented historically but that we inhabit an interdependent world which must be analysed as such.

Alarmingly, conventional approaches to the social sciences, based on rigid disciplinary demarcations, do not prepare us well for a world of interdependence. Political scientists deal poorly with economic variables, just as economists deal poorly with political variables. Moreover, domestically focused analysts deal poorly with international dynamics, just as international analysts deal poorly with domestic dynamics. In a world of spatial and sectoral *independence*, these deficiencies do not amount to a problem. Yet that is *not* the world we inhabit. In short, in an interdependent world that does not respect spatial and sectoral divisions of analytical work such divisions will simply not suffice.

This is the challenge to which the new political science of British politics is a response, and it has important implications for labour studies. First, it points to the obvious occupational hazards of disciplinary and sub-disciplinary boundaries which are, arguably, present in a most acute way in labour studies. Stated most bluntly, in a world of (acknowledged) interdependence, discipline- or sub-discipline-specific approaches to social, political and economic analysis will tend to rely on assumptions – the validity of which they are incapable of adjudicating – generated by other disciplinary or sub-disciplinary specialisms. This is nowhere more clear than in the literature on the political economy of New Labour and the imperatives globalisation supposedly summons. Here the debate circles endlessly around, without ever closing in on, the nature and the degree of negotiability of the constraints that Britain's external economic interdependence is seen to imply. Opinions vary wildly. Yet what is almost entirely absent from such discussions is any attempt to describe empirically, let alone to evaluate, the precise nature of Britain's external economic relations – with respect to trade, finance and foreign direct investment. Indeed, in the vast majority of accounts, a crude, simplistic and never more than anecdotally empirical business-school or hyper-globalist orthodoxy is simply internalised and assumed to reflect the limits of our knowledge on such matters, with scant regard to the now substantial empirical evidence. That evidence, for what it is worth, shows if anything a consistent de-globalising of the British economy over the last forty years associated with the process – almost wholly absent from the existing debate – of European economic integration (Hay 2002c).

This is but one example. What it, and others like it, suggest is that, as political analysts and political economists of Labour, we simply cannot afford, if ever we could, to get by without a rather more thorough grasp of the cognate disciplines on whose assumptions we have increasingly come to rely. Yet it is not only the interdependence of different spatial scales to which the new political science draws attention. Increasingly central to its analytical concerns has been the interdependence of political conduct, political discourse and political context – in short, the thorny perennials of structure and agency, the discursive and the material. It is to these that I now turn – drawing, for illustrative purposes, on the modernisation of the Labour Party and an argument first outlined in *The Political Economy of New Labour* (Hay 1999: chapter 1).

Structure and agency, context and conduct

The debate on the modernisation of the Labour Party provides yet further evidence of an academic truism: when engaged in abstract reflections of a theoretical kind, social scientists are keen to extol the virtues of a complex view of the relationship between actors and their context; yet, when it comes to more substantive concerns, the allure of actor-centred or context-centred positions often proves overwhelming. It is perhaps all too easy, then, to simply call for a more complex view of the relationship between structure and agency than that exhibited in much of the existing literature.

It is nonetheless important to contextualise political conduct, on the one hand, and consider the mechanisms by which political context is constantly shaped and re-shaped, on the other. To make such an appeal is not to imply that all previous accounts were guilty of one or other oversight: it would be fairer to suggest that they posit some relationship (however skewed or inconsistent) between conduct (for example, that of the party leadership) and context (say, that of the global political economy). It is, however, to emphasise the benefits of reflecting explicitly on the specific relationship between conduct and context; and to caution against the consequences of the structuralist and intentionalist positions to which many authors seem drawn. It is only by so doing that we can resist the tendency, characteristic of actor-centred accounts, to view Labour as being so radically unconstrained by its environment that pragmatic and contextual (as distinct from normative ethical) considerations simply did not enter into the equation when charting a course for the party's modernisation.

Similarly, it is only by so doing that we can resist the equally problematical tendency, characteristic of more context-centred positions, to imply such a rigidly delimited realm of political autonomy that the trajectory of the party's modernisation might almost be derived from a consideration of the environment in which it took place, independently of the actors involved. This latter view, it was earlier suggested, is closely associated with the uncritical acceptance of the 'hyper-globalist' thesis. Worse still, perhaps, is the vacillation between the two which allows New Labour to be presented, simultaneously, as the unwitting agent of the 'harsh economic realities' of the context in which it finds itself and yet as a principled exponent of a consistent, ethical, 'new' social democracy, freely chosen.

Such extremes are now thankfully rare. Indeed, even those approaches that tended to place their emphasis principally on structure–context or on agency–conduct have tended to do so without exclusively privileging the one over the other. Thus, for example, those analyses which sought to account for Labour's trajectory in recent years in terms of a strategic struggle for its soul (as reflected in the shifting balance of power within the party) have generally felt the need to introduce a range of contextual and structural factors – the balance of power itself at any given moment in time, the strategic resources at the disposal of particular actors, the constitution and the institutionalised practices of the party, and so forth. Similarly, accounts privileging the (invariably) harsh economic realities of a newly globalised political economy have nonetheless had to invoke *some* conception of agency – if only as the immediate mechanism by which the party's commitments might be brought in line with a new external environment. It might seem tempting at this stage to suggest some middle ground, or even a potential *rapprochement*, between these contending structural and more agency-centred accounts. Yet we should be extremely wary of any suggestion that essentially interpretive disputes over the assessment of Labour's modernisation can simply be adjudicated by importing abstract considerations of structure and agency. Empirical disputes cannot be resolved by theoretical *fiat*. In the end, choices must be made – about what's going on (empirically) and about how what's going on should be accounted for in terms of structural and agential factors. The best that can be asked is that, having made such choices, analysts seek to defend and develop them in terms of a consistent and explicit view of the relationship between the actors involved and the context they inhabit.

Rhetoric and reality: the discursive and the material

Equally significant, though the subject currently of less theoretical reflection, is the question of the relationship between political discourse and the environment in which that discourse is formulated and, arguably, on whose development it impacts (though see Berman 1998; Blyth 1997; Campbell 1998). The significance of the ideational (the realm of ideas) can easily be traced from the question of structure and agency itself. For, if we accept that actors inhabit an environment external to them, it is no large step to suggest that their conduct is influenced by the ideas they formulate about that environment. What is more, as we know from (often painful) experience, no one-to-one correspondence can be assumed to obtain between the ideas we formulate about our surroundings (immediate or more distant) and those surroundings themselves. If we want to understand how actors behave, it is essential that we give due consideration to their understandings of the context in which they are situated and the means by which they formulate and revise such understandings.

Consider the 'class dealignment' thesis (Franklin 1985; Särlvik and Crewe 1983). During the 1980s, a number of prominent psephologists claimed to identify a secular trend in the relationship between social class and voting behaviour – it appeared that a smaller (and an ever-diminishing) proportion of the electorate was voting for its 'natural' class party. Critics claimed that this conception of absolute class voting did not explain, but merely re-described, Labour's predicament. Any shrinkage in the size of the vote of a party like Labour, they protested, would result in an absolute drop in class voting. All that could be concluded, then, from such a measure was that Labour was not doing very well. What was required, to adjudicate the claimed weakening of the relationship between class and voting behaviour, was a measure of relative class dealignment. Moreover, such a measure showed no such secular trend (Heath, Jowell and Curtice 1985).

The influence of the dealignment thesis, however, did not wane in response to such criticism – far from it. This presents a certain difficulty in assessing its validity in the light of more recent evidence. For, since the mid-1990s a decline in relative class voting has come to be observed. We are presented with a stark choice between two rather different explanations in accounting for this phenomenon. The first is simple, intuitive, entirely conventional and gives no consideration to ideational factors. It is that proponents of class dealignment were right all along and have merely been vindicated by events subsequent to their initial hypothesis (Sanders 2002). The second, a more discursive explanation, would point to the direct influence of the dealignment thesis (as a thesis) on Labour's strategic thinking. Labour, in the early 1990s, became convinced of the validity of the thesis (whatever the relative class voting figures may have suggested). Consequently, it ceased to make a class-based electoral appeal, re-projecting itself as a catch-all party studiously courting the median voter. On this alternative reading, any subsequent evidence of dealignment might then be taken less as evidence of the validity of the thesis than of its influence. Quite simply, if Labour behaved as if the thesis were true (by abandoning its class-based electoral appeal), the predictions of the thesis would be confirmed. Moreover, this would be the case whether or not working-class voters would be inclined to respond to a more genuinely class-based appeal, should one have been made.

On the basis of the evidence it is impossible to adjudicate finally between these two contending and mutually incompatible explanations – with very different implications for electoral strategy and the prospects for class-based appeals. Nevertheless, while it remains plausible that recent evidence of both absolute and relative class dealignment may be a consequence rather than a cause of Labour's modernisation, it would seem dangerously presumptuous to conclude that socio-economic change has consigned class-based electoral politics to psephological history.

Similar arguments may be made about the impact of globalisation – and ideas about globalisation – on New Labour's perceptions of the limits of political and economic feasibility (for a further elaboration of the argument, see Hay 2001). Has globalisation constrained the parameters of political autonomy or has Labour come to constrain itself on the basis of its perceptions of such constraints? Or, indeed, has Labour come, somewhat duplicitously perhaps, to legitimise otherwise unpalatable social and economic reforms with respect to globalisation's convenient logic of non-negotiable external economic constraint?

What these two examples serve to highlight is that, convenient though it may be to do so, we ignore the realm of political discourse at our peril. Most social scientists now seem happy to concede that we do indeed *make* history, though not in circumstances of our own choosing. Perhaps it is now also time to concede that, very often, we make our history in the image of the theories we construct about it or – as perhaps in the case of New Labour – in the image of the theories deemed most convenient to justify specific strategic goals.

Political, economic and cultural factors

Political analysts should not restrict themselves to narrowly political variables. Yet neither should they seek to incorporate each and every conceivable explanatory variable to produce a saturated model in which no variance is left unaccounted for. Parsimony, given the choice, is no bad thing. Thus, although it is important to argue for the significance of political, economic and cultural factors and, above all, the complex nature of the interaction between them, it is perhaps equally important to caution against a crudely 'additive' conception of theoretical sophistication. The political, the economic and the cultural are not independent arenas. Accordingly, we should be careful to avoid the implicit theoretical one-upmanship of the claim that politicism is one-dimensional, political–economic explanations are two-dimensional, and that only an integration of the political, the economic and the cultural can provide the 'complete' picture – a three-dimensional view (of a, presumably, three-dimensional reality).

That having been said, it is equally important to caution against the dangers of politicism and economism, and to suggest that they may be countered by a consideration of the political conditions of economic dynamics and the economic conditions of political dynamics. Politicism, in the literature on the renaissance and the subsequent history of the Labour Party, tends to be associated with the blithe optimism which comes with intentionalism and a benign neglect of the external (above all economic) environment. Politicist accounts thus tend to emphasise the inherent contingency of the modernisation process, often as a means to celebrate the considerable foresight, conviction and strategic *nôus* of the modernisers.

Economism is no less problematical. At its worst, it tends to view the political as either altogether irrelevant or as a pale shadow of immutable and inexorable economic processes (such as globalisation). Not only does this frequently imply that there is simply no alternative to the policies that have been pursued (a dangerous and, as already argued, seldom defended assertion), it also fails to acknowledge the political 'authoring' of processes such as economic integration. For, as a growing number of authors have demonstrated, contemporary processes of economic integration owe their origins to a series of highly political decisions – associated with the deregulation of financial markets, the liberalising of capital flows, and so forth (Helleiner 1995). Once this is acknowledged, the logic of inevitability, which patterns of economic interdependence are so frequently seen to imply, appear somewhat less imposing. This is made very clear in the technical literature on financial re-regulation – a literature sadly unnoticed by mainstream political science (see, for instance, Akyüz and Cornford 1995; Eichengreen, Tobin and Wyplosz 1995; Ul Haq, Kaul and Grunberg 1996; Watson 1999).

If we are serious about resisting tendencies to privilege either the actor or the context it is imperative that we also resist the narrow privileging of the economic and the political with which they have become so intimately connected.

The domestic, the international and the transnational

Finally, I return to the complex question of the relationship between the domestic, the international and the transnational. It is tempting, as in the preceding discussion, to argue that we need to consider each moment, and each moment in its articulation with every other moment. In one sense, though glib, that is true. However, as in the previous discussion, it will not suffice. For, ultimately, the relative weight we should assign to the domestic, the international and the transnational, is both an evaluative and an empirical matter. If we are interested in Labour's economic and industrial policy the international may be of greater significance than if our principal concern is with the prospects for a democratically elected second chamber to replace the House of Lords. No meta-theoretical invocation to balance the domestic and the international can then be posited.

Yet, if we are to reach an even-handed assessment of New Labour's modernisation or, indeed, of its conduct to date in office, it seems plausible to suggest that we can begin to do so only by locating the party in some kind of international and comparative context. If we are to move beyond the twin poles of economism and politicism it is important to acknowledge the domestic conditions of existence of international political and economic dynamics and the international conditions of existence of domestic political and economic dynamics. That is easy to write, somewhat more difficult to say, and altogether more difficult to deliver. Nonetheless, political analysts are seemingly rather more prepared, these days, to accept that this is the nature of the task at hand. That is no bad thing if we are to rectify the still-glaring disparity between what we know we ought to do and what, for the most part, we still continue to practise.

In this chapter the aim has been to establish the potential contribution to labour studies of an emerging 'new political science of British politics' that is more reflective about its core analytical assumptions. The argument is stated simply, though its implications, if accepted, are more involved. Positions on the question of structure and agency, the ideational and the material, and the relative significance of political, economic and cultural variables on the one hand, and domestic and international factors, on the other, are implicit in all political explanations. Labour studies is no exception. While there is no single 'correct' answer to any of these questions, it is important that we strive for a high degree of internal coherence. A condition of so doing is a far higher consciousness of and greater reflexivity towards such analytical assumptions. If this can be achieved labour studies will be far better placed to focus attention on the strategies most appropriate to study labour and Labour alike.

References

Unless indicated, the place of publication is London.

Akyüz, Y. and Cornford, A. (1995) 'International capital movements: some prospects for reform', in Michie, J. and Smith, J. G. (eds) *Managing the Global Economy*, Oxford

Berman, S. (1998) *The Social Democratic Moment: Ideas and Politics in the Making of Interwar Europe*, Cambridge, MA

Bevir, M. and Rhodes, R. A. W. (1998) 'Narratives of Thatcherism', *West European Politics*, 21:1

Bevir, M. and Rhodes, R. A. W. (1999) 'Studying British government: reconstructing the research agenda', *British Journal of Politics & International Relations*, 1:2

Blyth, M. M. (1997) 'Any more bright ideas? The ideational turn of comparative political economy', *Comparative Politics*, 29

Brivati, B. and Bale, T. (eds) (1997) *New Labour in Power: Precedents and Prospects*

Brivati, B. and Heffernan, R. (eds) (2000) *The Labour Party: A Centenary History*

Campbell, J. L. (1998) 'Institutional analysis and the role of ideas in political economy', *Theory, Culture and Society*, 27

Clift, B. (2001) 'New Labour's Third Way and European social democracy', in Ludlam, S. and Smith, M. J. (eds) *New Labour in Government*

Coates, D. and Hay, C. (2001) 'The internal and external face of New Labour's political economy', *Government and Opposition*, 36:4

Drucker, H. (1979) *Doctrine and Ethos in the Labour Party*

Eatwell, J. (1992) 'The development of Labour policy, 1987–92', in Michie, J. (ed.) *The Economic Legacy, 1987–92*

Eichengreen, B., Tobin, J. and Wyplosz, C. (1995) 'Two cases for sand in the wheels of international finance', *The Economic Journal*, 105

English, R. and Kenny, M. (1999) 'British decline or the politics of declinism?', *British Journal of Politics & International Relations*, 1:2

Fielding, S. (2000a) 'Labour and its past', in Tanner, D. Thane, P. and Tiratsoo, N. (eds) *Labour's First Century*, Cambridge

Fielding, S. (2000b) 'A new politics?', in Dunleavy, P., Gamble, A., Holiday, I. and Peele, G. (eds) *Developments in British Politics 6*, Basingstoke

Franklin, M. (1985) *The Decline of Class Voting*, Oxford

Garrett, G. (1998) *Partisan Politics in the Global Economy*, Cambridge

George, S. and Haythorne, D. (1996) 'The British Labour Party', in Gaffney, J. (ed.) *Political Parties and the European Union*

Harris, J. (2000) 'Labour's political and social thought', in Tanner, D., Thane, P. and Tiratsoo, N. (eds) *Labour's First Century*, Cambridge

Hay, C. (1999) *The Political Economy of New Labour: Labouring Under False Pretences?* Manchester

Hay, C. (2001) 'The invocation of external economic constraint: a genealogy of the concept of globalisation in the political economy of the British Labour Party, 1973–2000', *The European Legacy*, 6:2

Hay, C. (2002a) *Political Analysis*

Hay, C. (2002b) 'British politics today: towards a new political science of British politics?', in Hay, C. (ed.) *British Politics Today*, Cambridge

Hay, C. (2002c) 'Globalisation, EU-isation and the space for social democratic alternatives: pessimism of the intellect . . .', *British Journal of Politics & International Relations*, 4:3

Heath, A., Jowell, R. and Curtice, J. (1985) *How Britain Votes*, Oxford

Helleiner, R. (1995) 'Explaining the globalisation of financial markets: bringing states back in', *Review of International Political Economy*, 2

Kerr, P. (2001) *Postwar British Politics: From Conflict to Consensus*

Marsh, D. (2002) 'Pluralism and the study of British politics', in Hay, C. (ed.) *British Politics Today*, Cambridge

Marsh, D., Buller, J., Hay, C., Johnston, J., Kerr, P., McAnulla, S. and Watson, S. (1999) *Postwar British Politics in Perspective*, Cambridge

Minkin, L. (1991) *The Contentious Alliance: Trade Unions and the Labour Party*, Edinburgh

Pontusson, J. (1992) *The Limits of Social Democracy: Investment Policies in Sweden*, Ithaca, NY

Sanders, D. (2002) 'Electoral competition in contemporary Britain', in Hay, C. (ed.) *British Politics Today*, Cambridge

Särlvik, B. and Crewe, I. (1983) *Decade of Dealignment*, Cambridge

Sassoon, D. (1998) 'Fin-de-siècle socialism: the united modern Left', *New Left Review*, 227

Smith, M. J. (1999) *The Core Executive in Britain*

Tanner, D., Thane, P. and Tiratsoo, N. (eds.) (2000) *Labour's First Century*, Cambridge

Ul Haq, M., Kaul, I. and Grunberg, I. (eds) (1996) *The Tobin Tax: Coping with Financial Volatility*, Oxford

Watson, M. (1999) 'Rethinking capital mobility, reregulating financial markets', *New Political Economy*, 3:3

Wickham-Jones, M. (2000) 'New Labour and the global economy: partisan politics and the social democratic model', *British Journal of Politics & International Relations*, 2:1

Guide to further reading

Chapter 1

For comparative studies of the ideological dynamics of social democratic parties see A. Przeworski, *Capitalism and Social Democracy* (Cambridge, 1985), T. A. Koelble, *The Left Unravelled* (Durham, 1991) and H. Kitschelt, *The Transformation of European Social Democracy* (Cambridge, 1994). R. Miliband, *Parliamentary Socialism* (1972), D. Coates, *The Labour Party and the Struggle for Socialism* (Cambridge, 1975) and L. Panitch, *Social Democracy and Industrial Militancy* (Cambridge, 1976) provide accounts of ideological change within the Labour Party from a Marxist perspective, while economic imperatives for ideological movement are also the focus of C. A. R. Crosland, *The Future of Socialism* (1963) and J. Gray, *After Social Democracy: Politics, Capitalism and the Common Life* (1996). R. Desai, *Intellectuals and Socialism* (1994) examines the role of Labour's intellectuals, while A. F. Heath, R. M. Jowell and J. K. Curtice, *The Rise of New Labour* (Oxford, 2001) carefully examine the electoral factors underpinning Labour's most recent ideological changes. S. Haseler, *The Gaitskellites* (1969) and M. Wickham-Jones, *Economic Strategy and the Labour Party* (1996) provide good examples of studies of the intra-party dynamics of Labour's ideological movements.

Chapter 2

Some books referred to in this chapter are now out of print, but most of the titles and all the journals are still available. Of the older works, T. Forester, *The Labour Party and the Working Class* (1976) and H. Drucker, *Doctrine and Ethos in the Labour Party* (1979) are still well worth consulting, as is, for its 'new' approach to writing political history (although about the Communist Party), R. Samuel's series in *New Left Review*, 154, 156, 165, published in 1985–87. J. Lawrence and M. Taylor (eds) *Party, State and Society* (Aldershot, 1997) provides the best guide to the 'new political history'. Studies which develop some of these themes and approaches for the Left include: S. Fielding, P. Thompson and N. Tiratsoo, *England Arise! The Labour Party and Popular Politics in 1940s Britain* (Manchester, 1995); L. Black, *The Political Culture of the Left in Affluent Britain, 1951–64* (2003); and I. Favretto, *The Long Search for a Third Way: The British Labour Party and the Italian Left Since 1945* (2002). R. McKibbin's *Classes and Cultures* (Oxford, 1998) and A. F. Heath, R. M. Jowell and J. K. Curtice, *How Britain Votes* (Oxford, 1985) are also important reading.

Chapter 3

For the history of the New Left and an assessment of its theoretical contribution, see L. Chun, *The British New Left* (Edinburgh, 1993). On the early New Left, see S. Hall, 'The first New Left', in R. Archer, D. Bubeck, H. Glock, L. Jacobs, S. Moglen, A. Steinhouse and D. Weinstock (eds) *Out of Apathy* (1989) and M. Kenny, *The First New Left* (1995). Among the many works produced by New Left writers, the following relate particularly to the themes discussed here: R. Miliband, *Parliamentary Socialism* (1972 [1961]) and 'Moving on', *The Socialist Register 1973* (1973); R. Williams, *Politics and Letters* (1979); R. Williams, S. Hall and E. P. Thompson (eds) *The May Day Manifesto* (1967); T. Nairn, *The Break-Up of Britain* (1977); S. Hall, *The Hard Road to Renewal* (1988); J. Saville, 'The ideology of Labourism', in R. Benewick, R. Berki and B. Parekh (eds) *Knowledge and Belief in Politics* (1975); P. Anderson, *English Questions* (1992); A. Barnett, *This Time: Our Constitutional Revolution* (1997). For criticisms of the New Left, see E. Meiskins-Wood, 'A chronology of the New Left and its successors, or: who's old-fashioned now?' *The Socialist Register 1995* (1995) and R. Samuel and G. Stedman Jones, 'The Labour Party and social democracy', in R. Samuel and G. Stedman Jones (eds) *Culture, Ideology and Politics* (1982).

Chapter 4

The interpretation in this chapter is developed more fully in M. Newman, *Ralph Miliband and the Politics of the New Left* (2002) which also includes a full bibliography of Miliband's works. *The Socialist Register: Why Not Capitalism?* (1995), contains several articles on Miliband, including L. Panitch, 'Ralph Miliband, socialist intellectual, 1924–94' and J. Saville, '*Parliamentary Socialism* revisited'. However, the best way to evaluate Miliband is to read his own work. The continuities and evolution in his analysis can be appreciated through the following: *The State in Capitalist Society* (1969); *Parliamentary Socialism* (1972); *Marxism and Politics* (Oxford, 1977); and *Socialism for a Sceptical Age* (Cambridge, 1994).

Chapter 5

For a fuller introduction to the approach discussed here, see D. Coates (ed.) *Paving the Third Way: The Critique of Parliamentary Socialism: A Socialist Register Anthology* (2003). On the Bennite Left and its aftermath, see L. Panitch and C. Leys, *The End of Parliamentary Socialism* (2001 [1997]). The second of the latter work brings the analysis through to the first term of the New Labour Government. For an important exploration of the socialist alternative and its attainment, see L. Panitch, *Renewing Socialism* (Boulder, CO, and Oxford, 2001); and the series of essays in L. Panitch and C. Leys (eds) *The Socialist Register 2000* (2000). For an introduction to the understanding of political economy associated with the Milibandian approach, see D. Coates, *Models of Capitalism* (Cambridge, 2000).

Chapter 6

The original key texts by Tom Nairn and Perry Anderson are contained in the collection P. Anderson and R. Blackburn (eds) *Towards Socialism* (1965). Anderson's historical overview is reproduced again, along with other papers, in his 1992 collection *English Questions*. Overviews of the Nairn–Anderson theses are contained in L. Chun, *The British New Left* (Edinburgh, 1993), G. Elliot, *Perry Anderson* (1998) and M. Kenny, *The First New Left*

(1995). For a sympathetic, if polemical, application to Labour history, see G. Elliott, *Labourism and the English Genius* (1993).

Chapter 7

There is an interesting video of Henry Pelling interviewed by Ross McKibbin, made in 1988 and available from the Institute of Historical Research. Clearly, the central work to consider is H. Pelling, *The Origins of the Labour Party, 1880–1900* (Oxford, 1954), which was so thoroughly researched and clearly presented that it remains a classic reference point. Pelling's further pursuit of the issues of the regional and ideological fragmentation of the working classes was published in *Social Geography of British Elections, 1885–1910* (1967) and *Popular Politics and Society in Late Victorian Britain* (1968). His approach has been influential on more recent work such as D. Tanner, *Political Change and the Labour Party, 1900–1918* (Cambridge, 1990), and many of the essays in E. F. Biagini and A. J. Reid (eds) *Currents of Radicalism. Popular Radicalism, Organised Labour and Party Politics in Britain, 1850–1914* (Cambridge, 1991).

Chapter 8

The interested reader should start with McKibbin's own books – *The Evolution of the Labour Party* (Oxford, 1974); *The Ideologies of Class* (Oxford, 1990); and *Classes and Cultures* (Oxford, 1998). McKibbin's treatment of the 'exceptional' development of working-class politics in Britain might be compared with Tom Nairn's earlier expositions of this argument in 'The English working class', *New Left Review*, 24 (1964) and 'The fateful meridian', *New Left Review*, 60 (1970). The argument is systematically questioned in Stefan Berger, *The British Labour Party and the German Social Democrats* (Oxford, 1994). McKibbin's treatment of the relationship between working-class culture and working-class politics is usefully compared with Gareth Stedman Jones's 'Working class culture and working class politics in London, 1870–1900', *Journal of Social History*, 7:4 (1974) and the same author's *Languages of Class* (Cambridge, 1982). Finally, those interested in the documentary sources for generalisations about working-class cultures should read Jonathan Rose's *The Intellectual Life of the British Working Classes* (2001).

Chapter 9

In terms of the historical debate, P. Clarke, *Lancashire and the New Liberalism* (Cambridge, 1971) makes the most convincing case for the existence of a viable 'progressive alliance', though this has been most recently challenged by D. McHugh, 'Labour, the Liberals and the progressive alliance in Manchester, 1900–14', *Northern History*, 39:1 (2002). R. Desai's *Intellectuals and Socialism* (1994) is a good place to start to acquire an overview of the place held by social democratic intellectuals within the Labour Party. P. Clarke's 'The social democratic theory of the class struggle', in J. Winter (ed.) *The Working Class in Modern British History* (Cambridge, 1983) provides a concise summation of their developing perspective until the formation of the SDP, while the essays contained in D. Marquand, *The Progressive Dilemma* (1999), are important to an understanding of the perspective from the later 1980s up to the formation of 'New' Labour. P. Gould, *The Unfinished Revolution* (1998), sketches out how 'New' Labour has appropriated the debate.

Chapter 10

Of the monographs on the unions–party link, Lewis Minkin's *The Contentious Alliance* (Edinburgh, 1992) is by far the most extensive and detailed, and focuses on the dynamics of the intra-party relationship. Pluralist perspectives on the link across much of the postwar period, and focused on unions–government relations, can be traced in Robert Taylor's *The Trade Union Question in British Politics* (Oxford, 1993), and, for a shorter but crucial period, in Gerald Dorfman's *Government versus Trade Unionism in British Politics Since 1968* (1979). Marxist analyses, again mainly of the unions–government relationship, are to be found in Leo Panitch's *Social Democracy and Industrial Militancy* (Cambridge, 1976), and in David Coates's *The Crisis of Labour* (Oxford, 1989). The best book-length treatment of the link during the key period on which the chapter focuses remains Andrew J. Taylor's *The Trade Unions and the Labour Party* (1987).

Chapter 11

Top of the list are Minkin's two magisterial studies *The Labour Party Conference* (1978) and *The Contentious Alliance* (Edinburgh, 1991. These are towering works which no serious student of the Labour Party can afford to ignore. Minkin's earlier treatments of the party–unions connection can be found in: 'The British Labour Party and the trade unions: crisis and compact', *Industrial Labour Relations Review*, October (1974); 'The party connection: divergence and convergence in the British labour movement', *Government and Opposition*, 13:4 (1978); and 'Leftwing trade unionism and tensions of British Labour politics', in B. E. Brown (ed.) *Eurocommunism and Eurosocialism: The Left Confronts Modernity* (New York, 1978). There are also some fascinating insights on Minkin's method and research techniques in his *Exists and Entrances* (Sheffield, 1997).

Elements of Minkin's interpretive framework have been applied to developments in the party–unions relationship over the last decade by Steve Ludlam. See 'New Labour and the unions: the end of the contentious alliance?' in S. Ludlam and M. J. Smith (eds) *New Labour in Government* (2001) and S. Ludlam, M. Bodah and D. Coates, 'Trajectories of solidarity: changing union–party linkages in the UK and the USA', *British Journal of Politics & International Relations*, 4:2 (2002). The topic of party–unions relations has also been treated in the following studies by John McIlroy: 'The enduring alliance? Trade unions and the making of New Labour, 1994–97', *British Journal of Industrial Relations* (1998), 36:4; 'New Labour, new unions, new Left', *Capital and Class*, 71 (2000); and 'The new politics of pressure – the Trades Union Congress and New Labour in government', *Industrial Relations Journal*, 31:2 (2000). The subject is discussed also in C. Howell, 'From New Labour to no Labour? The industrial relations project of the Blair Government', *New Political Science*, 22:2 (2000).

Chapter 12

The literature on the analytical techniques appropriate to labour studies is very limited indeed. There is, however, a broader political science literature on which labour studies might draw. That literature is introduced and reviewed in C. Hay, *Political Analysis* (2002), and D. Marsh and G. Stoker (eds) *Theory and Methods in Political Science* (2002). For an attempt to draw out the implications of this literature for postwar British politics, see D. Marsh *et al.*, *Postwar British Politics in Perspective* (Cambridge, 1999). For debates within labour studies which draw attention to these issues, see especially, D. Coates, 'Capitalist models and social democracy: the case of New Labour', *British Journal of Politics & International Studies*, 3:3 (2001), as well as C. Hay, *The Political Economy of New Labour* (Manchester, 1999) and 'Globalisation, EU-isation and the space for social democratic alternatives: pessimism of the intellect . . .', *British Journal of Politics & International Relations*, 4:3 (2002).

Index